D0505927

FIVE DAYS FROM DEFEAT

Other books by Walter Reid

Arras 1917: The Journey to Railway Triangle

Architect of Victory: Douglas Haig

Churchill 1940–45: Under Friendly Fire

Empire of Sand: How Britain Made the Middle East

Keeping the Jewel in the Crown: The British Betrayal of India

Supreme Sacrifice: A Small Village and the Great War
(with Gordon Masterton and Paul Birch)

FIVE DAYS FROM DEFEAT

How Britain Nearly Lost the First World War

WALTER REID

BIRLINN

First published in 2017 by
Birlinn Limited
West Newington House
10 Newington Road
Edinburgh
EH9 1QS

www.birlinn.co.uk

ISBN: 978 1 78027 490 4

British Library Cataloguing-in-Publication Data
A catalogue record for this book is available from the British Library

Typeset by Biblichor Ltd, Edinburgh
Printed and bound by Gutenberg Press, Malta

To the precious, vivid and ever-present memory of Flora

'I suppose history never lies, does it?' said Mr Dick, with a gleam of hope.

'Oh dear, no, sir!' I replied, most decisively. I was ingenuous and young, and I thought so.

Charles Dickens, David Copperfield

Contents

List of Illustrations

Field Marshal Sir Douglas Haig in his headquarters train.

Hindenburg and Ludendorff.

General Foch.

Crown Prince Rupprecht of Bavaria.

Henry Wilson.

Willy ('Wully') Robertson.

Haig after the Battle of Cambrai, from *Punch*.

Lloyd George practising water divining.

German propaganda poster.

Haig's Special Order of the Day of 23 March 1918.

A captured British soldier: a pitiful reminder of what defeat meant.

Some of the huge numbers of British captured by the Germans in the early stages of the offensive.

The *mairie* at Doullens.

Portrait panels of Foch and Haig on the exterior of Doullens town hall.

The room in which the Conference took place.

Haig and Clemenceau at Doullens station three weeks after the Conference.

Clemenceau's manuscript minute recording the appointment of Foch as Allied Commander-in-Chief.

One of the countless memorials that populate French villages and towns.

Acknowledgements

I owe a huge debt of gratitude to my dear friend John Hussey, OBE. Amongst many other things, John has written some outstanding articles on aspects of the First World War. They glitter and scintillate in the pages of many scholarly journals and illuminate this passage of history. In the course of researching them he amassed a considerable volume of fascinating material on the period which this book covers, and this treasure-store with immense generosity he handed to me.

His generosity was three-fold, perhaps greater. For one historian to make the fruits of his research available to another is a rare and kind act. To hand it to someone who might well place quite different interpretations on the material is even more generous: John is certainly not to be taken to be agreeing with my conclusions – he has his own views which can be strong and are based on rigorous logic – but he did not seek to influence my own analysis. Finally, he read this book in draft when he was very much involved in the final stages of work on his magisterial two-volume history of 1815 and the conclusion of the Napoleonic adventure, *Waterloo: The Campaign of 1815*, which will stand as a definitive account for many years.

I acknowledge with thanks permission from the Earl Haig and the Trustees of the National Library of Scotland to quote from the Haig Papers, of which they are respectively copyright owner and material owners; and from the Trustees of the Liddell Hart Centre for Military Archives, King's College, London, to quote from the Robertson and Kiggell Papers.

I have had the good fortune to have had two wonderful assistants who helped the book along its way, checking, researching and imposing order on my wayward working practices. Dawn Broadley took the first watch, and Gwen McKerrell the second. I am immensely grateful to both. They had much to put up with, but never said so.

As always, Hugh Andrew and Andrew Simmons, respectively Managing Director and Editorial Director at Birlinn, were wonderfully supportive and enthusiastic. It is always a great pleasure to work with them. Patricia Marshall was an outstanding copy editor, knowing apparently intuitively exactly when I was skating on thin ice, and humanely getting me off it.

Finally I record my gratitude to my wife, Janet, my gentlest and best critic, for all the fun and surprises of fifty years' companionship, and for her support at a time when I was the least of those who needed it.

Beauly, Renfrewshire
August 2017

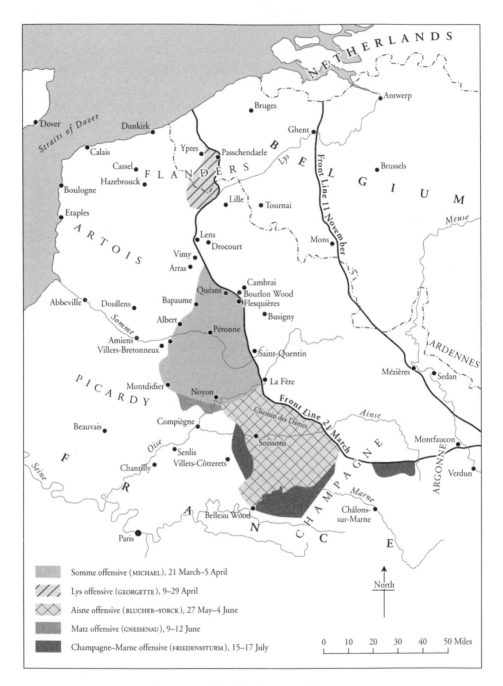

Legend

	Somme offensive (MICHAEL), 21 March–5 April
	Lys offensive (GEORGETTE), 9–29 April
	Aisne offensive (BLUCHER–YORCK), 27 May–4 June
	Matz offensive (GNEISENAU), 9–12 June
	Champagne–Marne offensive (FRIEDENSSTURM), 15–17 July

0   10   20   30   40   50 Miles

North

Ludendorff's 1918 Spring Offensive

Map labels

NETHERLANDS

Dover
Straits of Dover
Calais
Dunkirk
Cassel
Hazebrouck
Boulogne
Etaples
Ypres
Passchendaele
FLANDERS
Lille
Bruges
Ghent
Lys
BELGIUM
Brussels
Antwerp
Meuse
Front Line 11 November
Tournai
Mons
Lens
Drocourt
Vimy
Arras
ARTOIS
Abbeville
Doullens
Bapaume
Quéant
Cambrai
Bourlon Wood
Flesquières
Busigny
Albert
Péronne
Somme
Amiens
Villers-Bretonneux
Saint-Quentin
Mézières
Sedan
ARDENNES
Montdidier
Noyon
La Fère
PICARDY
Beauvais
Compiègne
Oise
Senlis
Chantilly
Villets-Côtterets
Soissons
Chemin des Dames
Ainse
Front Line 21 March
Montfaucon
Verdun
ARGONNE
Seine
FRANCE
Belleau Wood
Marne
Châlons-sur-Marne
CHAMPAGNE
Paris

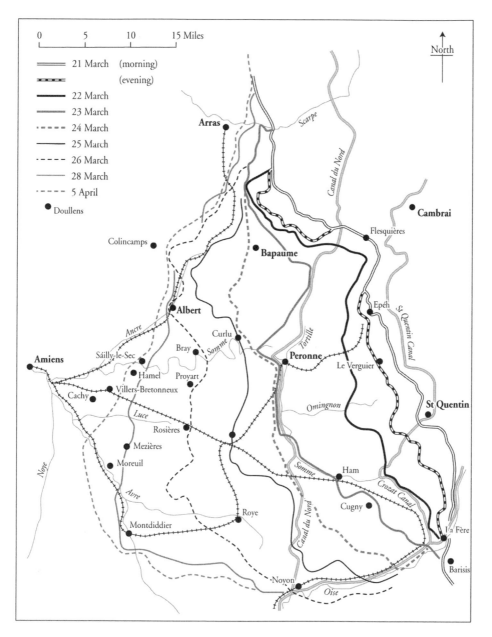

Movement of the Front, 21 March–5 April 1918

Prologue

21 March

The German army launched a massive attack on the British part of the Western Front. Aware that they might win the war now – before the Americans were present in force – and also aware that, if they did not do so, they would assuredly lose, the onslaught had all the berserk drive of what the Romans called *Furor Teutonicus* when they tried to describe the whirlwind attacks of the Germanic tribes in all their wrath. The assault was long prepared but had been well concealed. Ludendorff, the German commander, deployed tactics he had developed in Russia, essentially the storm-troop tactics that Hitler would use in 1940. His aim, like Hitler's, was to break the Allies by forcing Britain back to the Channel ports.

A devastating German artillery barrage opened at 04.40. By the time the infantry moved off, just five hours later, 3.2 million shells had landed on pre-registered positions. By the end of the day, Britain had suffered 38,512 casualties and lost 500 guns. The Cabinet secretary said that the day was one of the most decisive moments in the world's history.

22 March

Heavy fog continued to assist the advancing Germans. Fifth Army, defending the southern part of the British line, was penetrated as far as its reserve line. French troops moved in to bolster the dazed British. The fighting was fierce but the Germans, looking at the extent of their gains, said that the British must have run like rabbits.

1

23 March

By now the Germans had advanced 22 kilometres in an 80-kilometre breach in the British line. The British Commander-in-Chief, Sir Douglas Haig, requested very substantial aid from his French allies. British Fifth Army, falling back in confusion through inadequate defences, was disintegrating. It was put under French control. France complained that Haig was breaking contact, doing nothing for France except fleeing from her.

Haig feared that, if contact was lost, the British armies would be rounded up and driven into the sea. He began to talk of falling back to cover the Channel ports. There were fears in London that the government might fall. The Cabinet began to panic and contemplate evacuation. The Cabinet Secretary feared not only defeat in France but invasion of Britain.

24 March

Now Third Army, to the north of Fifth Army, was in retreat too. Fifth Army had fallen back a further eight kilometres and battlefield command had broken down. The Great Retreat of 1918, pretty much a rout, had begun. The Cabinet Secretary said that things were about as bad as they could be. In Paris, the president was adamant that contact must be maintained. Haig and his opposite number, Pétain, met late at night at Haig's forward HQ to try to coordinate plans. Little emerged from the meeting. Pétain was afraid that Haig was going to break away and head for the coast. Later, Haig was to allege that Pétain had ordered his troops to pull away to defend Paris.

25 March

By the fourth day of the offensive, the situation was pivotal. Third Army followed Fifth Army into a general retirement and the crucial defensive line of the Somme was lost. A German general said that the sun of Germany's victory was at its zenith.

Pétain estimated the likelihood of German victory at 96 per cent. The Cabinet Secretary described the day as 'the crisis of the nation's fate'.

The Chief of the Imperial General Staff and Lord Milner, soon to be Secretary of State for War, were sent out to France to address the crisis. They conferred with the French president and Pétain and it was agreed that the direction of the Allied military effort could no longer be divided between two independent and often antagonistic generals – there had to be a single commander. The war was being fought in France for French soil and preponderantly with French troops. To the French, it was obvious that a French general should have a united command. Indeed, the British Official History was to say of 25 March, the fourth day of a *British* battle, 'Everything now depended on the French.'

26 March

By now, Germany had taken 90,000 prisoners and advanced some 60 kilometres. The Allies had suffered 250,000 casualties, 178,000 of them British. Against this background French and British political and military leaders met in the town hall at Doullens, just a few kilometres from Haig's HQ, to try to avert defeat. Well within the sound of battle and with retreating British soldiers streaming through the town, the decision discussed on the previous day was formally adopted.

The French General Foch was appointed to the unified command of the Allied armies. In practice, the French prime minister, Clemenceau, now became equally involved in the direction of the war. Thus the unified command, political as well as military, was effectively French. The decision taken at Doullens arrested the German advance and Allied victory followed eight months later.

For the French, that decision was logical and necessary. They had felt let down by an uncommitted ally. The French president said of Doullens, 'It's good work – it was high time.' A French general said, 'It was time to put [the British] under our orders, for their own sake as much as ours.'

Britain saw things differently. Her generals had never had much time for the French and putting the British Empire under the orders of a Frenchman was far from palatable. How close defeat had been and the unconscionable step that had been taken to avoid it was never publicly acknowledged and has never truly registered in the national memory.

Introduction

THE FIRST WORLD War ended on 11 November 1918. A great, British-led advance in the last hundred days pushed the German army back close to the frontiers of France – the frontiers it had crossed in August 1914. There, broken and defeated in war and starved and demoralised at home, Germany, through the military dictatorship that now ruled the country, was compelled to seek terms for an armistice which, in the following year, crystallised into the most humiliating of peace treaties.

After four years in which France and Britain had poured out blood and resources to fight a war which they had not sought, it was inevitable that the Allies celebrated their victory. For Britain, in particular, only the triumph of what was so often described as 'right over might' could validate the sacrifices she had made in a war from which she had nearly stood apart. This unbroken series of victories leading to the one-sided armistice negotiations in a railway train at Compiègne on 10 November 1918 was thus elevated into a heroic climax to follow four years of suffering.

All that is hardly surprising. What is surprising is that, just eight months earlier, in March of that same year, all the indications were that the war would end no less dramatically but in a German and not an Allied victory. On 21 March 1918, Germany unleashed an attack of unprecedented vigour on the Allies, particularly on the British. They set their sights high. This was 'the Kaiser's War', no less – 'the *Kaiserschlacht*' – its phases given grandiloquent titles drawn from Christianity and the Norse Myths. The assault very nearly succeeded. Despite everything, the Germans failed. If they had not, Ludendorff's statue and not Haig's would stand in Whitehall and outside Edinburgh Castle.

Five days after the assault began, an Allied conference took place in the anteroom to the Council Chamber in the *mairie* of the little town of Doullens in northern France. The decisions that were taken there were confused and rushed but they represented a change in the way the war was directed. They arrested the German advance and created conditions in which the Allies and not the Germans would shortly celebrate victory.

The perilous state of Britain's affairs in these five days was known only to senior politicians and military men. These privileged observers wobbled or even panicked. They talked of withdrawing the British armies from mainland Europe. But their fears were not communicated to the public at large at the time and subsequent history took pains to conceal just how precarious the situation had been. This book tells the story of what happened in these five days when the Allies – and particularly Britain – nearly gave way. In the process, the extent to which the historical record was manipulated will be seen and how much, in that process, that which did not redound to Britain's credit was concealed.

The important thing about wars, of course, is who wins them; but that does not mean that it isn't important to investigate how close the Allies came to losing the war in March 1918. These pivotal events occurred not when, as in the early fluid months, France effectively stood alone between the Germans and victory, but after Britain was wholly engaged in the war and playing as large a part as she ever would – when, indeed, American troops were reaching the Western Front. The events of 21–26 March represent a hinge in world history.

Because the victors had to celebrate their victory, because what happened in November 1918 was historically more important than what nearly happened in March, historians have tended to treat the German advance as doomed. It is true that, by then, Germany did not have substantial resources in terms of men or *matériel*. Her civilian population was demoralised and starving as a result of the Allied blockade and she could not have sustained her drive for a protracted period. But she did not need to do so. If the attack had succeeded, as it so nearly did, Britain would have been driven back to the Channel ports. A Dunkirk miracle would have been unlikely in 1918. France would have been compelled to make peace and the terms that Germany had just imposed on Russia showed how humiliating a peace it would have been for both Britain and France.

The British Commander-in-Chief was Field Marshal Sir Douglas Haig. I have elsewhere written a study of his life and military career[*]

---

[*]   Walter Reid, *Douglas Haig, Architect of Victory* (Birlinn, Edinburgh, 2008).

and, taking that career as a whole, I believe still, as I did when I wrote that book, that he was a good general – in some respects, a great one and, almost certainly, the best British commander available. But he was not at his best in these critical days.* He certainly wobbled. He was inclined to let go the hand of his French allies and fall back. But that is not what history records. Largely because he was able to influence how the history of the war was written, his actions have been sanitised, his failings minimised and the extent to which he controlled events exaggerated. Haig put himself at the centre of events as the directing influence, the man who steered the Allies away from disaster and on to the path of victory, who steadied the French, threatening under the French Commander-in-Chief, Pétain, to break the Allied line and fall back on Paris. It was he, in his narrative, who convened the conference at Doullens and he who there magnanimously proposed that the British armies, for the common good, should serve under Foch, a French generalissimo.

In fact, Pétain was not in the funk which Haig described. Pétain was, as Haig had earlier acknowledged, a steady commander if not an inspirational one. He did not order his troops to fall back on Paris. It was Haig who, left to himself, would have withdrawn to the Channel ports and perhaps ultimately to Britain, if that were possible. Haig did not convene the conference. Haig was not responsible for Foch's appointment.

I have not thrown the Field Marshal out with the bathwater. I remain of the view that Haig was a very able commander – not the greatest that Britain has produced, but great all the same: great in his management of a huge military empire of a size that no British officer has commanded before or since, *usually* great in his ability to stand firm in the face of reverses and talented in his direction of the later stages of the war. His wobbles in March were excusable. The primary duty imposed on him by his government was to preserve the troops under his command and he would have been negligent if he had not considered all his options. If, as I argue, he was not impressive in the early stages of the *Kaiserschlacht*, that does not negate his achievements, and history is better served if he

---

* In the context of the space available for this vastly important but very short period of history in an account of his larger life, I gave the benefit of the doubt to Haig and concluded that, though he had been greatly stressed and concerned at this time, his nerve had held. Having now focused my research on this period, I have changed my opinion, unconstrained by consistency, that hobgoblin of little minds. When Keynes was accused of altering his position, he said, 'When the facts change, I change my opinion. What do you do?'

is not invariably regarded with either unalloyed contempt or uncritical admiration and nothing between the two.

In other respects too, a study of the history of the period overturns a number of assumptions that are taken as givens, certainly by anglophone students of the war. In particular, the respective contributions of the British and French armies, the notion that France had militarily and in terms of morale shot her bolt by 1918, and the question of which country was more robust and capable of standing firm in a crisis all require to be reviewed. What emerges is just how unreliable was the story that Haig created and was able to insert into the accepted history, both in France and in Britain, of these five days when the outcome of the war was in the balance.

That story involved the narrative that Britain was ill supported by the French as she faced the German onslaught. On the contrary, Pétain was generous and quick to supply Britain with reserves. British Fifth Army pretty well ceased to exist and its place was taken by the French at very short notice.

Recent histories have also played down the French contribution to the remainder of the war and suggested that a weakened France played little part in this phase, while Britain, on the other hand, delivered ultimate victory. The battles in the great advance to victory in the last hundred days of the war were very different from the Somme or Third Ypres. In 1916 in particular, lessons were being learned and the fighting that won the war was informed by these lessons. Infantry tactics no longer depended overwhelmingly on the rifle. Soldiers carried not only rifles but also Lewis Guns, grenades or rifle grenades. All-arms tactics in which the use of aircraft and sophisticated artillery techniques were closely implicated were complemented by trucks and tanks, armoured cars, camouflage and deceptive ruses, smoke and machine guns. Pre-calibrated artillery made use of sound ranging and flash spotting. This was the kind of war that would be waged until the 1970s. The achievement of Britain in these last three months of the war was certainly huge and this unbroken series of victories deserves to be better known than it is. All the same, France was far from inactive in this period and her achievements also deserve celebration.

In the great advance, the Allies fought well together, Foch coordinating, approving, encouraging, Haig directing Army Commanders who were by now experienced and competent. All this is in contrast to the reverses of March 1918. These reverses were, to a large extent, the product of dysfunctional squabbling on the Western Front on the one hand and, on the other, differences between the military commanders, French and British, and the political command in London and Paris.

The change in mood and organisation between March and the hundred days was due to the events that culminated at Doullens. These events disturb much of what British readers have been taught.

Part One

1914–17

1

A Council of War

BEFORE LOOKING AT the approach to the *Kaiserschlacht* and the events of five days in March 1918, it will be helpful to look briefly in this chapter at the nature of the war which Britain decided to fight in 1914 and of how the decision to fight in that way was reached, and in the succeeding chapter to look at the course of the war from its outbreak to the end of 1917. We shall see how the pieces were moved around the board to be ready for the game that opened in March 1918.

It is important to understand the different sacrifices and achievements of the French and the British, to look at one through the eyes of the other, to study the tensions between them. We shall also observe the way in which British politicians in particular, but French too, fought their own generals.

In the tense negotiations which preceded the war, Britain was almost an irrelevance. Germany hoped that Britain would stand aside. France was afraid that she would do so. And Britain came very close to doing just that. The decision to fight was only made at the cost of resignations from the Cabinet and after an important speech in the House of Commons on 3 August 1914 by the Foreign Secretary, Sir Edward Grey. Grey's contribution altered the political weather. It rallied his party's waverers on the back benches. Even then, it was far from clear that Britain would play a major, practical part in the war. Traditionally, Britain had fought her wars at sea, leaving land battles to her allies and mercenaries. This was what came to be called 'the British way of war'. Grey himself didn't know what Britain would do, even if technically belligerent. He bumped into the French ambassador, Paul Cambon, as he left the House after making that critical speech, and told him that Britain's role might well be limited to a maritime one.

On the following day, 4 August 1914, Britain declared war on Germany at 23:00 GMT (midnight German time). On 5 August, a quite remarkable Council of War took place at 10 Downing Street, an assembly of both key Cabinet members and a large number of eminent if slightly peripheral personages. Some of them – such as Sir John French, the Commander-in-Chief of the British Expeditionary Force, Sir Charles Douglas, Chief of the Imperial General Staff until his death in October 1914, Sir Archibald Murray, the Chief of Staff, Henry Wilson, the Sub-Chief of staff, Sir Douglas Haig, commanding I Corps, and Sir James Grierson, commanding II Corps – were certain to be involved in the conduct of the war. But a huge number of slightly less obviously military men were also present, including Sir Henry Sclater, the Adjutant General, and Sir Stanley von Donop, the Master General of the Ordnance. Even more extraneous were two more field marshals, Kitchener, not yet secretary of state, and 82-year-old Lord Roberts. The need for this extraordinary meeting arose from the fact that, amazingly, at this very late stage, no one knew what the British army was going to do.

The views expressed by Haig and French are interesting, and the discrepancy between these views has to be noted because of its bearing on the reliability of Haig's account of the events of March 1918 with which this book is principally concerned.

Haig's narrative of the Council of War is one of the parts of his records put together after the war, in this case to cast the role of Sir John French, his predecessor as Commander-in-Chief, in an unfavourable light and his own role as an heroic one. According to Haig, French suggested that the Expeditionary Force would best be sent off to Antwerp, a destination that had never been discussed, to liaise with the Belgian army and possibly the Dutch army. The Germans had not violated the neutrality of the Netherlands – indeed, Holland remained neutral throughout the war – but it was widely expected that the German advance would be through the Netherlands. Haig's own contribution to the discussion cannot be ascertained with certainty. Haig did not maintain his diary in these days. His account of the meeting is contained in a subsequent memorandum headed 'Mobilisation':

> Sir John French gave in outline a prearranged plan which had been worked out between the British and French General Staffs. Briefly stated it was hoped that the Expeditionary Force would move simultaneously with the French, and would be concentrated behind the French left at Maubeuge by the fifteenth day of mobilisation. Then the

intention was that we move eastwards towards the Meuse, and act on the left of the French against the German right flank. We were now however late in mobilising and so this plan was no longer possible. He spoke about his hopes of now going to Antwerp and operating with the Belgian, possibly Dutch armies.

Haig said, 'Personally, I trembled at the reckless way Sir J French spoke about "the advantages" of the BEF operating from Antwerp against the powerful and still intact German Army!'

One of those present at the meeting and, indeed, the individual who had most influence on its outcome was Sir Henry Wilson. His role in determining what Britain did in August 1914 is explored later. His diary sums up the conference as 'an historic meeting of men mostly ignorant of their subject'. As well as referring to 'the desultory talk and strategy', he records the ignorance of some of the speakers who believed 'that *Liège was in Holland*'.[1]

Wilson's diaries are entertaining but not always reliable. Haig's diaries do not require to be read with so much caution but they are certainly not always accurate. They are never entertaining. They will be mentioned quite a lot and it is worth saying a little about them. Haig wrote up his diary daily, in manuscript. He wrote in a notebook, seven and a half inches by five and a half, made up of top pages followed by two carbon copies. Every top copy page was detachable. Haig kept the carbon copies and sent the top pages to Lady Haig by King's Messenger (who sometimes carried soup from France to London when Lady Haig needed nourishment). The carbon copies which Haig retained sometimes had corrections and notes added. Other relevant information was occasionally pasted on the reverse.

After the war, Haig revised the manuscript diary and Lady Haig typed up a typescript version. The process was sometimes more complicated and John Hussey has analysed the procedures adopted by the Haigs.[2]

The royal household encouraged Haig to keep them in the picture and on occasions Haig instructed his wife to send extracts to the Palace. The first time this happened, the aim was to promote Haig's appointment as Commander-in-Chief in place of Sir John French. He did the same thing at other stages when he felt that he was being criticised by politicians. Copies of the diary were also sometimes discreetly made available to people with a key role in forming opinion. According to Denis Winter, the complete 1914 diary, for instance, was handed by

Lady Haig to Conan Doyle.[3] Given then that the diaries were intended to influence events and not simply to record them, they must be read in a critical spirit.

At the time, it was not unusual for political and military personalities to edit diaries before making them available to the public and most of the changes which Haig made were simply to clarify obscurities. On one or two occasions, however, there were more significant changes, clearly intended to alter the historical record to ensure that he was seen as acting as he would have wished to act, rather than as he necessarily had acted.

I return to the Council of War and Haig's differences with French. After the war, by which time he and Haig were bitter enemies, French wrote – or, more precisely, collaborated in – a ghosted book, his controversial and bitter memoir *1914*. There, he said that Haig, at the council, 'suggested postponing any landing until the campaign had actively opened and we should be able to judge in which direction our cooperation would be most effective'.[4] The strength of Haig's reaction reveals how important to him the historical record was. He resented and denied French's story. After the publication of *1914*, Haig wrote to the War Office saying that French had misrepresented him: he had not asked that the BEF should be kept in Britain, watching and waiting, simply that some of its officers and non-commissioned officers should be kept back to train new troops.

French's claim was possibly exaggerated but was not without foundation. On 5 August, Haig wrote to his old boss, Lord Haldane, formerly Secretary of State for War and now Lord Chancellor. He asked:

> Would it not be better to begin at once to enlarge our Expedy. force by amalgamating less regular forces with it? In three months' time we shd. have quite a considerable army so that when we do take the field we can act decisively and dictate terms which will ensure lasting peace.
>
> I presume of course that France can hold on (even though her forces have to fall back from the frontier) for the necessary time for us to create an army of say 300,000.[5]

Immediately ahead of the war, Haig had indeed come to think that the Expeditionary Force, the BEF, should be used as the nucleus of a much greater army rather than being despatched to France on its own. He had therefore a doctrinal background that supports the French contention. He wrote as late as 4 August 1914:

I agree that we ought not to despatch our Expeditionary Force in a hurry to France. Possibly had there been a chance of supporting her from the very beginning, our help might have been decisive. That moment seems to have been allowed to pass. Now we must *make* an army large enough to intervene decisively – say 300,000.[6]

Between 5 and 6 August Haig changed his mind. At the resumed War Council meeting on 6 August, he was for going to France at once. Later, he airbrushed out his wavering on the first day. In his 'Memorandum of Opinions expressed by me at the War Council meetings held at 10, Downing Street, on 5 and 6 August 1914', which dates from after the war, Haig declared:

I certainly never 'suggested', as Field Marshal Lord French states on page 6 of his book 'postponing any landing until the campaign had actively opened etc . . .' On the contrary, I definitely stated that 'our best policy' at the time 'was to be ready to do as the French wished us [*sic*]'.[7]

Haig says that his contemporaneous notes were given at the time to Maurice Hankey, the Cabinet Secretary. Hankey did not preserve them but, on 25 July 1919, sent his own notes to Haig, saying that he could not see anything to support French. His own summary used exactly the same words as those used by Haig quoted above.

Maurice, later Sir Maurice and later still Lord, Hankey is such an important actor and observer in the events of the First World War – including those of March 1918 – that he deserves a digression by way of introduction rather than a mere footnote, even if the crucial role he played in British public affairs was generally in the wings rather than at the front of the stage. From a naval background, at the age of just 31 he became, in 1908, naval assistant secretary to the Committee of Imperial Defence. He was set to steam ahead on an unbroken course of military and administrative service for the rest of his working life. He became Secretary to the Committee in 1912 and continued as such until 1938. He was Secretary of the War Council and then of the War Cabinet and of the Imperial War Council. He was Cabinet Secretary from 1919 until 1938, the first holder of an office that he moulded to his own design and which, in its turn, moulded the character of modern government to a shape that was again his own design. His influence on the nature and culture of twentieth-century Cabinet government was enormous.

In the Second World War, he was a member of Chamberlain's War Cabinet but not of Churchill's, though he was a member of the latter's government. His diaries and writings are an essential source for First World War history, though his closeness to and admiration for Lloyd George flaws some of his judgements. He was tactful and restrained in public, entertaining and critically acute in private. He was a family man and a happy man, despite an austere regime of cold baths every morning, outdoor eating in all weathers and a diet of whole-wheat bread, raw vegetables, fresh fruit, eggs and nuts.*

In his diary, Sir Henry Wilson, like French, says that Haig wanted to wait for up to three months before deploying in France or Belgium, to allow a build-up of forces from the Empire.[8] However Haig's account is supported not only by Hankey but also by John Charteris, Haig's intelligence officer for most of the war and always his loyal supporter, who says that all his chief wanted to do was to weigh the arguments for delay against immediate embarkation before making his decision. It may be significant that Haig was confident enough to appeal to third-party witnesses for support. As well as Hankey, he wrote to General Sir Ian Hamilton. Hamilton chose not to become involved but did not contradict him.

Whatever view one takes on this issue, it is important, in the light of the debate over the history of March 1918, to see the lengths to which Haig would go to ensure that the account of his war which history would preserve would be that of a heroic, decisive commander.

Though Haig and French did not know it, the outcome of the council had been predetermined and their proposals were irrelevant. The Chief of the Imperial General Staff, Sir Charles Douglas, told the meeting that plans had already been made for embarkation at Newhaven, Southampton and Bristol, with landings at Le Havre, Boulogne and other French Channel ports. The French had arranged rolling stock and railway time-tables to coordinate these plans, which could not now be changed. This outcome was the achievement of one man, Sir Henry Wilson, and

---

* Haig also favoured an unappealing diet, including an early version of yoghurt, in a search for the secret of prolonged youth.

his entirely personal initiative consisting of close cooperation with the French General staff over several years before the war. So personal was his role that the French referred to the British army as '*l'Armée Double-Vay*', 'W Army'. The First World War was indeed pretty much Wilson's War. If, without Henry Wilson, Britain had fought in the traditional way, had fought a naval war with a small military element, there would have been fewer names on our war memorials but Germany would have won the war.

Henry Wilson, who will play an important part in the five days of March 1918, was sometimes called the ugliest man in the British army as a result of a wound he received from Burmese bandits. He was intelligent, witty, tall and quizzical. He was characteristically to be found bent over his interlocutors, engaging them with irresistible geniality. He had failed twice for Woolwich and three times for Sandhurst and only obtained a commission by the back-door route of two years in the militia. But he was far from brainless, and passed for entrance to Staff College with no difficulty: by 1895 he was the youngest Staff Officer in the army. He was profoundly sociable and enjoyed the company of politicians, a trait that caused him problems during his military career. Haig and others were suspicious of him and considered him as unreliable. Haig regarded him as a politician and not a soldier and, for Haig, a politician was synonymous with crooked dealing and a wrong sense of values.[9] Haig was too suspicious of Wilson to realise it but the latter was generously supportive of Haig and never plotted against him. The affable, extroverted Irishman was very different from the withdrawn and silent Scotsman. Wilson could not understand why Haig did not engage with those outside the narrow confines of his staff and trusted confidants.

Haig was not alone in regarding Wilson with suspicion. His mischievous sense of humour, his intellectual reach and his love of the company of politicians – he was said to get an erection whenever he came within half a mile of one – were bad enough. To that was added the opprobrium of first appearing to foment the Curragh Incident and then failing to support the mutineers.* Sir Sam Fay, a civilian railwayman of independent mind who took over the post of Director of Movements at the War

---

* The Curragh Incident or Mutiny is the description given to events in March 1914, when some Army Officers resigned, or threatened to do so, rather than assist in implementing the government's Home Rule policy in Ireland or suppress resistance by the Ulster Volunteers.

Office in 1917 and refused to wear a military uniform or remove his beard although his post carried the rank of General, complained that Wilson could argue with total conviction that a horse chestnut was the same thing as a chestnut horse. Major-General Sir Edward Spears, at the heart of liaison between the British and French Armies, loathed him and compared him to Quint, 'the semi-spooky entirely evil valet in Henry James's *The Turn of the Screw*'.[10] Wilson's command of big and broad ideas, as in his masterly lectures as Commandant at Camberley, drew enthusiastic audiences but separated him all the more from his more pedestrian colleagues.

After the war, Churchill recalled the skills that made Wilson popular with politicians and his ability at making complicated military issues clear to the layman:

> He wantonly pronounced grotesquely the names of French towns and Generals. In discussing the gravest matters he used the modes of levity. 'Prime Minister,' he began one day to the War Cabinet, at a meeting which I attended, 'Today I am Boche.' Then followed a penetrating description of the situation from the standpoint of the German Head-quarters. On another day he would be France or Bulgaria, and always out of this adaption there emerged, to my mind, the root of the matter in hand. But some Ministers were irritated. He did not go so far as Marshal Foch, who sometimes gave a military description in panto-mime; but their methods of displaying a war proposition had much in common.
>
> I can see him so clearly as I write, standing before the map in the Cabinet Room giving one of his terse telegraphese appreciations. 'This morning, Sir, a new battle ... This time it is we who have attacked. We have attacked with two armies – one British, one French. Sir Haig (his flippant name for the Commander-in-Chief) is in his train, Prime Minister, very uncomfortable, near the good city of Amiens. And Rawly is in his left hand and Debeney is in his right. Rawly is using 500 tanks. It is a big battle, and we thought you would not like us to tell you about it beforehand.'

Churchill then permits himself to stray from his narrative:

> We should be thankful that the future is veiled. I was to be present at another scene in this room. There was no Henry Wilson. The Prime

Minister and I faced each other, and on the table between us lay the pistols which an hour before had drunk this loyal man's blood.[11]

After the war Wilson did what he should perhaps have done earlier and went into politics, saying that he wanted to make mischief. He became Irish Secretary. He left that office hated by the Fenians and, on 21 July 1922, having performed the official unveiling of a war memorial at Liverpool Street Station, returned to his flat, wearing full military uniform and carrying a sword. As he reached his doorstep two Fenians closed with him. A pistol was fired at short range but missed its target. Wilson did not take advantage of the missed shot to take refuge in his flat. He turned and advanced on his assailants with a drawn sword, was hit by six bullets and was killed. A Roman death.

There is a touching little note in the manuscript papers of Brigadier-General Launcelot Kiggell* that tells us something about Wilson's charm – how, unlike Haig, he was loved by the French even when he was laughing at them – and something too about Kiggell's own lack of confidence:

> A spell-binding lecturer – always joking and amusing and informal – the only General who could meet politicians ('the frocks') on equal terms – he fascinated the French and could say outrageous things to them (eg 'we can't trust you French an inch' caused much laughter coming from him. What would have been the effect from Haig?!) I think the only VIP I ever felt completely at ease with. [12]

Staff talks had begun between Britain and France in 1906 under Grierson but gathered impetus in 1910 when Wilson became Director of Military Operations. Wilson became intimately involved in the talks in a very personal way. In a vacuum of planning, he and his colleagues enjoyed considerable freedom. The War Office and the Admiralty and many in the army were unaware of what was going on. His philosophy was that of two armies operating in the same theatre and in very close proximity – the British Expeditionary Force on the left flank of the French army. He spent much of his leaves in the years running up to war visiting France and cycling over the Franco-German frontier. He came to know France and the French countryside and the French people as a

---

* Haig's Chief of Staff for much of the war – we shall meet him again.

result of these visits, studying in great detail the topography of the land where fighting might be expected.

Before the war, military thinkers had tended to divide into 'with Belgium' and 'with France' schools of thought. The first of these reflected the traditional view and was favoured by Sir John French. It essentially involved strategy based on the northern flank of a joint line. The 'with France' school was a more modern development. It was less limited than the 'with Belgium' approach and was favoured by the general staff and especially Henry Wilson. His approach was a careful development of this philosophy. If it had not been for his work, it is difficult to see how mobilisation would have succeeded – no one else gave the matter of the geographical deployment of the Expeditionary Force any great thought.

Thus, at a meeting of the defence committee in 1911, in response to the Agadir crisis,* there was a great deal of squabbling between the Admiralty and the War Office. Wilson then set out the General Staff Plan for the deployment of the Expeditionary Force. This was the first the defence committee had heard of it. Maurice Hankey, in his capacity as Secretary of the Committee of Imperial Defence, recorded that Wilson had carried the day[13] and John Terraine, Haig's most devoted biographer, acknowledged the significance:

> The result was the acceptance of the (Henry) Wilson plan, *and without any full discussion or realisation of its implications* [Terraine's emphasis]. That this is what occurred is shown by the facts that, when war broke out, and those implications came closer into view, it transpired that neither the recent CIGS (French), nor the C in C of I Corps (Haig) were fully aware of what had been decided; two cabinet ministers (Morley and Burns) resigned as soon as they understood; and a number of other ministers (chief among them Churchill and Lloyd George) were never able to bring themselves to accept those implications, with which they should have been familiar for years.[14]

The facts that Morley and Burns resigned at the outbreak of war and that Churchill and Lloyd George did not embrace the implications of what Wilson had been arranging were due to the pre-war staff talks with the French having been – quite amazingly – kept secret from the rest of

---

* When a confrontation between France and Germany in Morocco threatened a general war.

the Cabinet by Asquith, the prime minister, and Sir Edward Grey, the Foreign Secretary. The plans that the two staffs evolved were not binding and there was no formal treaty; but they were the only plans in existence and it was thus that Sir Henry Wilson dictated the nature of the war which Britain was to fight.

2

The War to the End of 1917

Thus *l'Armée W* went to France, as Henry Wilson had envisaged, to fight where he intended it to fight. The British Expeditionary Force, the BEF, was possibly the best-trained army that Britain ever sent to war, but it was a very small army – four infantry divisions and one cavalry division with two more infantry divisions following fairly swiftly. Wilson knew how insignificant his little force was. When he was Commandant of the Staff College, he made his point with typical punch: 'There is no problem in European politics to which the answer is six British infantry divisions and a cavalry division.' At the end of the war, Haig would command not six but sixty divisions. In the long run, the size of the early BEF, the army that the Kaiser was alleged to have described as 'a contemptible little army', was not important. Before the war, Foch was once asked, 'What is the smallest number of British soldiers that you would require?' He replied, 'One – and we shall make sure that he is killed.' The presence of even a very small British army on European soil represented a commitment to a land war, an abandonment of the 'British way of war'.

The BEF may have been a small army but it was Britain's only army. The nation was proud of it, and what it did in 1914 dominated British coverage of the war news. But, in 1914, the fight on the Western Front was largely a conflict between Germany and France. France had 62 infantry and 20 cavalry divisions and Germany 87 and 11. By the time the first British shot was fired, near the Mons-Condé Canal, the French and Germans were already locked in what is known as the Battle of the Frontiers, in Alsace and Verdun. In the course of these awful engagements, France lost almost 250,000 men, 70,000 of them dead. Daily losses exceeded those of Britain on the first day of the Somme in 1916.

In open, Napoleonic warfare – not yet the war of the trenches – in the five months from August to December 1914, France suffered well over one million casualties. Germany suffered 800,000. It is extraordinary that France, with a smaller population and a lower birth rate than Germany, was able to accept punishment on this scale and go on to sustain the conflict throughout the years that followed.

When the BEF finally linked up with French Fifth Army in late August, the French Chief of Staff greeted them: 'At last you are here . . . If we are beaten we will owe it all to you'.[1] Sir John French, commanding the BEF, was no more generous to his allies – he blamed the French for the retreat which followed, saying that the Commander of Fifth Army had started to retreat without telling him.

That retreat followed Britain's first engagement, at Mons. At the time, Mons was hailed as a great victory. It was neither that nor really a set-piece battle at all. It resulted from an encounter with von Kluck, who commanded Germany's formidable First Army. The encounter was followed, as far as Britain was concerned, by a series of uncoordinated actions which delayed the German advance by no more than a day, for British losses of 1,600 men, many of them taken prisoner. Elsewhere that day, the French were engaged in far greater battles with far larger casualty counts, at Charleroi and in the Ardennes.

Mons was a comparative sideshow but its consequences were serious. Sir John French lost such confidence as he may have had in his allies and, in particular, in General Lanrezac, on his right, 'a Staff College pedant' who was withdrawing his Fifth Army, forcing the BEF to retreat or risk exposing a flank. Withdrawal was pretty well inevitable in the face of von Kluck's well-supplied juggernaut.

French's reaction was to plan to take his men back from the front to rest and recuperate – going, indeed, as far as Le Havre from where they could, if needed, be taken safely back to Britain. This default reaction should be remembered – we shall have to consider whether Haig, French's successor, also planned for a similar retreat in 1918. I shall argue that he did, informed by the same instincts and indeed constrained by essentially the same government instructions, to preserve the army he commanded, as French had in 1914.

Johnnie French, as he was still known even after he became Field Marshal Lord French of Ypres, was loved by his men as Haig never was. He was, indeed, an attractive character. He was not of obviously military appearance. He would have been a sailor had he not been defeated by seasickness. In formal dress, he was always said to resemble a walrus, still essentially a marine creature – he was short and chose to wear an unusually long tunic that emphasised his lack of stature. He was nonetheless a ladies' man.

He contracted an unwise early marriage. Had he been divorced, that would have been the end of his military career but his wife – possibly for a financial inducement – agreed to appear to be the guilty party. He subsequently got married again – this time to Eleanora Selby-Lowndes, one of eight sisters known as the Belles of Bletchley. Affairs preceded and followed his marriage, none of which appears to have bothered his wife. He did, however, break the rules by having affairs with the wives of brother officers. When he was Commander of the 19th Hussars in India, he took what wits called 'French Leave' and went off to the hills with one of the wives. He was cited for adultery and, for the second time, was lucky that his career did not end. During the First World War he had a final affair with Mrs Winifred Bennett, as tall and elegant as he was portly and absurd. Unperturbed by their ill-matched appearance, they found strength in an ardent, romantic love affair – 'two shipwrecked souls', as French said, 'who have found one another'.[2] On the eve of the Battle of Neuve Chapelle, he wrote to her: 'Tomorrow I shall go forward with my war-cry of "Winifred".'[3]

The next threat to French's career was financial mismanagement. He was imprudent, invested unwisely when he had money and borrowed when he had not. In 1893, he was on half-pay, possibly as a result of the Indian divorce scandal. Had he continued on half-pay for two more years, he would have been compulsorily retired and his military career would have been over. He filled his time with long walks and, as he could not afford a horse, took up cycling. 'He was too self-conscious to be seen practising on a road, so he would march his sons to a secluded spot and then enlist their aid. He never mastered the process of mounting, and would disappear into the distance, hopping wildly alongside his machine, but failing to get astride it.'[4]

At one stage the young Douglas Haig, who saw French as a wagon to which his star could be hitched, made a substantial loan to him, instructing his trustees not to press for repayment. It was a wise investment. It came to French when he was within about twenty-four hours from bankruptcy. It was not repaid until about 1909. In the meantime, Haig and French had gone to the South African War, where Haig was French's protégé. Haig had very real abilities and would have risen high in the army even without French, but French's friendship during the war certainly accelerated his rise and thus helped to create the circumstances that would result in Haig's superseding his mentor in 1915. Haig and French fell out dramatically and irrevocably during the First World War but, in 1902, the older man gave his young colleague a gold flask inscribed: 'A very small memento, my dear Douglas, of our long and tried friendship proved "in sunshine and in shadow". JF'.

The South African War made French. He came to popular attention largely as the result of a successful but small engagement in the course of the war at Elandslaagte. Successes in the war were few and far between and French, like Roberts and Kitchener, but not like Haig, was idolised by the public at large at a time when the photographs of successful generals were circulated like those of footballers in a later age. After his success in Kohlsberg in South Africa, an appalling verse was published:

> 'E's so tough and terse,
> 'E don't want no bloomin' nurse:
> And 'e ain't 'ad one reverse,
> 'Ave yer French?

As the war approached, French was appointed Chief of the Imperial General Staff (despite his lack of staff experience) and was promoted Field Marshal on the king's insistence. He was designated as the commander of British troops in France in a war which was expected pretty much on an annual basis. At the last stage, there was another setback. He was implicated in the Curragh Incident. His future became precarious. Ramsay MacDonald, the future Labour prime minister, reported that on the night of 2 August 1914, two days before war was declared, he was at the house of Sir George Riddell, the newspaper proprietor. 'After supper they want upstairs to Riddell's smoking room. The telephone bell rang, and Riddell picked up the receiver. All they heard was: "That you Johnnie? How are you? . . . Oh yes it is going to be war . . . Oh yes, fancy you not having heard. You are to command it all right." It was Sir John French at the other end, who was learning of his command from the Proprietor of the *News of the World*.'⁵

So French's luck had held out. He was to command the British Expeditionary Force. But the qualities that had endeared him to his men in South Africa made him a very unsuitable commander of part of an allied force. He disliked his French allies and spoke very little of their language. He remained a good regimental commander. Even as Commander-in-Chief, he took time to visit wounded men, and their plight and anguish caused him great pain. But that was not the correct role for a Commander and, indeed, in the chaos of the Retreat from Mons, much confusion derived from the fact that he was often away from his headquarters, visiting hospitals or units in the line. He liked to get out and put heart into his troops (which he was good at). As a consequence, the two corps commanders, Smith-Dorrien and Haig, found it difficult to obtain instructions. GHQ staff work was appalling, intelligence was frequently not shared with the two corps that constituted the British army, orders were often issued too late. Thus the Great Retreat was uncoordinated, rapid and executed in conditions verging on panic.

French felt betrayed by France, a nation which he did not regard as a reliable ally with whom to continue fighting a war. His allies thought no more of him than he did of them. They regarded him as irresolute and nervous, hesitant to commit his army, always looking to his rear. He rarely actively supported them and then only under pressure from London or in the face of emotional appeals from the French commander, Joffre, a strong imperturbable man of the south.

Following the Great Retreat, Joffre's liaison officer at French's GHQ reported that the BEF 'has lost all cohesion', was finished as a fighting force for the time being and could not be relied on. This was pretty much French's view too. He could see no option other than to escape to the Seine or, preferably, the coast, to rest and regroup. One of his telegrams to the War Cabinet caused such alarm that Kitchener, now Secretary of State for War, was sent out on 1 September 1914 to stiffen his backbone and order him not to desert his French allies. Kitchener and French had never got on and French was particularly angry that Kitchener, here in his civilian capacity and not as French's superior officer, chose to come out wearing his Field Marshal's uniform – as he did throughout the war until he went down with the *Hampshire* in 1916 (when the ship sank, he was wearing a Burberry trench coat).

Joffre made his stand on the River Marne. Von Kluck had made a potentially fatal mistake, wheeling to the east and, in doing so, leaving his right flank exposed to a counter-attack from the south. Despite the opportunity offered, the pleas from the French commander and his directions from Kitchener, French continued to stand back from the engagement. Finally, on 5 September, Joffre called in person to persuade French to keep his forces in the field in support of the French stand. The encounter was emotional and pivotal. Joffre gave an utterly convincing picture of how he could turn back the Germans and passionately appealed to Sir John's honour. French rose to the occasion. He attempted to reply in French, failed and said to an aide, 'Damn it, I cannot explain. Tell him that all men can do, our fellows will do.'

The BEF spent the next eight days pursuing the retreating German Armies, albeit at a judicious distance behind the French. Finally, the Germans stopped and turned, and pursuit turned into confrontation on the River Aisne. There, the armies fought to a standstill and dug in. The war of movement was over. Trench warfare began at the Aisne and, by the end of the year, the trenches extended, in the phrase to which historians are always drawn, to the Swiss border in one direction and the English Channel in the other.

1915

In the following year, 1915, Joffre attacked the German salient near Compiègne. Britain fought to the north, at Neuve Chapelle. A month later, in April, the Germans opened the second battle of Ypres, when the British line threatened to break and a gap of six kilometres was created in the Allied line. Germany failed to consolidate their success and, at the cost of withdrawal, the Franco-British line was repaired.

In September Britain attacked at Loos. This battle set records for the British army in terms of the number of men engaged and the level of casualties suffered. It was a battle which the British and in particular Haig did not want to fight, and it was fought on ground which both he and Sir John French thought unsuitable. The battle took place for the sake of the Alliance, acknowledging that France's contribution to the war had been far greater than Britain's. Indeed, in 1915 alone, nearly as many French soldiers died as British soldiers did throughout the whole of the Second World War.[6]

To demonstrate Britain's commitment, French agreed to participate at Loos in the joint attack, placing his forces in the extreme right of the French First Army. John Terraine described the battle of Loos as 'the true beginning of the martyrdom of the British Army'. By the end of the battle, almost a third of the Staff College graduates in the Expeditionary Force had been killed. The BEF was now being bulked up by the addition of lightly trained and unseasoned Territorials and volunteers.

At Loos, Britain did make something of a breakthrough but, like the Germans at Second Ypres, they were unable to consolidate it. Fifteenth Division made the furthest advance of any division since the outbreak of war. The problem was a lack of reserves. Loos was Haig's battle and Haig thought that what should have been his victory had been denied him by the way in which French, as Commander-in-Chief, had handled the reserves. French was now vulnerable to the ambitions of this younger officer, a better French speaker, though also with little liking for the French race.

The issue of the reserves at Loos was more complicated than Haig allowed but French was done for by now. Haig, so impressed by French before the South African War, had concluded that his benefactor had to go. As early as 11 August 1914, he recorded in his diary that he had been speaking to the king about French:

> I felt it my duty to do so, that from my experience with Sir John in the South African War he was certain to do his utmost to carry out orders which the Government might give him. I had grave doubts, however, whether his temper was sufficiently even or his military knowledge sufficiently thorough to enable him to discharge properly the very difficult duties which will devolve upon him during the coming operations with our Allies on the Continent. In my own heart, I know that French is quite unfit for this great command at a time of crisis in our Nation's history. But I thought it sufficient to tell the King that I had 'doubts' about the selection.

Two days later he went further:

> [French's] military ideas often shocked me when I was his Chief of Staff during the South African War . . . With all this knowledge of the Chief . . . behind me, I have grave reasons for being anxious about what happens to us in the great adventure in which we are now going to start this very night.

Now, after Loos, Haig briefed against his old Chief much more widely. He wrote to Kitchener and, when Haldane, the former Secretary of State for War and Haig's old chief, was sent out by the

Cabinet on 9 October to find out what had gone wrong at Loos, Haig spoke to him at length.

He also remained in touch with the Palace. The king's secretary made enquiries of Sir William Robertson, French's Chief of Staff, to see whether he felt it was time for French to go. A week or so later, the king was in France and asked Haig to dine with him. Haig's diary: 'I ... thought strongly, that, for the sake of the Empire, French ought to be removed. I, personally, was ready to do my duty in any capacity and of course would serve under anyone who was chosen for his military skill to be C in C.' What was Haig truly up to? He was an ambitious man and ambition is perfectly honourable. He certainly believed, and most observers would have agreed, that French was a good regimental commander but not a good Commander-in-Chief. He also knew that, if French were deposed, he would get his job. Before the year ended, he had it and a friendship proved and celebrated in sunshine had dissolved forever in sorrow.

The man charged to see whether it was time for French to go, William Robertson, always known as 'Wully', is the only man in British military history to have proved Napoleon right about the marshal's baton in every soldier's knapsack. He not only rose from the rank of private soldier to become field marshal but also did so from an unpromising social background. His parents were said to have been illegitimate. Robertson left school at the age of thirteen and went into domestic service as a footman. When he went into the army he was – pretty unusually for those days – recognised for his ability and given a commission. He chose to be gazetted into the cavalry, where the gap between his background and those of his colleagues was particularly marked. He seems to have had no chip on his shoulder. Unlike his fellow officers, who lived on private incomes and enjoyed their pig-sticking, Robertson applied himself to his career, with a self-disciplined focus on his profession, working while others slept. He learnt not only Hindi, but also Urdu, Persian, Punjabi and Pashtu. To all these, he added French and German. He also had time to win prizes for tent-pegging, swordsmanship, fencing and other contests, including the prize for the best officer at arms.

> These achievements [he said], such as they were, were mainly due to keeping myself physically fit – not an easy thing to do in the plains of India unless one is blessed with a strong constitution, and is careful to safeguard it by temperate habits and suitable exercise.

I claim no credit for pursuing these habits, because I had not the wherewithal to do otherwise. Water was the only drink I could afford, while for smoking I had to be content with a fixed amount of tobacco and cheroots at two shillings a hundred. It was not altogether agreeable to be seen drinking water at the mess when others were drinking champagne, or to defer smoking to leaving the mess because pipes were not allowed, but it had to be done.[7]

After India he went to Staff College and then to the Intelligence Staff of the War Office. He worked in Intelligence at the start of the South African War.

Despite the wide range of foreign languages in which he could express himself, he never lost his regional English accent. When, in the early years of the First World War, Horace Smith-Dorrien was told that he was being removed from command of Second Army, Wully is said to have announced, ''Orace, y'er for 'ome.'[8] His colleagues had lots of fun with variants such as, 'Well, 'Orace, I'm afraid you 'ave to 'op it.'

At the outset of the First World War, Wully, as Quartermaster General, came out of the Retreat from Mons with credit, having taken pains to ensure that the retreating army was properly fed and supplied. In January 1915, he became Chief of Staff in France and, later in that year, he moved to London to become Chief of the Imperial General Staff, CIGS, the military overseer of the British armies. By then, Haig had superseded French as Commander-in-Chief of the armies in France and, until Robertson was deposed at the beginning of 1918, the two men worked closely together. Although their names tend to be associated in histories of the Great War like a music hall double act and, although their views on strategy were similar – both were convinced 'Westerners', believing that the Germans could only be defeated on the Western Front and that men and *matériel* should not be wasted on what they regarded as side-shows like Italy – they were very different. Robertson had a sense of humour and could be self-deprecating as Haig never was. Haig, for his part, had no great affection for Robertson. When he heard of his appointment as CIGS, Haig's diary response fell far below any acceptable level:

I am sure that it is good for the Government and the country to have such a man in authority at the War Office at this time. He means very well and will succeed I am sure. How much easier, though, it is to work with a gentleman.

Robertson's chief difficulty, as increasingly was Haig's, was in dealing with Lloyd George, Minister for Munitions, Minister for War and then prime minister, and those like him who opposed what seemed to them an unimaginative persistence in the bloodletting on the Western Front. Robertson was laconic and abrupt. In Cabinet, when Lloyd George would say to him, 'I have heard it said that . . .' and put to him a proposition with which he disagreed, Robertson simply slammed his ruler on the table and said, 'I've 'eard different.'

But, like Haig, Robertson was a good organiser and the general staff under him was an efficient machine. He held it to be his duty to have complete strategic control over all fronts and he had that control. The complaint against him was that his knowledge was entirely book-learned and that he would not deviate from those principles which he expounded so slowly and deliberately. Churchill was particularly irritated by Robertson: 'He had no ideas of his own, but a sensible judgement negative in bias. He represented professional formalism expressed in the plainest terms.'[9] On another occasion, when he discovered that Robertson had described the Cabinet as 'poltroons' (defined in the *Oxford English Dictionary* as 'spiritless cowards, mean-spirited, worthless creatures'), Churchill responded by referring to 'General Robertson (who had never himself at any time led even a troop in action, and whose war duties involved him in no more risk than many clerks)'.[10]

French politicians were frustrated by Robertson's stolid intransigence and called him 'General Non Non'. To the mercurial and imaginative Lloyd George, Robertson's principles were platitudinous. But, to balance the record, it is worth remembering that Hankey, who as Secretary to the War Cabinet knew Robertson and understood him as well as anyone and who, because of his closeness to Lloyd George, might have been expected to have been blinded to Robertson's good qualities, said that 'taking him all in all he was within his limitations a rugged, dogged, able and likeable man'.[11]

Throughout his time as CIGS, Robertson never failed to defend Haig. He tried to alert the Commander-in-Chief to criticism from the politicians and never did anything to fertilise these criticisms. When Robertson himself was being forced out, even a threat of resignation on Haig's part would have saved him. No muscle moved.

But, by that time, at the beginning of 1918, Haig's support for Robertson was distinctly lukewarm – he thought that he was proving unreliable on Western Front policy. Haig wrote to Henry Wilson on 5

February 1918, saying that Robertson 'has not resolutely adhered to the policy of concentration on the Western Front – he has said that this is his policy but he has allowed all kinds of resources to be diverted to distant theatres at the bidding of his political masters'.

1916

In 1916, Haig, though he had now superseded Sir John French, had, all the same, to fight French's battle. The Battle of the Somme, which opened on 1 July 1916, germinated from a seed planted at the Allied conference at Chantilly at the end of 1915 when French was still Commander-in-Chief. The conference was a pretty desperate one. Britain and France had done badly in 1915. Some say that their strategy was in shambles.[12] Although Italy had joined the Allies, Bulgaria had joined the Central Powers. The naval assault on the Dardanelles had failed, as had the landings at Gallipoli.

When Joffre talked through the Chantilly plans with Haig on 29 December 1915, what was intended was a great Allied attack on either side of the Somme, on a front 60 miles wide. But the purpose of the Somme and the nature of the battle, and the nature of Britain's role in it, changed with the opening of the Battle of Verdun early in 1916.

This battle was the outcome of the conclusion by the German commander, Erich von Falkenhayn, that the way to victory lay in knocking 'England's best sword [out of her hand by] bleeding France to death' at Verdun. His decision to attack the very strongest fortress in the whole of France was, on the face of it, bizarre but he knew that France would defend this iconic citadel to the last man. A huge offensive on the French line 200 miles east of the Somme began when the Battle of Verdun opened on 21 February 1916. By the time it ended on 18 December, it was the longest battle of the First World War. The total casualties are estimated at 714,231 – 377,231 French and 337,000 German. One estimate puts the number of casualties closer to one million.

And, yet, while France was haemorrhaging at Verdun in late March, Wully Robertson was so biased or uninformed as to declare that Joffre had 'no idea of ever taking the offensive if he couldn't get other people to take it for him'.[13] This is an astounding reflection of national self-preoccupation, a phenomenon which did not end with the end of the war. At Verdun, France fought alone. For France, the defence of Verdun was essential not only for tactical reasons but for strong symbolic reasons too. It is to the enduring credit of the French army and nation that morale never cracked fatally but the effect of Verdun on France for the rest of the war and, indeed, between the wars was immense. Its legacy was the defeat of 1940.

In British mythology, the Somme was Britain's battle and Haig commanded it. In fact, Foch was appointed to coordinate the battle. As it became clear that the main effort, although far from the only one, would come from Britain, 'French generals understood that the change in preponderance of force from the experienced French to the novice British would likely lead to a "narrow-front battle".'[14] The French doctrine, reinforced by their observation of German tactics at Verdun, was that broad-front battles were best but that narrow-front ones were easier to run. The French Official History recorded that Joffre found Britain's insistence on narrow-fronts frustrating. Haig would not have warmed to France's condescending assessment of her inexperienced ally.

British proprietorship of the Somme in the national memory shows just how partial such traditions can be. By the end of the battle, more French soldiers had taken part than British and Commonwealth troops combined.[15] Britain remembers the Somme (where her casualties were about 420,000) much more than Verdun. The fact that eight French divisions took part in the Somme, suffering about 194,000 casualties, is very often overlooked. So too is the fact that, on the first day of the Somme, not only was there a major British offensive in which casualties totalled some 60,000 but also an important defeat of the German Second Army by French Sixth Army in the south. Britain now sees the first day of the Somme as a disaster. But Joffre was said to be 'beaming' with France's success on 1 July.[16] France captured most of the goals for the day and took 8,000 prisoners in the first 72 hours.

Haig's great error was to continue the battle for far too long for any good that it was doing; but it had done some good. The battle was notable for the use of air power, and the tank also appeared on the battlefield. Kitchener's New Armies were now present in numbers. By the time the battle was closed down, Allied forces had penetrated 10 kilometres beyond the German front line, taking more ground than at any time since the battle of the Marne in 1914. Perhaps most important of all, as far as Britain was concerned, British commanders, at every level, were learning lessons and drawing conclusions which caused changes in tactics which would deliver results later in the war.

1917

By 1917, the British army in France and Belgium had grown to its maximum size. It was still, however, only two-thirds of the size of the French army. The French troops, having borne the main burden of the war, were now weary and, after a huge offensive in April 1917 on the Chemin des Dames, prolonged in the face of very heavy losses – 100,000 casualties in a week – French soldiers refused to take part in further offensive action. The French Commander Nivelle was replaced by Pétain. Pétain combined pretty severe disciplinary action with an acknowledgement of the state of the morale of his troops. France stood on the defensive for the rest of the year to avoid casualties and to rebuild its spirit.

Pétain is important to this narrative because he was Haig's fellow-commander in March 1918, when together they faced the onslaught of the *Kaiserschlacht*. His strengths and weaknesses there will be discussed later, together with what he did and did not do, as opposed to what Haig said he did. For the moment, by way of general appraisal, it can be said that he was an able manager of warfare who understood his men. He had tactical insight. Although he remained committed to broad-front attacks, he was even more committed to limited objectives. Alastair Horne has observed:

> It might well be said that without Foch and his spirit of *l'attaque*, the war would not have been won in 1918; on the other hand without Pétain in 1917 it would almost certainly have been lost . . . Pétain may have had no strikingly original strategic views on how the First World War should be fought; however, he knew better than most of the other war lords on either side how it should *not* be fought.[17]

Finally, it would be wise for historians to remember, as *ex parte* Haig supporters do not when they study the events of March 1918 and as almost everyone does not when the events of 1940 and succeeding years are taken into account, that, after the end of the First World War, Pétain enjoyed, perhaps even more than Joffre or Foch, senior Marshals of France, the adulation of his fellow countrymen.

Britain had taken part in the April 1917 offensive, her contribution being at Arras, which met with success which could not be exploited. The main British offensive during that year was at Third Ypres, beginning with an attack on Messines Ridge on 7 June and continuing until

November. This offensive had originally been planned as a combined operation, involving army, navy and air force. In the event, the naval element was omitted. British casualties were more than 300,000 and Germany's about 260,000. It is estimated that the battle cost the lives of 35 British men for every metre of ground gained. Haig was much criticised for prolonging the offensive. There remains a question posed by Tim Harrington, the very able Chief of Staff to General Plumer, who commanded Second Army at Third Ypres, that no one has been quite able to answer. Once the offensive had been launched, '[w]here', asked Harrington, 'short of the [Passchendaele] Ridge, could the offensive have been halted?' The question is a good one. But even Haig's most loyal supporters admit that Third Ypres went on far, far too long. The Somme, in the previous year, was not at the time regarded as the disaster it is so often represented as nowadays – it was Third Ypres that damaged Haig's reputation. After it, he never had the confidence of the government in London, whose primary objective was now to limit his capacity to preside over bloody and unprofitable offensives.

As Third Ypres ended, Britain used massed tanks for the first time at Cambrai. British forces got further in six hours than they had done at Third Ypres in four months. There were, however, no resources available either to exploit the Cambrai success or to launch more Cambrais.*

A significant and appropriate note on which to conclude this brief summary of the principal operations on the Western Front from 1914 to 1917 is the fact that, in a German counter-offensive on 30 November (which recovered all the ground gained at Cambrai), the Germans, for the first time on the Western Front, used massed storm troopers and infiltration tactics – a warning of what would be faced in 1918.

---

* But the reaction to the lack of follow-up to Cambrai reveals how ready, by this stage in the war, even supporters of Haig and the High Command were to wonder if the war was being directed competently. *The Times*, owned by Haig's champion, Northcliffe, while recognising that too often '[t]he merest breath of criticism on any military operation is far too often dismissed as an "intrigue" against the Commander-in-chief', demanded on this occasion a 'prompt, searching and complete' investigation into what had gone wrong.

Part Two

The Approach to the Spring Offensive

3

Haig

BEFORE STUDYING WHAT he did in the critical days in March 1918, let us look briefly at the personality of the British Commander-in-Chief. John French's successor, Sir Douglas Haig, was very different from his predecessor. Where French looked unmilitary, even absurd, Haig was every inch a general. He was tall and good-looking in an impassive way, his face dominated by a meticulously groomed moustache. His uniform was always immaculate. He carried himself with dignity. Without charisma, he was all the same an impressive figure.

Haig was a Lowland Scot from the family of the whisky firm that carried his name. Some have suggested that he remained conscious of an association with trade which was unusual in the Victorian professional army but it is more likely that it was his unconcealed ambition that kept him aloof and apart from his brother officers. When he was at Staff College, they scrambled to avoid sitting beside him at breakfast. Where French was loved by his men, Haig was respected. Where French believed that war was waged by intuition, for Haig, the art of war lay in learning lessons from the past. He uncritically accepted what he read, even in the quarterly magazines, and, for him, the lessons he learned from diligent study of Napoleon's campaigns and the American Civil War were to be applied and not to be criticised. Above all, they told him that conflict consisted of three phases – encounter, wearing down and breakthrough. He looked for this tripartite sequence in all of the great battles he fought in the course of the war and when, one after another, they failed to produce breakthrough, he applied the analysis to the war as a whole. In his Final Despatch of 1919, he simplified the convulsions of the war years by characterising them as an encounter in 1914, a wearing down for the next four years and a breakthrough in 1918. Thus he never needed to revise his opinions.

Douglas Haig's reputation has undulated over the years. When he died in January 1928, there was a massive outpouring of sympathy.

Two thousand, five hundred people passed his coffin in St Columba's Church, Pont Street, London, where it lay for two days. The official funeral on 3 February was, to all intents and purposes, a state funeral. The three eldest sons of the king walked behind the gun carriage that bore the coffin, together with two marshals of France. Huge crowds attended the ceremonial. Nothing remotely similar had taken place or would take place for any of the other First World War leaders. Indeed, among the Second World War leaders, only Churchill's funeral eclipsed Haig's.

While the ceremony took place at Westminster Abbey, simultaneous services took place throughout the United Kingdom – something that did not happen for Churchill. The coffin was then taken to Scotland and lay in St Giles Cathedral while 70,000 of Haig's countrymen passed by.

Britain had won the war that threatened to bring down the Empire on which the sun never set and Haig was the soldier who had won it. In the aftermath of the war, to criticise Haig would have been to criticise the effort in which so many men had died. There was no criticism. Streets and railway engines were named after Haig. Children were given his names. Statues were erected.

Little change took place in his assessment until the 1960s. Then scattered volleys which had been fired in the interwar years by people like Basil Liddell Hart and Major General JFC Fuller* were reinforced by an impenetrable critical barrage. The publication in 1952 of Haig's private papers provided some ammunition. They were followed by Alan Clark's *The Donkeys* and *Oh, What a Lovely War!*, first in Joan Littlewood's Theatre Workshop Production and then in Richard Attenborough's film. The new critical approach to Haig was carried forward into much of the literature of the next 20 years, both in the form of history and in fiction, and the picture of the First World War commanders which emerged was largely pure satire, a picture of stupid, callous, vain technophobes. Haig presides, personally ambitious and uninterested in finding an alternative to fighting methods which slaughtered his men and the Germans in indiscriminate confusion. The myth was consolidated in *Blackadder Goes Forth*. Very funny, but not history, incredibly the programme was recommended for the GCSE syllabus.

---

* The military theorist Basil Liddell Hart is the subject of a later footnote. JFC Fuller was also a military commentator of great influence, arguing, like Liddell Hart, for the mechanisation of war. During the Second World War, he was suspected of fascist sympathies. After the war, he maintained that the wrong side had won – the suspicions appear to have been well founded.

So powerful is the image which has been created and so frequent is an approach to the history of the First World War made through the writings of the war poets that it remains to be seen if revisionist historians will ever succeed in establishing a more nuanced portrait. There have been a number of such historians. The first was John Terraine. His book, *Douglas Haig, The Educated Soldier* (sometimes described even by Terraine's admirers as 'Haigiography'), published as far back as 1963, has been followed by others. An 'educated' soldier, in the jargon of Haig's youth, meant a serious soldier who sought to study and master his profession. Most of the officers who joined the British army in Haig's time had no such pretentions – they were moneyed amateurs whose aim was simply to live an agreeable, gentlemanly life, with time for country pursuits. The subtitle to the French translation of Terraine's book, '*soldat de métier*', 'Soldier by Profession', describes Haig's approach. Others have described Haig as the 'Architect of Victory'.

This revisionist approach has demonstrated that a huge change took place in the nature of the British army between 1915 and 1918, a 'learning curve' which resulted in the all-arms approach that allowed the British army to deliver victory in 1918. In 1914, the infantry relied very heavily on rifle, and gunnery was elementary and worked on line-of-sight. Within two years of the start of the war, the old, professional British Expeditionary Force had largely been replaced by raw troops, volunteers and conscripts who had to learn to fight a kind of war that had never been envisaged. In the course of the next two years, they learned. This amalgam of various trends and new tactical thinking came together to favour the intelligent use of small, multi-skilled units, relying far less on the rifle than before, adapting movements to terrain and exercising individual initiative. It has been said that, by the last months of the war, 'British tactics had effectively reached a pitch that would scarcely be surpassed for at least thirty years thereafter'.[1] The war that was being fought in these last three months was very much the kind of war that would be fought between 1939 and 1945. Haig was not personally involved in every detail of the technical change but he presided over it and he was fascinated by it.

In addition, he was responsible for nearly three million men and half a million animals. The British military presence in France was equivalent to a conurbation six times more populous than the Birmingham of the time and only a third less populous than London, then the largest city in Europe. Haig had to feed, supply and move this huge body of men. To do so he had to build roads and lay railway tracks.[2]

Whether those who approach the history of the Great War through the war poets or *Blackadder* will ever agree with more serious historians is questionable but those who study the war as history are now largely agreed that Haig was a good Commander-in-Chief. Lloyd George and Churchill, who would both have greatly loved to dump Haig, each admitted that there was no one to match him. Smuts* and Hankey, who were sent out to France by the Cabinet to find an alternative, came to the same conclusion. And that is not to say that Haig was simply the best of a bad bunch. It would be fatuous so to characterise the leaders of one of the major armies of the world at that time. Even if the criticisms I make of Haig in this book are held to be proved, that will not significantly diminish his status.

We have seen something of the respective contributions to the war of the two Allied armies on the Entente side.† Before considering how together they faced the spring onslaught, we shall examine the tensions between them and how each army saw the other.

---

* Jan Christiaan Smuts, the Boer commander who accommodated so well to the outcome of the South African War that he became a loyal servant of the Empire. A member of the British War Cabinet in the First World War and of the Imperial War Cabinet in the Second, he was the only man to sign treaties that ended both of these global conflicts. Smuts was prime minister of the Union of South Africa from 1919 to 1924 and again from 1939 to 1948.
† The Entente Powers were France, Britain and (until 1917) Russia. They confronted the Central Powers, Germany and Austro-Hungary. The Triple Alliance consisted of the Central Powers plus Italy but, despite the alliance, Italy chose to stand apart from the war until 1915, when she opted to join the Entente. In 1939, after some similar wavering, she made the wrong choice.

4

How the French Saw the British

WHEN FRANCE LOOKED at her ally, she inevitably started on a premise that focused on the fact that the British army historically had been a small army, largely used for colonial skirmishes. It had only recently been reshaped as a Continental war was seen to be approaching and the most effective Secretary of State for War Britain has ever had, Lord Haldane, sought to create a modern, professional and effective army. The institutions of such an army, the Committee of Imperial Defence and a Staff College, for instance, had been established only a few years before the war. By the time war broke out, as a result of Haldane and a small number of serious officers who worked with him – including, notably, Douglas Haig – Britain's army was highly trained and competent.

But it was unproved and it was very small. Although it displayed great professionalism, even in the first year of the war, it was almost insignificant during that year by comparison with the size of the French army and the role that the French army played in halting the German advance. Moreover, as has been seen, Sir John French, as Commander-in-Chief, gave a very poor account of himself and did not deploy his army to best effect.

In these circumstances, the French were very dismissive. They thought the British did not understand 'solidarity, were slow on the move, obsessed by the importance of the Channel ports and generally simply did not take the war seriously enough'. The British saw the war, said the French, as a bit of a game. They had gone off to play football on the beach after being relieved by the French in the First battle of Ypres. General Fayolle, commanding French Sixth Army beside the British on the Somme in 1916, touched on the long-held view that Britain liked to stand aside and watch her neighbours destroy each other: 'It is Britain who will reap the main benefits of this war. Once again, she will have induced the continental nations of Europe to cut each other's throats for her greater profit'.[1]

The French may have underestimated what Britain did at the Somme. At the time, Lord Esher, in Paris, wrote to Haig urging him to make sure the French knew more about what Britain was doing.[2] What is certain is that there was much greater ignorance on the part of Britain about France's enormous sacrifices at Verdun. Britain was repeatedly attacked in the French press and accused of standing aside while France bled to death. The military historian Paddy Griffith has concluded that, in the generality, 'most of the serious fighting ... was left to our French allies, with whom we were often on terms of such cordial hostility that their absolutely vast contribution has never to this day been fairly laid before the British public'.[3]

France was still very critical of Britain when the March offensive was unleashed. In the second phase of the *Kaiserschlacht*, in April 1918, GEORGETTE, directed against lines in Flanders occupied now by French troops, there were serious losses, including the loss of the Passchendaele salient that had been won at the cost of so much blood in a previous year. Lord Esher, occupying a fairly unofficial position in Paris, was not unhappy about the scale of French reverses: 'This will make [the French] less critical of our gallant troops ... [T]he gossip in Paris has been on the usual lines of depreciation & criticism.'

In total, by the end of the war, France, with a smaller population than Britain, had lost 1.4 million men – 14 per cent of her men between the ages of 15 and 49. Britain had lost 720,000 men – 6 per cent of those in the same age group.

5

Haig's Support Circle and his Enemies

LORD ESHER WAS mentioned at the end of the last chapter. Because he was – only *quasi*-officially – a conduit almost as important as the British ambassador in Paris for the maintenance of discreet communications between the two governments, I shall look briefly at this unusual personage. It is worth doing so because he is an example – there are others in this book – of the importance in the development of policy in these years of rich dilettantes who had the time, resources and inclination to serve their country unencumbered by appointment, election or responsibility. More importantly, he fits in to the mechanism which supported Haig and others – such as Robertson – and fought to limit the power of the government to control the military.

Very few people were so intimately involved in the preparation for – and, to an extent, the conduct of – the First World War as Reginald Baliol Brett, Second Viscount Esher. One of the oddest features of his career is that he achieved so much without holding any public position. He had toyed with politics but a year or two in Parliament reassured him in a preference for operating from the shadows. He was parliamentary private secretary to Lord Hartington and must have been the only PPS ever to have driven his chief by sleigh through the snow to a Cabinet meeting. He declined offers of Cabinet positions on several occasions. The *Dictionary of National Biography* described him as 'possessing all the attributes of success except the conviction that it was worthwhile'.

He was an unlikely companion for senior officers and other men of action. He loved elaborate costumes and ceremonial. He was responsible for a marquee erected in the garden of Buckingham Palace for the reception of visiting heads of state at Queen Victoria's Diamond Jubilee celebrations. Ladies found the atmosphere stuffy and started fainting. Esher seized a ceremonial sword and with a fine, slashing gesture deftly sliced the canvas flaps to make windows. In doing so, he impaled the bottom of a housemaid on the tip of his sword. His friends regarded this man who moved so swiftly from gilded youth to elder statesman with some amusement, although they could become irritated by his capacity for finding excuses for wearing his beloved uniforms. He obtained a militia commission immediately after Cambridge but this elaborate dandy, smoking his rose-scented aromatic cigarettes, never himself achieved a martial aspect.

He was partly French and could recall sitting on the lap of a wizened old man who had played the violin for Marie Antoinette. He himself had an enormous respect for royalty. As Secretary of the Office of Works, he saw much of the old Queen Victoria and, on her death, Edward VII came to rely on him increasingly for all sorts of advice. At the end of 1903, he met or corresponded with the king every day. When Edward died, Esher fulfilled the same role for George V. For the rest of his life, he was unofficially but, in fact, the royal family's most trusted adviser.

Apart from the monarchy, Esher's particular interest was defence. His close contact with the Palace – involving, at times, three or four meetings a day with courtiers – was resented by those with responsibility for military matters. St John Brodrick, Secretary of State for War, felt that very often, before a matter even reached the Cabinet, 'the issue had been largely pre-judged on the incomplete premises of an observer who had no official status'. The objection is valid as a constitutional observation but, in fact, Esher was pretty sound. George V, indeed, would have liked to have had him as Secretary of State for War.

Esher was appointed to chair the War Office Reconstruction Committee ('The Esher Committee') after the South African War, to advise on the creation of an Army Board. It was on the advice of the committee that the Committee of Imperial Defence, the CID, was at last reconstituted on a proper basis. In 1905, he joined the CID as a permanent member. From the previous year, all appointments to the War Office were agreed by Esher and were often suggested by him. From the same years he, Haldane, Secretary of State for War from 1905 till 1912, and Haig worked closely together. Esher accompanied Haig on army manoeuvres in 1906 when he was disturbed by Haig's snoring on the palliasse next to him. Esher and Haldane were particularly concerned with the establishment of the Territorial Force. These three men were more important than any others in preparing Britain for war of a sort she had never fought before. Haldane and Haig did so by virtue of their political and military appointments, Esher, in an entirely unofficial and unpaid role, was regarded simultaneously as a repository of wide advice and far-seeing judgement and an unwise follower of the turf.

During the war, he occupied a position, as usual entirely unofficially, as *de facto* head of British Intelligence in France, a point of contact for the Cabinet, the military and the king. His son asked him what position he was to hold. Position, his son said, was important in France: 'People opened doors much more easily in [France], where the first question is always "What position does he hold?"' Esher's response was the epitome of his approach to life: 'I am not going to put myself out. I never do. Nor am I going to *regularise* my position which means that someone can give me orders. I never have . . . It's such a new idea for the French and it makes them sit up'.[1]

Esher had a close working relationship with the remarkable young man whom Haig appointed as his private secretary at GHQ immediately he became C.-in-C., Sir Philip Sassoon. On the face of it, Sassoon was everything that Haig should not have liked – intellectual, brilliant, an exotic and artistic millionaire. But, even if Haig himself did not contribute to the gaiety of his headquarters, he enjoyed wit in others and liked the sophistication that Sassoon lent to his circle. Sassoon became an integral part of the retinue at GHQ until the end of the war – and even after it, when he continued to act on Haig's behalf in delicate negotiations.

Sassoon was totally loyal to Haig, despite their differences in background and attitudes. He was a darling of London society, humorous, with a love of harmless gossip. He was amused, in a kindly way, by Haig's earnestness and by his habits and tastes. His own love was for the treasures and *objets de vertu* with which he filled his houses in Park Lane, Port Lympne in Kent and Trent Park in Enfield. Kenneth Clark described Sassoon's 'idiosyncratic and infectious *style*. He moved quickly and always seemed to be in profile, like an Egyptian relief.'

His mind moved equally quickly, and as his most unexpected comments were made without any change of inflection, they often took people by surprise. He saw the ridiculous side of Port Lympne. Going round the house we came upon a particularly hideous bathroom, panelled in brown and black zig-zags of marble. Philip said without altering his tone of voice. 'It takes you by the throat and shakes you.'[2]

Sassoon wrote of himself:

Of course the sort of house I like & pine for has no comforts, nothing
but stone floors and stone walls, moth-eaten 14th century fragments –
draughts – and a few still chairs against the wall with a string attached
across to prevent anyone from sitting down on them. You would think
it easy to realise this ideal. But it isn't, and I find myself the reluctant
possessor of Park Lane with its *leitmotiv* of sham Louis XVI, Lympne
which is Martini *tout craché*, and Trent which isn't even Lincrusta
when my period is Merovingian or Boiling Oil. *Le Monde est toujours
mal arrangé.*[3]

This marvellous Third Baronet, of Indian and Sephardic Jewish
decent, comes straight from the pages of Saki and there must have been
a huge part of his life which he could not share with Haig.

Sassoon had been placed on French's staff at the start of the war and
then became aide-de-camp to Sir Henry Rawlinson.* He did not arrange
or necessarily wish to spend the entire war as a staff officer. Indeed,
although this exquisite epitome of taste and discernment seems an
improbable warrior, he had, even before the war, perhaps in continuation of his father's desire to assimilate to English society,† joined the
Royal East Kent Yeomanry so, on the outbreak of war, he expected and
was ready to fight at the front. His political and social connections and
the perfect French he had acquired from his French mother's family
made him more useful on the staff than he might have been in the field –
on one occasion, he tripped over his spurs (silver, of course), falling
full-length in the street.

On the staff, he worked very hard and efficiently. After the war, as
Lloyd George's parliamentary private secretary, he went on to display
similar diplomatic skills. What this super-sensitive aesthete truly thought
about the bluff and practical Haig will unfortunately never be known.
He was totally discreet and left no helpful records. He gave voice either
explicitly or implicitly to not the faintest criticism of his chief. On the

---

* Rawlinson successively commanded Fourth Army, Second Army and Fourth Army again. He
ended his career as Commander-in-Chief, India, dying in office.
† Philip's great-grandfather, David Sassoon, had been imprisoned in Baghdad in 1828 as a Jew.
He fled with just a money belt and some pearls sewn into the hem of his cloak, and established
himself first in Bushire in Persia and then in Bombay, where he continued to dress in turban and
robes as he would have done in Baghdad.

contrary, he served him loyally and used his initiative to protect his interests.

Not all of Haig's circle appreciated the presence of this exotic, semi-oriental, semi-civilian bird of paradise in their nest. Esher did. He told Sassoon in 1916 that 'the real crux now is to erect a barbed wire entanglement round the fortress held by K[itchener], old Robertson and the C in C. But subtly, propaganda is at work.'[4]

The propaganda was a two-way trade. Lloyd George and Churchill and others disparaged Haig and the other 'westerners' and briefed against them. They tried to enlist the support of the press but, like all conspirators, they feared conspiracies. They believed that the generals were using the press to undermine the authority of the government, seizing on any pretext, shortage of men or shortage of shells. Churchill complained about 'the foolish doctrine ... preached to the public through the innumerable agencies that Generals and Admirals must be right on war matters and civilians of all kinds must be wrong. These erroneous conceptions were inculcated billion-fold by the newspapers under the crudest forms.' A bit rich from someone so ready to use the newspapers for his own purposes.

Haig used the press to bolster his position. He didn't like doing so but he realised he had no choice and his advisers told him he must. Sassoon particularly understood the necessity and, to deal with it, he built up a particular relationship with the press baron Lord Northcliffe, whom I shall introduce properly very soon. Haig condescended to deal with Northcliffe, invite him to dine at GHQ and allow him to visit the front. He would not, however, fawn over him. Sassoon did that not because it was in his nature but because he understood Northcliffe's nature and Northcliffe unburdened himself to him. Thus, on the Cabinet: 'They are a pack of gullible optimists who swallow any tale ... [T]he generality of them have the slipperiness of eels, with the combined vanity of a professional beauty.'[5] Haig, by contrast, was a man of action, a man of 'push and go', as Toby mugs of the period described him, and the public seemed to think all the more of him if they were privy to what he had had for breakfast.

Sassoon was kept advised by the Palace on what the 'Churchill Cabal' was up to and he, in turn, told Northcliffe. The result was articles in the Northcliffe press, contrasting Haig's achievements with the interference of 'shirt-sleeved' politicians. Lloyd George disparaged Northcliffe as Haig's 'kettledrum' and complained to Esher about '"intrigues" against him. Philip Sassoon was the delinquent conspiring with Asquith and the press.'[6]

Esher's position in Paris – and more generally his role as an elder statesman with particular access to and influence on the Court – made him important but he was only one of many who, from the wings, played a key part in the covert politics of the period. Historians are familiar with 'court parties' in the eighteenth century but the existence of such factions in the early twentieth century is surprising, and yet they were there. There was a perception that the Army and the Crown had an identity of interest that was inimical to that of the liberal left, of which Lloyd George was the symbol.

As a result of the war, Lloyd George had come to occupy a novel position. He was a prime minister of an entirely new type. He was often described as a 'dictator' and not in a critical sense. Desperate times required novel methods. Thus Bonar Law, although leader of the Conservative Party and close to the Army–Crown nexus, told Hankey on 2 March 1917 that 'he regarded Lloyd George as dictator and meant to give him his chance'.[7] This was very far from the conventional role of the prime minister as no more than *primus inter pares*, the role still occupied by Asquith a year earlier.

It was a role that worried the court party. When Bonar Law made his remark to Hankey, there was a possibility that Haig might resign as a result of machinations by Lloyd George at the Calais Conference in February 1917 to subordinate him to the French general, Nivelle. Clive Wigram, Assistant Secretary and then Principal Secretary to the king from 1910 to 1936, and quintessentially a representative of the court party, visited GHQ on 9 March 1917. He reported his fear that, if Haig did resign, it might allow Lloyd George to go to the country and 'come back as a dictator' – by which, he meant more than Bonar Law had done.

There is a risk today of thinking of these times as an extension, only disrupted by war, of mellow Edwardian days of prolonged summer and privileged display. The pre-war years had, in truth, been difficult ones, characterised by tense constitutional crises (precipitated, of course, by Lloyd George's controversial budgets and his provocative Limehouse speeches which appeared to challenge the social status quo), talk of abolition of the Lords, labour unrest and the likelihood – indeed, pretty well the perceived certainty – of civil war over Ireland.

The ship of state sailed in uncharted waters. Among the new features she had to navigate past, the new Labour Party and threats from anarchists and syndicalists, were the newly appeared press barons, mostly self-made men like Max Aitken, Lord Beaverbrook and the Harmsworth brothers – Harold, who became Lord Rothermere, and, above all, Alfred, later Lord Northcliffe. They took possession of the new literate working classes by offering them cheap journalism. Playing to public opinion made them enormously rich, and manipulating it made them hugely powerful. Well before the war, they were, only half-jokingly, being referred to as semi-official advisers to the Crown. In 1904, W.T. Stead, formerly the editor of the *Pall Mall Gazette* and now of the *Review of Reviews*, wrote a piece entitled 'His Majesty's Public Councillors: To Wit, the Editors of the London Daily Papers'. The article was inspired by the Dogger Bank incident, when Russian warships on their way to Japan unwisely fired on British trawlers. Stead identified features in the newspaper reaction which would be evident ten years later – xenophobia, over-reaction and imbalance.[*]

Churchill assessed Northcliffe thus:

> There can be no doubt that Lord Northcliffe was at all times animated by an ardent patriotism and an intense desire to win the war. But he wielded power without official responsibility, enjoyed secret knowledge without the general view, and disturbed the fortunes of national leaders without being able to bear their burdens. Thus a swaying force, uncertain, capricious, essentially personal, potent alike for good or evil, claiming to make or mar public men, to sustain or displace Commanders, to shake policies, and to fashion or overthrow Governments, introduced itself in the absence of all Parliamentary corrections into the conduct of the war.[8]

It was press power much more than parliamentary opinion or the workings of democracy that had pulled Asquith down and replaced him with Lloyd George. The press by and large supported the generals against the politicians – a good patriotic stance. Northcliffe, greatest of all the barons, had enormous power as the proprietor of a vast press and he used that power overtly, in a direct way that is unimaginable today. Moreover, he was unpredictable, mercurial and, by the end of his

---

[*] Stead was a man of protean interests and energy, unassailably the creator of modern journalism, investigative and campaigning. His spiritualism included some thoughts that came oddly close to previsions of his own drowning on the *Titanic*.

life, clinically insane. He was interested in phrenology. Kitchener was no use: 'A tall man with a narrow forehead.' Lloyd George, himself an amateur phrenologist, was not acceptable: 'It's his big head on a little body that I don't like.' The conformation of Haig's cranium was, however, ideally that of a general: 'Lithe and alert, Sir Douglas is known for his distinguished bearing and good looks. He has blue eyes and an unusual facial angle, delicate features, and a chin to be reckoned with.' Haig hated submitting himself to Northcliffe's appraisal. His classical concept of a great military leader precluded him, like Coriolanus, from submission to the approval of the public. An appeal to the press was something unworthy of a great general. Sassoon convinced him that it was, however, necessary.

During the First World War Northcliffe's papers (*The Times, Daily Mail, Evening News*) made up 28.9 per cent of total circulation figures of the London-based nationals. If his brother's *Daily Mirror* is added in, the total is 46.7 per cent. Even if the *Mirror*'s line could deviate from his, Northcliffe's reach was unique. *The Times* (along with the *Westminster Gazette*, an evening paper with a much smaller subscription) was essential reading for top people. Further, to his quality papers, Northcliffe could add his popular prints. More than anyone, he could address both the classes and the masses.[9]

Northcliffe had been unimpressed by Asquith: 'We are not at law with Germany, we are at war with her.' He brought down Asquith's ministry but soon tired of Lloyd George. Even before the end of Asquith, he had, on one occasion, burst into Lloyd George's War Office and roared at his secretary, 'I don't want to see him – you can tell him from me that I hear he has been interfering with strategy and that if it goes on I will break him.' Lloyd George was conscious that he could indeed, like Asquith, be broken by Northcliffe, who he thought was planning a bid for his own dictatorship, a risk which he took seriously. It was partly to keep Northcliffe harmlessly busy that Lloyd George first sent him to the United States as a leader of the British War Mission and then appointed him Director of Propaganda in Enemy Countries.[10]

Lloyd George was, indeed, not immune from the power of the press just because he was, to an extent, its creator and its creation.* He was apprehensive about a link between the War Office and certain sections

---

* Indeed the press played a part in his downfall in 1922 and nearly ended the premiership of Stanley Baldwin soon afterwards.

of the press. His reaction was not paranoid but perfectly reasonable. Howell Gwynne, who was editor of the *Morning Post* from 1911 until 1937, adopted a fiercely patriotic, anti-Semitic and well-nigh paranoid position through the war. In 1916, he wrote to his proprietor, Lady Bathurst, saying, 'There are times when one feels that a military dictatorship is the only thing for England.'[11] And, in 1918, he attempted to organise a coup which would have replaced Lloyd George with Sir William Robertson. He and his military correspondent, Charles Repington,* were prosecuted and found guilty of contravention of the Defence of the Realm Act.

---

* See footnote, p. 60, for more about Repington.

6

British Views of the French

THE FIRST BRITISH Commander-in-Chief of the BEF, Sir John French, was pretty typical of his class and time. He said, '*Au fond* [Basically] they [the French] are a low lot, and one always had to remember the class these French generals mostly come from.'[1] His successor, Haig, wrote them off equally superficially but perhaps more reprehensibly, as Haig was more intelligent and better educated.

France, since Revolutionary times, had the experience of being a nation in arms. Britain had used very small, professional armies and had paid her allies to do much of her land fighting. She was a maritime nation and had no experience of *levée en masse* (mass military conscription). French military service was organised on principles of national solidarity – all men at the age of 20 had to spend three years in the army, followed by eleven years in the Reserve, then seven years in the Territorials and then seven years in the Territorial Reserve. Thus between 1914 and 1918 20 per cent of the population was engaged in military service – more than 8.19 million men.[2]

There were many barriers to effective communication between the Allies. It was quite some time before a common time system was adopted. Language was another problem. Very few French officers spoke English. More Englishmen spoke French, even if pretty badly. When Asquith attended a meeting at Calais in July 1915, he wrote to his wife that he had never heard 'such a quantity of bad French spoken in all [his] life – genders, vocabulary, & pronunciation equally execrable'.[3] At the French Military Academy of Saint-Cyr, it was compulsory to study German. Seventy-one per cent of the French officers promoted to the rank of general between 1889 and 1914 had language qualifications in German and only 21 per cent qualifications in English.[4]

Sir John French could speak almost none of his ally's language. Haig was reasonably good and took French lessons during the war. All the same, he too had a bias towards Germany. He had attended far more German manoeuvres before the war than French ones and had, indeed, met the Kaiser and exchanged toasts with him.

There was always a fear amongst the British that France's political or military morale would fail. Since the extent of the French efforts wasn't fully recognised, any problems were clearly due to lack of moral fibre. Hankey recorded in his diary on 8 June 1917 that Henry Wilson had come to the War Cabinet that morning to warn that the French could not stick it much longer. Esher, in Paris, had said the same thing.[5] It is now accepted that Pétain's army, after the problems caused by Verdun had been addressed, was, on the whole, efficient and well led but, during the war, '[a]ccording to the prevailing Anglo-Saxon narrative, [the French army] was past its best after 1917, a dispirited mob, accustomed to defeat and in need of the support of its more virile British allies'.[6] It is on this prejudice that Haig builds, representing France in 1918 both in March and later as being too weak and dispirited to take the initiative.

In the course of GEORGETTE one of the components of the *Kaiserschlacht*, Mont Kemmel was captured from the French. Haig was unimpressed: 'The French have lost Kemmel – a position of extraordinary strength. How they managed it I don't know.' He was even worse in his comments after the war, when he should have had time to reflect: 'Between 21 March and 15 April, the French did practically nothing and took no part in the fighting.' The period he is dealing with covers not only the early part of GEORGETTE, but also MICHAEL, when the British line only held because of the reserves which France poured into it.[7]

In Haig's view, the French generals were 'a queer mixture of fair ability (not more than fair) and ignorance of the practical side of the war'. 'Some Frenchmen find it hard to conceal their jealousy of Great Britain. They hate to think that the British army is on French soil saving French!!'[8] This he wrote while France was fighting at Verdun. Sir John French was equally smug in his memoir, *1914*: what would Napoleon have thought of 'this friendly invasion of France by England's "good yeomen", who are now offering their lives to save France from possible destruction as a Power of the first class'?[9] The French contribution to the war remains underestimated in popular British thought even to this day. The Somme continues grimly to fascinate but it is remembered as a purely British battle. We have noted that Britain does not acknowledge more than 200,000 French casualties in that battle. Similarly, we shall see that the French contribution is written out of British accounts of the Hundred Days.

The French army was not without faults. Attempts by radical politicians from the turn of the century to reform the army had weakened morale. So had the Dreyfus Affair.* Some officers left because career prospects were unappealing. France was committed to the doctrine of the offensive. So was Britain, but France carried the theory further. Foch and others, such as General de Grandmaison,† stressed the importance of the offensive at all costs and others, like Pétain and Fayolle, who thought that firepower should be met by firepower, rather than the almost metaphysical concept of the offensive, were ignored. A consequence of this was that sophisticated artillery tactics, such as pre-registration at indirect targets and counter-battery work, received little attention.

But, as in the British army, new ideas were developed to meet the new situation. While Joffre, like Haig, continued to favour decisive confrontation, Foch moved fairly early to the idea of limited attacks, rather like Henry Rawlinson's 'bite and hold', but with an important additional element in thorough artillery preparation and with the aim of continuing, successive advances. Pétain tried to move the conflict from relentless attacks on defended positions to a confrontation on open ground where exposed flanks could be attacked.[10]

Very broadly speaking, both France and Britain learned the same lessons from 1914 to 1916. The irony is that the country which learned most and was readiest to innovate was the country which lost the war – Germany. It lost the war not because of military failures but because of blockade, material deficiencies and disintegrating morale at home.

---

* In 1894, Alfred Dreyfus was accused of handing secret documents to the Germans. He was convicted of treason and sentenced to life imprisonment. His innocence was protested, notably by Emil Zola in his open letter, '*J'accuse ...*'. After serving almost five years on Devil's Island, Dreyfus was brought back to metropolitan France and, after much controversy, was demonstrated to have been entirely innocent. Dreyfus was Jewish and much of the animus against him was certainly the product of widespread anti-Semitic prejudice. The whole affair destabilised society painfully and left scars for a generation. In the process the army and its standing in France suffered. The republican element in France, always antagonistic to the pro-army establishment section was, initially at least, ascendant and military esprit suffered.

† General Louis de Grandmaison was one of those (Nivelle and Joffre were others) who favoured *attaque à outrance* – unlimited attack in the face of and in reaction to the challenge of modern defensive weaponry. For all its appeal to French notions of *élan* and dash, it was a philosophy rather than a logical doctrine.

The post-war idea of 'a stab in the back', the army's attempt to blame the civilians for defeat, was skewed but, all the same, defeat was not the army's fault.[11] Or, if it was, it was only the fault of the leadership – Hindenburg and Ludendorff.

7

Starving Haig

THE NEXT ELEMENT of the matrix for the events of March is the tripartite question of British manpower: Why was the army on the Western Front kept short of men when an expected offensive took place? Who was responsible for the deficiency? Was the problem ever remedied? The question bears on both responding to the offensive and on exploiting the subsequent allied counter-offensive.

The manpower question goes to the heart of an assessment of how the British army performed in March 1918. The government certainly kept Haig short of men. His supporters see this as criminally wrong-headed. But, as far as the government was concerned, if in, say, November 1917, Haig had been supplied with the sort of numbers that he wished, he would have used them to resume the bloodletting of Third Ypres. Haig told the war correspondent Charles Repington* that 'the continuation of the Flanders offensive is the best way he knows of attracting and using up the Boches, [but] he cannot go on with it if he is not adequately supplied with drafts'.[1]

Haig was to a large extent to blame for being kept short of drafts. He had justified the prolongation of the Flanders campaign in the autumn of 1917 by saying that Germany was being weakened to the extent she would offer little threat in 1918. He had urged the government for men in 1917. He complained in May 1917 to Robertson that he needed drafts and that the government was failing to rise to the occasion (his letter reveals his assumptions about France's deficiencies): 'For the last two years most of the soldiers have realised that Great Britain must take the necessary steps to win the war by herself, because our French allies have

---

* Charles à Court Repington, a brilliant soldier with a contempt for his colleagues. He left the army after breaking his word given 'upon his honour as a soldier and a gentleman' to end an affair (his parole was given to Henry Wilson). He worked for *The Times*. To the Liberal left he was known as 'the gorgeous Wreckington'.

already shown that they lacked both the moral qualities and the means for gaining victory. It is thus sad to see the British Govt. failing at the XIIth hour.'[2]

He had predicted that the Flanders campaign would mean that, by 1 April 1918, the Allies would outnumber the Germans by 30 per cent even after allowing for divisions brought over from the Eastern Front.[3] On the basis of such promises he was given in 1917 at least in large measure the men he wanted.

But after Third Ypres had ended Haig had to face up to the fact that, despite his promise that all would be well in 1918, he very much needed fresh troops. He needed them to make up deficiencies and because he was very aware of the tiredness of his men after the long Flanders campaign of 1917. He wrote to the War Office on 12 December 1917 urging the necessity of leave for his men: 'They have earned it, and it is a valuable means of keeping them in good heart.' Additionally, his command was well aware that French soldiers got much more leave. On 15 January 1918, the Chief of the Imperial General Staff told the War Cabinet that there were about 350,000 French soldiers on leave as against 80,000 British soldiers. Geographical considerations obviously affected British personnel in a way that the French were not affected and there was a shortage of cross-Channel transport.[4]

By now, however, the government was determined that Haig shouldn't get more men. First of all, Lloyd George didn't *want* to believe that he needed them. Haig was losing men but not winning the war. Better to fight on another front in a more imaginative way. Better perhaps just to mark time and wait for the arrival of the Americans. To Lloyd George, almost anything seemed preferable to what he regarded as stubborn and perverse continuation on the Western Front. We can now see that he was wrong to see Eastern Europe as a fruitful alternative. At the end of the day, it was true, as the Westerners argued, that the Germans could only be defeated 'where they were', in the west. Moreover, the railways had their logic. The strain on the central powers' interior lines of railway communication to the west was very evident by 1917[5] but the Entente powers had much poorer communications to the east. The Allies had to stay in the west.

But one can understand how Lloyd George's mind was working – there was little evidence that a continuation of Haig's offensives in Flanders would have defeated the Germans in 1918 any more than it had done in 1917. Moreover, the prime minister could point out that

Haig had said earlier in the year that he would not need additional troops. He had not only played down the numbers of German troops that would be available but also stressed the low quality of the German reserves: 'The German losses are being replaced now in large proportions by quite inferior material, and the proportion of such material in the German ranks will increase rapidly in the future, while by May or June [1917], the German reserves will be exhausted.'[6] Lloyd George's later comment was: 'When Haig discovered his mistake it was too late for any rearrangement. The Government had by then apportioned the national man-power. Not a single battalion could be added to the trained men available for the Western Front in the spring.'[7] The prime minister could add that the Cabinet were being required at this time to consider the demands for additional men for the fleet, for transport services and for the production of coal and food supplies.

After the war, Lloyd George rejected the argument that it was the government's fault that sufficient numbers of troops were not supplied to the army in March 1918. On 8 October 1917, he had asked for an appreciation of the role that the British armies could adopt if Russia were forced out of the war. Haig misread the significance of the elimination of Russia. He replied via Robertson that his troops were in good form while those of Germany were broken. German reserves would be exhausted by May or June 1918. Very shortly after 8 October, Haig had changed his position radically and came to predict a shortage on the Western Front by 31 October of 460,000 and of 250,000 by 31 March 1918.[8]

Lloyd George blamed Haig and Robertson. He said that Robertson had required 130,000 men to cover the losses which would be sustained at Third Ypres but that the drafts actually sent totalled 376,000 men. 'The ghastly massacres of the Flanders Campaign completely falsified the estimates of the Chief of the Imperial General Staff; the total casualties on the whole British front during the progress of the battle mounted up to the appalling figure of 399,000 men – three times the official military estimate . . . when we discovered what the actual deficit was, no conceivable measures taken by us then could have closed that bleeding gash before the end of March [1918].'[9]

Lloyd George was not the only one to be sceptical about Haig's pleas. Hankey reflected this scepticism. He recorded on 6 December 1917 that the War Office had warned that 'if large numbers of men are not recruited and sent out at once Haig's army would not be able to hold the line.' His reaction was: 'This is inconsistent with Haig's continual reports of bad German morale and that the German divisions had been put through the mill in Flanders and knocked out one by one.'[10]

Haig continued to appear inconsistent. His apparent belief, when he spoke to the War Cabinet in January 1918,* that the Germans were likely to attempt only limited attacks in the west in 1918 could be used to resist demands for more men.

Added to all this is the fact that the figures which Haig and the War Office supplied were not convincing. Hankey was fairly typical in his view of War Office figures: 'Utterly unreliable, as their facts are twisted to support their arguments.'[11] David Woodward has analysed the War Office's manipulation of figures – a manipulation which ultimately served to reduce the credibility of their claims.[12]

In December 1917, a Cabinet Committee had been set up to decide on the allocation of available manpower. It had no confidence in the figures presented to it. '[The] figures supplied through the War Office were being constantly altered, and the Cabinet were quite unable to get any stable and reliable estimates as to the actual position.'[13]

The lack of reciprocal confidence on the part of generals and politicians is pretty well impossible to exaggerate. It is tempting to say that each had more regard for the Germans than for their fellow countrymen. Haig and other generals thought that Lloyd George was intent on bringing down constitutional rule and establishing a republic. Lloyd George had huge contempt for what he saw as the intellectual poverty of the commanders who produced demands which 'were not estimates carefully prepared by officials who understood the elements of accountancy but merely a succession of grouses from generals who had failed to achieve what they had hoped for and had promised and were anxious to put the blame for their discomfiture on the politicians who had dared to predict the failure'.[14]

And so, when Haig talked at the beginning of 1918 about 'the fatigue of his forces . . . [weary and depleted units that had] been engaged in the offensive since the spring',[15] his pleas were received with little sympathy.

As Third Ypres went on, Britain was faced with increasing complaints about manpower not only from Haig and Robertson but also from France.

---

* See p. 86.

Both the French government and French headquarters, *Grand Quartier Général* (*GQG*), demanded a bigger contribution from Britain – more men and extensions of the British front. Haig cooperated but to nothing like the extent the French wanted. In the French Chamber, there were demands which the French government found difficult to resist that Frenchmen should be released from the army to work in the fields and Pétain wanted more troops to cope with the consequences of Russia's disappearance from the war – a reserve of 40 divisions. Lloyd George and the French prime minister, Paul Painlevé, met at Boulogne on 25 September 1917, when Britain accepted that the British line should be extended. The details were avoided and it was left to the two Commanders-in-Chief to decide how great the extension should be and when it should take place.

It is time to say something more of Pétain, who took over as Commander-in-Chief after the failure of Nivelle's offensive on the Aisne in 1917. He was born in 1856. His parents were modest country people. His mother died when he was just two and he went initially to a Jesuit College and then to the Military Academy of Saint-Cyr. At the outbreak of war, he was only a colonel and about to retire in that rank. He had bought a pair of secateurs for the next phase of his life. As with many of the commanders, the war provided an Indian summer, the prolongation of a career that would otherwise have ended without distinction. He was not a flamboyant man, despite a colourful love life. His realism verged on pessimism.

The two commanders didn't rush to meet and talk about mutual support after the meeting of the prime ministers on 25 September. It was not until 18 October that they discussed the matter at Amiens. Haig did not accept, as a matter of *principle*, that he should take over more line but he did undertake, as a matter of *practice*, to transfer four divisions from the coastal sector. There was no great meeting of minds. Each Commander-in-Chief handed a convoluted paper to the other. Haig reported back to Robertson and matters progressed no further for the time being.

On 14 December, Pétain pressed again for a movement of British troops and a further meeting took place between him and Haig on 17 December. Haig said that he had not been given troops to replace the losses from Third Ypres. On 10 January 1918, he did promise two divisions and said he would try to take over part of the French line. On the same day, the military representatives at the Supreme War Council

(SWC) at Versailles* said that the British should man the front as far as the left bank of the Ailette, the exact point of junction to be decided by the two Commanders-in-Chief, who fixed it at five and a half miles east of the River Oise.

THE IMPLICATIONS FOR 1918

In January 1918, the Cabinet Committee on Manpower, which had been set up in the previous month, sent an advance copy of its draft report to the Army Council.† There were two elements to the report. In the first place, the Committee recommended that manpower should not be wasted now but rather hoarded until American troops were present in numbers and there was a prospect of victory. Secondly, the Committee said that Britain was bearing, and was bearing unrecognised, a significant manpower burden in the shape of providing Allied sea power, transporting food and supplies in general and coal, ordnance and ammunition in particular. Additionally, the availability of British shipping for the transport of American troops was going to become critical in 1919. Hankey echoed this: 'Our resources had to be doled out with great care, in order to tide us over until the arrival of reinforcements from America on a substantial scale, and to ensure that, when the time came, the seas should be sufficiently safe and the tonnage adequate to ensure their transport'.[16] He went on to add, rather weakening the case for restricting drafts, that the army was suffering from morale problems as well as numerical ones. He referred to war weariness and general discontent after the fighting in Flanders. Men at the front resented the pay that civilians were receiving.

The army, which was not represented on the Cabinet Committee, was unhappy with the outcome. Senior officers reckoned that they needed 615,000 men for 1918 and that, on the basis of the Cabinet Committee's report, the Ministry of National Service would not be able to find much

---

* The establishment, function and failure of the Supreme War Council will be dealt with in Chapter 9.

† The Army Council was established in 1904 as part of the reforms which involved the creation of a Chief of the General (later Imperial General) Staff. The Council was the supreme administrative authority for the army and was the final stage in reforms which had started after the Crimean War, continued through the Cardwell Reforms of 1870 and had been reinvigorated after the experiences of the South African War. Elgin's Commission which investigated into these experiences, Esher's sub-committee of the Committee of Imperial Defence and Haldane's work at the War Office came together to instil a new professionalism into the army. Haig personifies that new professionalism.

more than 100,000 category 'A' men.* There was a strong protest from the military members of the Army Council, which the War Cabinet ignored. Lloyd George made much of the fact that the army was to stand on the defensive for most of 1918 – he was convinced that losses in defence would be lower than those in offence, a doctrine which does not invariably apply in practice. The War Cabinet persisted with a plan, opposed by the Army Council, to reduce the strength of divisions from twelve to nine battalions. This change appears to have been encouraged by France. There was some expectation that American personnel could bring divisions back to twelve battalions. The Army Council was not so much against the principle of the change, which increased the proportion of guns to infantrymen, as against the fact that it was being implemented at the very time that a German attack was expected.

The army's demand for 615,000 category 'A' men was unrealistic. Once the German attacks began and the government had no choice but to find fresh troops, they could only bring together 372,330 category 'A' men between January and November 1918. The intricacies of Britain's extraordinarily complicated classification system have very understandably confused many historians and created the myth that there was a huge pool of men available for the front. There was a view, for instance, that there were numbers of Home Defence men who could have gone out to France. General Sir Arthur Paget,[†] however, reported that '[t]he men lining the beach [on Home Defence duties] were cripples, all B and C men, and the mobile reserve behind were largely boys of 18 to 19, very good boys, but impressionable and partially trained, with bad officers'.[17]

At Versailles, when the Supreme War Council met at the end of January 1918, Foch attacked Lloyd George, claiming that Britain was not making as great a military effort as she should. Lloyd George responded that, since the opening of the Battle of the Somme on 1 July 1916, British losses had been greater than those of any of the Allies.[18] By the end of 1917, British casualties totalled over two million. That was, of course, a huge number and made such an impression on Britain that little attention was paid to what had happened to France. France, with a slightly smaller population, had lost over a million more.

---

* That is the fittest men available. That may seem obvious but the methodology of classification is far from straightforward.

† An unappealing, blustering man whose social connections rather than his abilities carried him to high office, he was never made to account for his role in the Curragh incident.

Lloyd George's reaction to the scale of Britain's sacrifice does credit to his humanity but was, to an extent, an emotional response which caused him, in despair at what was happening on the Western Front, to see alternatives elsewhere that were chimerical – the expressions of hope, not reality. In his *War Memoirs*, he wrote:

> Every nation was profligate of its man-power in the early stages of the war and conducted its war activities as if there were no limit to the number of young men of military age who were fit to be thrown into the furnace to feed the flames of war. The Allies, who had an enormous superiority in the number of fit young men available, nearly threw away their advantage by the reckless prodigality of their military leaders ... The idea of a war of attrition was the refuge of stupidity.[19]

Recrimination continued. The French conscription system had been in place since 1913 and was quite differently based from the British system. Additionally, there were differences in the way in which manpower was used. The BEF held a shorter length of line per head. There are a number of reasons for this: the concentration of Germans was usually stronger on the British sectors; and French civilians could carry out work which had to be done by British soldiers. All the same, it rankled with the French, who calculated that, in 1916, 30 British divisions held 142 kilometres whereas France held 632 kilometres with six to seven divisions. Pétain suffered from manpower shortages just as Haig did and was bitter about what he saw as an inequitable arrangement between the two armies.[20] This was the sort of resentment that brought Clemenceau to say that Lloyd George was '[t]he greatest liar he'd ever met'.

The March offensive shone a spotlight on the manpower issue but didn't resolve it. The question was vigorously debated between the British and the French at a conference at Abbeville in April 1918. Clemenceau asked that two French officers might be sent to London to look into things for themselves. The request was initially refused but was agreed to a few days later when Clemenceau returned to the attack at the Supreme War Council. A Colonel Albert Roure was sent to London. He contrasted the 91.9 per cent of the French 1904–15 classes who had been called up with much lower British statistics. One of the differences was that, in France, men did not, in general, avoid conscription by working in essential industries – there were only 45,000 men under the age of 42 doing such work who had not already fought.[21] Roure reported to Lord Milner, now Secretary of State for War, who asked him for advice about the number of uniformed personnel to be seen on the streets of London.

There were, indeed, about 80,000 BEF soldiers on leave when the German attack took place – at a known place and at a known time. A myth persisted that there were a million enlisted men in Britain who were playing no part on the fronts. Foch got very excited and waved his arms around at meetings. Clemenceau said that the British Empire had mobilised six million men: 'They must be somewhere or other and they ought to be forthcoming.' Roure's report did not help a great deal. He concluded that Britain was not contributing fairly or making use of her available manpower. France had mobilised 702 men out of every 1,000, whereas Britain, he said, had mobilised only 572, even allowing for the retention of a million men for essential services.

There were flaws in Roure's methodology. He failed to acknowledge that coal sent to France was mined by British miners, almost half a million of them, and carried to France in British ships manned by British personnel, thus allowing France to maintain her production of munitions. He failed to recognise the importance not only of Royal Naval personnel but also of the Merchant Marine, in which there were 560,000 men between the ages of 18 and 43. Roure unfairly concluded that the British were less interested in the present war than the 'great Colonial expeditions which render [her] history illustrious'.[22] The reference to colonial expeditions touches, perhaps unconsciously, on the rivalry which had informed relations between France and Britain until the formation of the Entente. What is surprising about the wartime alliance is perhaps that it was not uneasier than it was.

But Clemenceau considered himself vindicated by Roure's report. Derby, as Secretary of State for War, promised more men but Clemenceau was never satisfied that Britain truly pulled her weight in terms of contribution of personnel. He was asked in the Chamber of Deputies on 3 June 1918 whether it was not the case that there were numbers of unused men in Britain and he said that was so.

If France thought that Britain was not fully committed in terms of personnel, it is no less true that Britain never really understood the scale of France's sacrifice of blood. What can certainly be seen is that Pétain, no less than Haig, felt that he was fighting a war without adequate resources.

Lloyd George's sense of injustice about French claims that Britain was not pulling her weight was still burning when he wrote his account of 1918, all of 18 years later:

The British man-power problem differed in some essential respects from that of our Allies. In a special measure we had to carry the burden of maintaining, not ourselves alone, but our Allies as well. The command of the seas, without which Allied victory would have been impossible, was preponderatingly our charge, and our Navy had the supreme task of keeping the seas clear, hunting down the German submarines, holding the enemy warships pinned to their harbours, and convoying the merchant shipping which bore supplies not only for ourselves but for our Allies. The French and Italian Fleets made their contribution to this work, but compared with ours it was insignificant, and involved no serious drain on the man-power of those two countries. Men were needed not only for the manning of our immense Navy and Mercantile Marine, but for the building of new ships and swarms of new craft to patrol the sea, and to keep these constantly repaired and refitted. There was a difference equivalent to several army corps between the numbers absorbed by the manning and equipment of our naval and mercantile marine and those employed by France, Italy, Russia or Germany in the same tasks. The occupation of the corn-growing and cattle-rearing plains of Northern France by the Germans deprived Frenchmen of a large proportion of their wheat and meat resources. Without our ships, neither Italy nor France could have carried on for a single year. They would have been starved into surrender. Nor could we have conveyed our troops and theirs – including American troops – to the various theatres of war and maintained them there. But the manning of our naval and mercantile fleets, the provision of men for their docks, their building and repairing yards, their arming and munitioning, the maintenance of minelayers and minesweepers and of the endless contrivances invented to fight the deadly submarine – all these demands in the aggregate absorbed well over a million of our man-power. If the men of military age and fitness amongst these were counted, it would be the equivalent of at least thirty divisions. There is no greater proof of the exclusiveness of a profession than the fact that great soldiers of exceptional intelligence like General Foch could never understand how essential sea power was to the very existence of the alliance.[23]

THE MAURICE DEBATE

Moving ahead of the narrative, the issue of the adequacy of troops in France in March 1918 became a public one when Major General Sir Frederick Maurice,* until recently the Director of Military Operations, believing that Lloyd George was trying to bring Haig down, accused the prime minister in the press of misleading the House of Commons and holding back reinforcements from the Western Front, thus contributing to the German success in the March offensive. There was now a fairly open battle between the generals, who blamed the prime minister for what had so nearly happened, and the politicians, particularly Lloyd George, who claimed that the problem lay in Haig's incompetence. This issue mattered hugely to Haig and Lloyd George. Haig wrote a despatch in July 1918, saying in three separate places that his preparations for the German offensive had been sabotaged by the government's deliberate withholding of troops. When the despatch was finally published, the government deleted the relevant passages. In 1919, Haig's complete Despatches were published. His Private Secretary, J.H. Boraston, showed the deletions by asterisks. He also set out the text which had been deleted.[24] A settling of scores.

Maurice's allegations were described in the *Star* as 'Gen. Maurice's bombshell'. Lloyd George defended himself in Parliament duplicitously but effectively by holding back the most recent information that was available to him regarding troop numbers.[25] He believed that Maurice's true purpose was to bring down the government. He was wrong and he behaved badly, and everyone knew that, but he got away with it. Maurice resigned and was never allowed the public enquiry which he expected to vindicate him. He needed no vindication: his career in public service, though now civilian rather than military, continued unchecked.

Sir James Edmonds, the general editor of the Official History† said, 'It is obvious that the British armies in France could have been brought up to full establishment before 21 March without unduly weakening the forces

---

* Maurice was an outstanding example of commitment to variegated public service, who was both a soldier (he and his father served together in the Tirah campaign, 1897–98) and a professor of military history. After his dismissal by the Army Council Maurice *fils* had a distinguished career as a writer, academic and promoter of adult education. His son-in-law, Sir Edward Spears, said that he was '[a]s imperturbable as a fish, always unruffled, the sort of man who would eat porridge by gaslight on a foggy morning in winter . . . just as if he were eating a peach in a sunny garden in August'.

† Both Sir James Edmonds and the Official History are introduced more fully in Chapter 18.

elsewhere had the government so willed.'[26] Lloyd George's main motive for withholding troops was not concern about other theatres but concern that Haig would waste recruits. To an extent, Haig himself was the source of the problem because of the losses incurred in his prolonged campaigns in 1916 and 1917. His successes in the Hundred Days and the sudden collapse of Germany in October–November 1918 were not expected by any observers. Criticism of Lloyd George for withholding drafts is accordingly based on hindsight.

Or is it? By the end of 1917, there were grounds for thinking that Germany would not be wise to launch a major offensive in 1918, when labour unrest and the effect of blockade were causing problems at home which, together with industrial problems, difficulties in supply and in transport, particularly in the railway systems, inhibited her ability to sustain offensive as opposed to defensive operations. Against that, there were grounds for thinking that, despite all that, she might make a desperate and perhaps final throw. Robertson strongly argued that the evidence supported this thesis and General John Charteris, Haig's likeable, loyal but finally hopeless intelligence chief, sacked by Lloyd George in December 1917 for the poor quality of his work, made an uncharacteristically accurate assessment of German plans in two appreciations just before his deposition, 'A Note on German Intentions' and 'A Note on the Situation from a German Point of View'.* If someone else had written them they might have had more traction.

I shall return in a later chapter to the manpower question and how the Supreme War Council, established to deal with it, threw a web over the actors on the Allied side in the months running up to March 1918 but, first of all, I want to examine the political and military developments that determined the events which Robertson and Charteris predicted.

---

* Published as appendices to his *At GHQ*, Cassell and Company, London, 1931.

8

German Imperatives and Preparations

THE GREAT GERMAN advance that began on 21 March 1918 was the product of two events that took place in 1917. In Russia, the Bolsheviks seized power in the October Revolution and immediately decided to end the war with Germany. Although the formal treaty was not signed until 3 March 1918, fighting stopped in December of the previous year when an armistice was concluded. A week later, the peace negotiations at Brest-Litovsk began. In terms of the Treaty of Brest-Litovsk, Russia lost Poland, Lithuania, Estonia, Livonia and Courland. Finland, though not awarded to the Central Powers, seceded, as did Ukraine. The Ottomans recovered those parts of the Caucasus that they had lost in 1878.

In all, Russia lost about a million square miles of territory containing most of its prime industries and mineral resources, together with about a third of its population, 55 million people, and about a third of its agricultural reserves. Benjamin Ziemann described the savage terms of the treaty as '[t]hat abyss of defeat, dismemberment, enslavement and humiliation'.[1] It was a cruel blow to the new Bolshevik Republic. Russia lost 34 per cent of her population, 32 per cent of her agricultural land, 85 per cent of her beet-sugar land, 54 per cent of her industrial undertakings and 89 per cent of her coalmines.[2] As *The Times* said, Britain could now see how Germany treated those whom it defeated. What was done to Russia in 1917 should be remembered when we see what Russia did to the continent of Europe in 1945.

The second event took place in the United States of America. On 20 March 1917, three days after the Tsar abdicated in the aftermath of the February Revolution, President Woodrow Wilson called a meeting of his Cabinet. A year earlier he had said, in phrases that were not well received, 'There is such a thing as a man being too proud to fight. There is such a thing as a nation being so right that it does not need to convince others by force that it is right.' Now, after the announcement of unrestricted submarine warfare in the German 'war zone', the sinking of several US ships and the revelation in the Zimmermann telegram that Germany was prepared to secure an alliance with Mexico by giving that country bits of Texas, New Mexico and Arizona, his mood had changed. When they met, his Cabinet saw things even more clearly – he had to ask Secretary of State Lansing to calm down and lower his voice.

He asked for a special joint session of Congress on 2 April and started to type out his speech on his old Hammond portable. At 8.20 p.m. on 2 April, he got into his car and was driven along Pennsylvania Avenue, escorted by mounted troops. The strictest security had been maintained but no one was in any doubt about what was happening. Despite light rainfall, his route was lined by solemn crowds. The men took off their hats as the president passed. The Capitol was heavily guarded but the mood within was less subdued than outside. When the Speaker introduced Wilson there was an eruption of cheering and waving of flags that lasted for two minutes. At 8.35 he spoke in his usual calm, didactic style, telling the nation that the world must be made safe for democracy. Four days later, Congress declared war on Germany. In the Senate, the resolution was passed by 82 votes to 6 and in the House by 373 votes to 50.

The implication of these occurrences was twofold: Germany could not win the war if it was still being fought in 1919, when the full weight of the American contribution could be deployed; but, given that the deployment could not take place until then and that, in the meantime, she was fighting on only one front, she could win the war now.

The direction of Germany's war was no longer in the hands of the Kaiser or his ministers but rather was controlled by the warlords Erich Ludendorff and Paul von Hindenburg. In the course of 1917, they secured the dismissal of the chancellor, Bethmann-Hollweg, and his replacement by a much less powerful successor. The German people looked for deliverance to the High Command – effectively these two men.

Although he came to symbolise high Junkerdom, Hindenburg's background was fairly unremarkable. His father was no more than a lieutenant in the army and of modest means. Hindenburg's own career was about as military as it could be – he went to Cadet School at the age of eleven, fought in the Austro-Prussian and Franco-Prussian Wars and married a general's daughter. His career was distinguished, rather than glittering, and appeared to have come to an end when he retired in 1911. The outbreak of the war three years later brought him back to the army, first as an Army Commander at Tannenberg, then as commander on the Eastern Front. From that, he moved to become Chief of the General Staff and, in effect, Commander-in-Chief. His self-control and ambition established him, with Ludendorff, as ruler of Germany from 1916 onwards. The two men overturned the constitutional convention that their responsibilities were limited to advising the Kaiser on military affairs. They argued that military interests embraced foreign and domestic policy. While they did not seek political office, they dominated political life by securing the dismissal of any civilians with whom they disagreed.

Ludendorff, like Hindenburg, was raised near Posen, now Poznań, in West Prussia. His background was even less elevated. He was unpopular with his colleagues and with the Kaiser, overtly ambitious, unappealing and febrile. His career in the war was intimately associated with that of Hindenburg, whose Chief of Staff he was both at Tannenberg and on the Eastern Front. When Hindenburg became Commander-in-Chief, Ludendorff was his First Quartermaster General. In reality he was Hindenburg's equal and his success was not dependent on Hindenburg's patronage – for all the dislike he engendered in the army, his imagination and organisational ability could not be ignored.

By 1917, Ludendorff was exhibiting signs of paranoia and had become deluded by Napoleonic ideas of world domination. Despite Brest-Litovsk, he maintained a million soldiers in the east. There were expeditionary forces in Finland and at Batoum, Baku and Odessa, and the Ukraine and Romania were occupied. Nonetheless, there was a massive shift of troops to the Western Front. While there had been 150 German divisions on the Western Front at the beginning of November 1917, by 21 March there were 192. A further 16 arrived thereafter.

It was not simply a question of the *quantity* of men brought to the Western Front – it was much more the quality. In those divisions which were moved from Russia to the Western Front, only men under the age of 35 and fit for the kind of war that was to be fought in the *Kaiserschlacht* were included. And the divisions that remained on the Eastern Front had to give up those under the age of 35 for the benefit of the Western Front. And so when, in March 1918, the army in the west had been brought up to a strength of 136,618 officers and 3,438,288 other ranks, those officers and men were of a much higher calibre than the Allied troops on that front.[3]

What was the calibre of those Allied troops? At the beginning of 1918, Cyril Falls,* liaising with the French, asked himself, 'Was the French army's recovery complete?' He replied, 'I should answer that in the best formations and units it was but on the whole not.'[4] In the British armies, most troops were very, very tired after the prolonged campaign in Flanders in 1917. A high proportion was overdue for leave.

The implications of all of this were clear. As early as 9 May 1917, Sir William Robertson, in a paper, 'The Military Effect of Russia Seceding from the Entente', said, 'We should be prepared for the worst, namely that the Central Powers will be free to concentrate their forces against their remaining enemies ... It must be assumed that the whole of the German army on the Eastern Front will be available for operations on the west.' He recognised that, while they would be *available* for operations in the west, not all of them could physically be in the west, as the railway systems would not be adequate to supply them. 'The surplus numbers would be kept in rear and used to relieve divisions in the Front Line.'[5]

There were American troops in Europe by March 1918 but they contributed little in the response to the March offensive. The American Commander-in-Chief, Pershing, of whom Haig said, 'I was much struck with his quiet, gentlemanly bearing – so unusual for an American', was instructed by the US Secretary for War that the United States Armies must be maintained as a separate and distinct component of the combined forces, subject only to minor exceptions in particular circumstances. Pershing took this instruction very seriously, to the extent that he told Foch that he would prefer to see France defeated in battle than compromise his orders – despite the fact that the final paragraph of his instructions, which he always chose to ignore, read, 'But, until the forces of the United States are in your judgement sufficiently strong to warrant operations as an independent command, it is understood that you will cooperate as a component of whatever army you may be assigned to by the French government.'[6]

The imperatives that bore down on Germany were not dictated only by the entrance to the war of the United States and the exit of Russia. At home, while there were some war profiteers who were doing very well out of the war, the mass of the people were close to starvation and perhaps revolution. The Executive Committee of the Workers' Councils

---

* Falls, who served through the First World War and became a military writer, journalist and Chichele Professor of the History of War at Oxford, also worked on the Official History.

called a strike on 27 January 1918 and, on just one day's notice, one million workers came out, 600,000 in Berlin itself.[7] The soldiers called the strikers and demonstrators the 'rowdies'. 'We have to thank these Berlin whelps for lengthening the war by at least half a year.'[8]

An extra propellant to High Command's desire to see the war finished sooner rather than later was the effect on German domestic politics of the revolution in Russia. Workers, hungry as a result of food shortages, were angered by hearing of the huge profits being made out of the war and unskilled workers resented the difference between their wages and those of more skilled men.

The coal shortage, bad in France, was even worse in Germany. Fuel consumption was limited to one third of normal, non-essential industries worked part-time, lights went out in Berlin flats at 9 p.m., the rail network broke down, riots, sabotage and strikes were commonplace and even the navy was threatened by mutiny. The majority of the parties in the Reichstag passed a 'peace resolution' in 1917 but the Reichstag was powerless. The Kaiser himself was a mere figurehead.

The reaction to the 1918 strikes was severe, with long prison sentences pronounced by Special Courts Martial. The *Bureau für Sozialpolitik* reported on them to the War Ministry, which copied on to Army Corps. But, in reality, labour relations were much less disruptive in Germany than in Britain. In 1918, there were 391,000 strikers in Germany who caused the loss of 1,452,000 days of work; in Britain, there were 923,000 strikers and 6,000,000 work days lost.[9] The Associated Society of Engineers, a craft trade union, decided to call an all-out strike for the very day the *Kaiserschlacht* began. But tricky labour relations were not a novelty in democratic Britain – they were in Germany. High Command was concerned by the breakdown in solidarity and by the unpatriotic content of pamphlets circulating amongst the troops.

THE ORIGINS OF THE SPRING OFFENSIVE

On 11 November 1917, exactly a year before the armistice, there was an important conference at Mons, Headquarters of Crown Prince Rupprecht's Army Group (as opposed to the German Crown Prince's Army Group).* It is a reflection on the reality of rule in Germany that

---

* Rupprecht was Crown Prince of Bavaria. There is scope for confusion. He was theoretically a claimant to the British crown through the Stewart succession. Though he forbade any discussion

the Kaiser was not invited to the conference and probably not Rupprecht either. Ludendorff met a variety of Chiefs of Staffs. He proposed an attack on the British element of the enemy line which would separate them from the French and trap them against the sea. His proposal was not immediately accepted.

There was debate about whether to launch an attack westwards against the British sector of the allied line or southwards against the French. There were advantages and disadvantages. The main drawback about an attack to the south was that the French had plenty of room to retire and Germany could be drawn deeper into France, as had happened in 1914. Furthermore, Ludendorff, with an evident scepticism about Britain's loyalty to her Allies, thought that Britain might well refrain from assisting a retreating French army, which would mean that Germany would have to conduct a second offensive against the British in Flanders. There were not resources for two offensives.

He was opposed by Major Wetzell, Chief of the Operations Division of the General Staff, who argued for an attack on the French at Verdun, with the aim of an outright victory rather than victory by separation. Colonel Count von der Schulenburg, Chief of Staff to the German Crown Prince's Army Group, also took that view. After three hours of discussion, the British option was agreed on. After the war, Ludendorff sought to justify his decision, saying that he had thought that Britain would sue for peace more readily than the French, who were defending their native land. In any event, he regarded the French as more skilful and flexible soldiers.[10]

The brunt of the attack would accordingly be directed against Britain:

> The situation in Russia and Italy will, as far as can be seen, make it possible to deliver a blow on the Western Front in the New Year. The strength of the two sides will be approximately equal. About 35 divisions and 1,000 heavy guns can be made available for *one* offensive; a second great simultaneous offensive, say as a diversion, will not be possible.

---

of that idea, he was entitled to style himself Duke of Cornwall and Duke of Rothesay. He was also a descendant of William the Conqueror, Louis XIV and more recently 'mad' King Ludwig of Bavaria. He regarded Hitler as also being insane and would have nothing to do with the Nazis, who caught his wife and daughters during the war and imprisoned them in Sachsenhausen and then Dachau, experiences which they survived. He lived on till 1955, hoping always for the restoration of the Bavarian monarchy.

Our general situation requires that we should strike at the earliest moment, if possible at the end of February or beginning of March, before the Americans can throw strong forces into the scale.

We must beat the British.[11]

Ludendorff's plan was refined in the month that followed the conference of 11 November 1917, partly as a result of productive argument with Hermann von Kuhl, Crown Prince Rupprecht's Chief of Staff. By the end of January, the initial plans were more or less settled. Three prongs of MICHAEL were to be launched on 20 March, from the northeast of Bapaume to the south of Saint Quentin. Since this book deals with what happened, rather than what did not happen, the detailed evolution of the plan and the changes that were made and then abandoned can be left aside.[12] Similarly, the series of operations which were finally agreed upon other than MICHAEL is not directly relevant to this book and how they developed will not be considered.

What is important in the story of 21–26 March is that the final decision, which Ludendorff did not make till 21 January, was to select MICHAEL as the principal attack, with MARS as an optional extra. Rupprecht only accepted Ludendorff's choice with reluctance. There had been a great deal of continuing argument after the meeting of 11 November 1918. But Ludendorff got his way and the main objective for the first part of the attack would be an assault on the British front on the line Albert-Bapaume. It was envisaged that Britain would then move troops from the Ypres front, when Germany would attack the salient there and descend from the north in GEORGE I and II. It is thought that emphasis on the MICHAEL front, occupied by British Fifth Army, was due to the knowledge that Britain was dangerously stretched, having agreed to extend her line to Barisis, taking over that part of the line from the French in circumstances which have been mentioned and which will be developed later. On 16 January, the Chief of Staff of Oskar von Hutier's Eighteenth Army wrote very perceptively that, because of the extension of the British line:

[t]he [German] *Eighteenth Army* will therefore have only British opposite to it. This will make the situation more favourable to us.

The offensive is principally intended to strike the British. They now stand opposite to us on the whole front of the Group of Armies which is to make the offensive. It need not be anticipated that the French will run themselves off their legs and hurry at once to the help of their entente comrades. They will first wait and see if their own front is not attacked also and decide to support their ally only when the situation has been quite cleared up. That will not be immediately, as demonstrations to deceive the French will be made by the German Crown Prince's Group.[13]

Forty-four divisions were initially allocated. They were known as 'mobile' or 'mob' divisions and, at the end of 1917, were withdrawn from the front to be trained in accordance with Ludendorff's handbook, *The Offensive in Trench Warfare*. The nub of the approach was a move from traditional infantry tactics with reliance on the rifle. A mob division had a machine-gun sniper unit, air support and a communications unit. Soldiers carried light machine guns, flame-throwers and mortars. Rifle grenades and mortars firing in low trajectory were favoured for use against machine-gun nests. The superior resources of the Entente Allies were thought to be at least counterbalanced by leadership training and motivation underwritten by surprise and deception.

TACTICS

Ludendorff had developed his tactics on the Eastern Front. His troops in the March 1918 Spring Offensive were already called *Sturmabteilung*, 'Storm Troops' – exactly the name Hitler's soldiers were to carry. Their instructions were to exploit advantage and to regard their objectives as unlimited: 'Infantry which looked to the right or left soon comes to a stop. Touch with the enemy is the *desideratum*; a uniform advance must in no case be demanded. The fastest, not the slowest, must set the pace.'

Troops were ordered not to concentrate on points of defence but to bypass them and try to get through to the enemy's artillery. Advancing tanks were simply avoided. The aim was always infiltration. Dictation of the pace by the movement of a creeping barrage was avoided because the barrage was to be controlled from the advancing infantry in front and not by the artillerymen in the rear. The Storm Troopers were followed by multi-weapon teams which included sections of field artillery. A great emphasis was put on flexibility of function and speed of movement. There was much more stress on secrecy than in the past. Significant troop movements were carried out under cover of darkness and concentrations of troops were concealed so that, as far as possible, attacks took place unannounced. Use was made of camouflage and aerial inspections ensured that there were no signs of tracks left by advancing units. Railheads were cleared the moment troops were detrained. This approach, so similar to that of Hitler's armies in 1940, was to characterise an offensive which consisted of five separate thrusts, MICHAEL from 21 March to 5 April, followed by four others.

Much of the change in German tactics was prompted by the experience of the Somme, and the Allies' use of huge preparatory artillery barrages. German infantry now deployed in a fairly light front line, with two reserve forces behind it, at least some of the men out of the range of artillery. Deployment in depth was supported by a greatly increased use of machine guns. Storm-troop tactics can be seen to be evolving even in the course of 1917 in the shape of infantry squads offensively used in counter-strokes (*Gegenstöße*).[14] While it was Falkenhayn who learned the lessons of 1916, it was Hindenburg and Ludendorff who were to apply them in 1917 and 1918.

Britain had refined her tactics too. Some lessons had been learned from the Germans but Britain learned others by herself. Experience in the South African war had shown that there were circumstances in which fire and movement was preferable to linear advance. Much more was learned from the Somme, with the use of multi-weapons tactics to enable infantrymen to find their own way forward. Manuals such as *Instructions for the Training of Divisions for Offensive Operations* (SS135) and, in particular, *Instructions for the Training of Platoons for Offensive Action* (SS143), published in December 1916 and February 1917, have been described by Paddy Griffith as a 'Storm Trooper's Handbook'.[15]

By 1917 and 1918, British Ninth Division (it's interesting to note how often these tactical advances were pioneered at divisional level) had found that, in some circumstances, section columns should advance in single file. A pamphlet issued by Fourth Seaforth Highlanders in 1917 advocated counter-attacking by 'dribbling' forward in columns 'on the German model' rather than moving in waves. A firing line would then advance in what was rather well described as 'controlled irregularity'. This was infiltration. General Ivor Maxse, always a forward-looking commander, approved these tactics for his XVIII Corps.[16]

Sectional attack in 'blobs' rather than in lines was supplemented by squares or diamonds. In this way, sectional advances could adjust the line of attack to facilitate infiltration. Again, Maxse picked up these ideas and included them in his 1917 pamphlet *Hints on Training Issued by XVIII*

Corps, which was circulated widely in August 1918 in time for the Hundred Days, when it was known as 'the Brown Book'. Maxse's dictum was 'When in doubt go ahead. When uncertain, do that which will kill most Germans. Don't fear an exposed flank.' He is pretty close to the German storm-troop orthodoxy.

CRITICISM OF LUDENDORFF

It is clear from what has been said that Ludendorff's scheme did not enjoy the enthusiastic proposal of all senior officers. Von Kuhl complained about the lack of operational goal. Crown Prince Rupprecht, viewing matters in a similar way, could not see that the operations could succeed and, indeed, was coming to the view that there should be a negotiated peace.

The essential objection to Ludendorff's plan was that he abandoned the classical principle that strategy must be based on political aims or, indeed, that he had abandoned true tactics in favour of tactical opportunism. Instead of identifying the point in the enemy line at which an attack could achieve most operational success, he chose to break through where he could advance most easily. The criticism is not entirely reasonable. It is advanced best with hindsight but it is important to recognise, as he himself acknowledged, that Ludendorff had *chosen* to place tactics above strategy.[17] It was all he could do. He did not have the resources for the sort of set-piece battle that the classical theorists envisaged – and which had proved so unproductive in the course of the long years of the war. In the limited time he had and with limited men and *matériel* at his disposal, an exploitative breakthrough was the best he could hope for and it came pretty close to success.

Ludendorff's aim should have been, according to the classical view and in ideal circumstances, to destroy the British army by an all-out attack culminating in seizing the Channel ports. To do that, he would leave aside the deep Fifth Army Amiens-Somme front, where he would advance into a sack. Instead, he would attack Ypres, Arras and Vimy and expose Boulogne and Calais. Haig could see the logic of this and had concentrated his defences accordingly. Ludendorff, seeing the density of the British forces facing him there and aware of his own limited resources, compromised from the ideal and chose the opportunistic alternative.

At a planning conference, Rupprecht pressed Ludendorff to identify the operational objective of the attack. Ludendorff's response was: 'I object to the word "operation". We will just blow a hole in the middle. The rest will follow of its own accord.'[18] Ludendorff's approach is criticised in modern studies for its lack of attention to the operational level, the planning that enables tactical victory to flow into the strategical victories that win wars. German planning in the First World War had been based on the belief that victory had to be won quickly in a single, decisive battle – Schlieffen's Battle of Annihilation (*Vernichtungsschlacht*). The essential sequencing was absent from their planning. (In the Second World War, Alanbrooke, the Chief of the Imperial General Staff, criticised Churchill for a failure to sequence. He said, 'If you are going to the barber, you think about where he is before you head out of your front door.' Churchill's childish response was 'No I don't.'[19])

Germany identified the BEF in 1918 as the Clausewitzian Centre of Gravity (*Schwerpunkt*) – the critical hub of the Franco-British line. The assumption was that, if the BEF could be knocked out and chased off the continent, France would speedily collapse. In the event, as will be seen, Ludendorff left off attacking the BEF to exploit the fact that Britain and France were falling apart. Haig's initial disposition of forces forced Ludendorff's compromise. That was Haig's achievement. His failure lay in his delay in realising that the compromise had taken place. Because of that failure Ludendorff's gamble almost came off.

9

The Supreme War Council

PREPARATION FOR MEETING the Spring Offensive was damaged almost irretrievably by the existence of a body sitting at Versailles, just outside Paris, called the Supreme War Council. It was the physical expression of Lloyd George's frustration with the military.

It evolved by stages. In June 1917, Lloyd George set up something new and distinct from the War Cabinet – the Cabinet War Policy Committee. It consisted of Milner, Curzon, Bonar Law, Smuts and the two Chiefs of Staff, Robertson for the army and Jellicoe for the navy. It proved an unhelpful invention and increasingly the prime minister tended to take his advice from Henry Wilson.

Wilson had been British Liaison Officer at the French General Headquarters, *GQG*, until June 1917. It was a good place for this Francophile to be. But, when Pétain was appointed French C.-in-C., he came to the conclusion that Wilson was too chummy with his predecessor, Nivelle, and Wilson was sent back to Britain. After a few months on half pay, when he toyed with the idea of going in to Parliament as a Conservative, he was appointed as commander of the UK Eastern Military District. The job doesn't seem to have absorbed a great deal of his time or energies but it was based in London and so kept him conveniently close to the centres of political power. He used his opportunity to build up a plan to bring the Allies together into closer strategic and political unity – a scheme which appealed to Lloyd George.

In September 1917, frustrated by the bloodletting and stasis on the Western Front, and dissatisfied by the advice he received from Wully Robertson, his constitutional military adviser, the prime minister took the irregular step of calling for what he called 'a second opinion'. He consulted Lord (formerly Sir John) French, who had been, as Haig put it, sent home in disgrace in 1915, and Henry Wilson, whose mind was working in the same direction as the prime minister's: 'Really we must change in 1918 our puerile, useless, costly strategy of 1916 and 1917.'[1] 'Wilson,' it has been said, 'was the man who took Lloyd George's critique and made it a fully fledged alternative grand strategy.'[2] That seems to be pitching Wilson's role a bit high. Low politics rather than grand strategy were his speciality. What he did do was understand that, in an age of mass democracy, generals were subordinate to politicians.

In itself, working more closely with allies was not a bad idea. But the covert element in the plan was to provide Lloyd George with military advice independent of what he received from Wully Robertson. Whether or not that too was a sensible objective, it was certainly an unconstitutional one. Wilson proposed an Inter-Allied Supreme War Council to meet once a month, supported by joint strategic staff. On 24 August 1917, Leo Amery 'motored down with Lord M[ilner] and Henry Wilson and went for a walk along the edge of the Downs near Tatsfield. Had a long talk after dinner . . . I discovered that there was a new suggestion afloat which [Wilson] had put to Lloyd George. This is that the Italians, French and ourselves should form a small committee consisting of the three prime ministers or leading politicians and three soldiers under the Chief of Staff to arrive at a command plan for the whole Front.'[3] These proposals were first officially mentioned on 14 October, when Lloyd George suggested that an Inter-Allied War Council and a Permanent General Staff should be set up in Paris. Hankey was 'horrified' at the thought of how Haig and Robertson would react.[4]

Leo Amery, almost forgotten today, was one of the most influential politicians of his time. If he is remembered at all it is because of a famous speech in the Norway debate in 1940 which resulted in the downfall of Neville Chamberlain. But he held many of the most important offices, including that of Secretary of State for India. Indeed, it was said that he might have been prime minister if he had been half a foot taller and his speeches half an hour shorter. But what was perhaps most interesting about him was the extent to which he influenced policy and events from the wings, without substantial control or ostensible authority. He was a protégé of Lord Milner and, like him, used All Souls' College, Oxford as a resource for research and a platform for the dissemination of his views, particularly in connection with a forward policy for the development of the Empire.

In the first half of 1917, he was Political Secretary to the War Cabinet, a creative role – he was entitled, indeed expected, to submit proposals to the War Cabinet. Technically, he was Assistant Secretary to Hankey, who was Secretary to the War Cabinet (and, indeed, to the Cabinet itself). He relished the situation, which was 'delightfully vague'. Along with Mark Sykes,* he provided a weekly summary of the world situation for the War Cabinet. The privilege of creating such a report involved the prerogative of creating an agenda.[5]

Because of his role in the War Cabinet, Amery was intimately involved in the negotiations for the establishment of a Supreme War Council, a project of which, in any case, he wholeheartedly approved. His position was all the more interesting because the Secretary of State for War, Derby, had appointed him to his personal staff. Derby had threatened to resign over the establishment of the Supreme War Council because he could see it was an attempt to sideline Robertson. Amery sought to reassure Derby (entirely dishonestly).[†] In due course, Amery was sent to work with the Supreme War Council at Versailles.

The Supreme War Council proper was finally set up by agreement between the British, French and Italians at a conference at Rapallo on 7 November 1917. The Americans joined thereafter. In the period up to the Doullens Conference, the Supreme War Council met for just four sessions: at Rapallo, on 7 November 1917; at Versailles, on 1 December 1917; at Versailles again, from 30 January to 2 February 1918; and in London, on 14 and 15 March 1918. After Doullens, the Council met much more frequently. There were fourteen more sessions before its final meeting in Paris on 17 March 1919.

The different countries represented on the Council were supported by Permanent Military Representatives, PMRs. The stress on the fact that *they* were military men reflects the fact that the Council itself was not intended by its creators – certainly not by Lloyd George – to be a military body. Quite the reverse – it was devised to wrest control of the

---

*   Sir Mark Sykes was a sport of nature – another young man who had huge influence without official authority. He had little formal education and left Cambridge after just two years, spent largely in the dramatic societies. He is remembered today for his part in negotiating the Sykes-Picot Agreement, which still causes problems in the Middle East but helped the Allies to win the First World War. He died of Spanish influenza in 1919. Because he was buried in a lead coffin, he was exhumed in 2007 to see whether examination of his body could help create remedies against another pandemic – a rare example of public service, working for the good of mankind after his death.

†   Amery had no time for Robertson. His diary for 12 November 1917: 'Looking back over the best part of a year at the cabinet, I cannot recollect Robertson on a single occasion indicating what he thought the enemy was really likely to do or what we might do ourselves, beyond expressing the general hope that we were going to obtain our objectives in the West.' Amery was distinctly a Wilson man.

war from professional soldiers and hand it to democratically responsible politicians. The PMRs were only there to advise. The agreement for the formation of the Supreme Inter-Allied War Council, signed at Rapallo on 7 November 1917, said that the 'executive function' of the permanent military representatives was 'to act as technical advisor to the council'. The American Commander in Chief, Pershing, went out of his way to say in his memoirs that the organisation of the council was designed to give Lloyd George greater control over operations. He noted that the Commanders-in-Chief, though they were expected to attend meetings, were not members and had no vote. He was not alone among the military men in his suspicion of the council.[6]

When the Council met on 1 December 1917, it gave the Military Representatives the enormous brief of examining the entire military situation from Nieuwpoort to Baghdad, not just the Western Front, considering plans and reporting their recommendations. The Council did not sit again until the end of January 1918. Between 13 December and 23 January 1918, the Military Representatives produced a series of Joint Notes.

At the same time, back in London, the War Cabinet took time to review what would happen in another year of war. They asked Robertson and Haig for their views. Robertson made the logical suggestion that Germany would try for a decision before America could deploy her forces in numbers. He thought that Germany would attack the Channel ports, Paris and northern Italy. The War Cabinet, in about as pessimistic a mood as they had known, seemed to doubt that the Allies could win the war. They asked whether the prospects of success were sufficient to justify a continued struggle. Robertson's reply was in effect that it all depended on how determined the Allies were and, in particular, what manpower was available. The critical thing was not killing Germans or Austrians but increasing the number of Allied soldiers.

Haig's opinion was now sought at a meeting of the War Cabinet on 7 January 1918 which is briefly mentioned above (p. 63). He was asked what the position would be in six or twelve months' time. This inarticulate man, eloquent on paper but tongue-tied when speaking, performed about as badly at this meeting as he ever did. Lloyd George described his performance as 'wooden-fisted, club-footed and without imagination'.[7] The consequences were disastrous for him and for Britain's stance ahead of the *Kaiserschlacht*.

There was a political dimension to the antipathy between the Commander-in-Chief and the prime minister which had crystallised into something close to personal hatred.[8] Haig, the uncritical monarchist, deluded himself in the belief that Lloyd George was working to establish Britain as a republic. In March 1918, he told his wife that, if the prime minister 'reorganised' the House of Commons, he would have popular support. Lloyd George was equally fanciful, suggesting that Haig and Robertson wanted to overthrow the government and rule through military control.[9]

Lloyd George used his *Memoirs* as an opportunity, long after the war had finished, for settling scores and having the last word. They are not to be relied on factually but they do reflect his opinions accurately enough. In his chapter on the 'Outlook for 1918', he states baldly:

> The heroic if unintelligent and ill-coordinated efforts put forth in 1917 by the armies of France and Britain to drive the Germans out of Belgium and the occupied territories of France had been sanguinary failures . . . As to the British army, it kept on fighting doggedly [at Third Ypres] right into the December mists, but it was tired and without confidence in the wisdom of the leadership which was responsible for the stupid and squalid strategy of the last two months of Passchendaele, and for the egregious muddle which threw away the great opportunities of Cambrai.[10]

This was how he saw things when Haig was questioned by the Cabinet.

Haig appeared to say that the Germans would not attack. On the following day, he said that what he had been endeavouring to say was that he thought that the German Armies *would* attack but that, if *he* were in charge of them, he would not. He tried to correct the impression he had given by sending a corrective written message on the following day in which he said:

> In my opinion the crucial period for the Allies is the next few months. During this period the Central Powers may make a determined effort to force a decision on the Western Front, i.e. on the Italian, French or British Front. I regard such an effort on the part of the enemy in the light of a gamble with a determination to risk everything in order to secure an early and favourable decision. Provision must be made to meet such an eventuality and to replace the losses which would certainly be incurred in withstanding a heavy and sustained attack.[11]

The minutes of the meeting undermine his argument that he had been trying to say what he would do if he were Ludendorff rather than what the real Ludendorff would do. After some introductory remarks by Amery and Lloyd George, who mentioned that the French refused to accept that the British were doing their share, 'whereas it was common knowledge that the brunt of the fighting in 1917 had been borne by the British, thus enabling the French Army to recover', Sir Edward Carson, Minister without Portfolio, asked whether Haig thought:

> [i]t would be possible for the Germans to break through our lines in France in the near future.
>
> Sir Douglas Haig replied that nothing was certain in war. A long-continued offensive by the Germans would use up all our present reserves, and our losses would continue to be heavy; but, after consultation with his Army Commanders, he was satisfied that the condition and morale of the British Army was such as to give him every confidence that the British Army would hold its own, as it had always done in the past.

Shortly afterwards, Bonar Law put the critical question, in a form which caused Haig so much trouble:

> If you were a German Commander, would you think there was sufficient chance of a smashing offensive to justify incurring the losses which would be entailed?
>
> Sir Douglas Haig replied that it seemed to him that an expensive offensive would not pay the Germans. If they failed, they were so much worse off, while the present position gave them little hope of substantial success. There were two ways of effecting victory in a war like this:
>
>   a) by destroying the enemy's Army;
>   b) by destroying the moral[e] of the enemy people.
>
> The latter course had proved successful in Russia and seemed now to be the enemy's game. However, he was taking no chances and was making every preparation in case the much-advertised offensive materialised. We were now in possession of all the main ridges which the Germans had held last year, and we were therefore in a much better position to deal with an enemy offensive.

That was the exchange as recorded in the draft minutes. Although the question had focused on what Haig would do if he were the German commander, his reply did not rest on that assumption. He had an opportunity to read and amend the draft. What follows is the amended handwritten re-script of the passage, with Haig's own underlinings:

> Sir Douglas Haig replied that it seemed to him that there were two ways of effecting victory in War:
>
>   a) by destroying the moral[e] of the enemy's <u>Army</u>; or
>   b) by destroying the moral[e] of the enemy <u>people</u> by attacks of limited scope such as against Chalons, Arras, or some salient.
>
> The latter seemed to him to be the more probable course for the enemy to adopt because an offensive on a large scale made with the object of piercing the front and reaching Calais or Paris, for instance, would be very costly. Moreover the German manpower situation did not seem very satisfactory: he had about one million Reserves for the whole of the coming year. If he attacked and failed, his position would thereupon become critical in view of the increasing forces of the Allies in August ... We must expect to be seriously attacked, to be pressed back in places, to lose ground and also guns possibly. But he felt confident of holding his front provided his Divisions were maintained at proper strength.[12]

The amendments are of little moment. Haig expected no more than attacks of limited scope which he was confident of repelling. It is impossible to sustain the argument that he had inadvertently misled the War Cabinet because, at Bonar Law's request, he had been wearing a German cap rather than a British one. Only later did he realise that he had talked the Western Front out of a job in 1918 and try to row back in the corrective message referred to above.

His misconceived remarks and this apparent about-turn provided delightful ammunition for his enemies in their purpose of denying him reinforcements. The prime minister demanded to know what was to be thought of a man who was now expressing an opinion totally at odds with what he had said two days earlier.

HENRY WILSON'S WAR GAMES

Unlike Haig and Robertson, who kept telling the prime minister that the war must drag on in France and Flanders without any prospect of a resolution, Henry Wilson, Britain's man at the SWC, was prepared – indeed, anxious – to tell Lloyd George what the prime minister very much wanted to hear.

In parenthesis, it is worth mentioning that, while Wilson and Lloyd George are always treated as being entirely sympathetic one to the other, never separated in their views, in reality, the former's influence on the prime minister was limited. Lloyd George regarded him as unduly facetious and frivolous, 'whimsical almost to the point of buffoonery'. He respected his lucid mind and capacity for expression. 'But he had no power of decision. That is why he failed on the field.* For the same reason, he was not a complete success in council. He shrank from the responsibility of the final word, even in advice. I was always perplexed to know what to think of him'.[13] His instinct was to doubt what Wilson said. Wilson's influence was stronger with other members of the War Cabinet than it was with the prime minister.

At Versailles, the French always knew that Wilson was basically a Francophile (not a common thing among British officers) and so they accepted or favoured many of his opinions, but there is some evidence that they too found his professional competence poorer than expected. Even his friend the French Chief of the General Staff, Foch, whose assistant Maxime Weygand was the French PMR, expressed himself as being disappointed in Wilson. He said, 'General Wilson was not as good as he had thought he was, and required a great deal of close support and help; were it not for General Weygand Versailles would be in a bad way as General Wilson kept giving "free rein" to his fancy.' He said that Wilson needed to be informed about many things.

In December 1917, while almost everyone expected a major German attack on the Western Front, Henry Wilson ran a war game at Versailles. Wilson's career had been passed mainly in staff work and liaison and teaching. His time as Commandant of the Staff College at Camberley (1906–10) has briefly been referred to. He was famous there for evaluating global trends and military options and, while Director of Military Operations (1910–14), for invaluable work on mobilisation timetabling and scheduling. War games had been a feature of his time at Camberley. He liked the intellectual stimulus of war games, in which paper battles were fought by two sides in order to try to get an insight into how the enemy would be viewing matters.

---

* It's not clear what failure Lloyd George had in mind. Wilson's critics are inclined to mention that he didn't spend much time in the field.

Now at Versailles, to make the exercise more convincing, he required the section of the staff playing the part of Germans to wear their caps back to front. The game was intended to evaluate the various options the Germans might have for offensives on the Western Front in 1918 and thus to help formulate a British and Allied riposte. It would also help to define whether and to what extent Allied moves in other theatres could be risked.

The most important of all his war games was in finished form by mid December 1917 and underwent a degree of revision a month later. The conclusion of the game was that there would be no decision on the Western Front in 1918 and the Allies should therefore concentrate on Turkey. Haig should also be asked to extend his front by 40 miles. The game was very popular with Lloyd George and others and was rerun to packed houses for visitors who came to the SWC during the two and a half months when he was British Permanent Military Representative Versailles, from late November 1917 to early February 1918.

During Wilson's time at Versailles, he frequently spoke of this game to his *British* contacts but it is unclear whether the French and Italians saw it played or how much they knew of it. We do not know if they were involved in collecting and analysing the basic data or whether they accepted the conclusions of the game. But, at any rate, the conclusions strongly influenced the War Cabinet's thinking during the winter and early spring of 1917–18. The game's arguments were influential in deter-mining the point to which the British line should be extended in relief of the French. It was not, however, decisive in this because the French and British Cs-in-C. had, meanwhile, come to a personal compromise on the point of junction.

The war game was a powerful weapon in forming policy. It exerted great influence on the War Cabinet's assessment of the risks and oppor-tunities in Western Europe and the Middle East in 1918 and in 1919. It confirmed their prejudices about the security of the Western Front and helped in pushing for a decisive campaign at the eastern end of the Mediterranean. And this was despite quite different formal advice from the CIGS, Robertson, and the C.-in-C. in France, Haig.

Wilson developed his views further in a paper of 1 January 1918, amended on 28 January, on 'A German Offensive in France'. Looking at the numbers available on each side, he concluded that, from a military point of view, the Germans would be likely to postpone their offensive until 1 May. The areas which Wilson forecast as being the most probable places for a hostile attack did not include the points on which Ludendorff concentrated his forces in March 1918.

Haig viewed the Supreme War Council and its Executive War Board as an ineffective talking shop. Originally the Executive War Board was to be attended by the Chiefs of the General Staffs. Haig was unhappy that, in Britain's case, Lloyd George had, in effect, a personal representative in Henry Wilson. The other PMRs were responsible to their armies and governments. Wilson was not.

The French were ambivalent. Clemenceau, the prime minister, was not in favour of the SWC. The two commanders on the Western Front, Pétain as much as Haig, were unimpressed. They were aware that an attack was imminent but they did not use the Council as the conduit for their reactions. Pétain told Foch, the French PMR, that he would assist Haig but did not formally communicate the details to the Executive War Board – or, indeed, at a formal level, even to Haig himself. The SWC tried to inject some rigour into these arrangements by saying that '[t]he agreement arrived at between the Commanders-in-Chief of the Allied Armies in France for mutual support should be communicated formally to the permanent Military Representatives at Versailles'. But that never happened. In these circumstances, the Supreme War Council and the permanent Military Representatives did almost nothing to meet the German assault of March 1918. The Council did not meet as a whole between the launch of the offensive on 21 March and 1 May. It was an irrelevance which damaged rather than aided the Allied war effort.[14] It need not have been if Haig and Pétain had chosen to make it work.

THE SWC AND THE END OF WULLY ROBERTSON

For constitutional reasons, the establishment of the SWC led directly to the downfall of Wully Robertson. This was exactly what Lloyd George and, no doubt, Henry Wilson had wanted. Lloyd George had absolutely no regard for Robertson, whom he had long written off as being 'merely the echo of 'aig'. By Christmas 1917, Lloyd George had begun to prepare the press for the dismissal of Robertson together with the Secretary of State, Derby, and Haig. It should not be thought that Lloyd George was engaged on a purely personal vendetta. Lord Milner was threatening at this time to resign if Robertson were not removed.[15]

This war within the war gravely weakened control on the Western Front at precisely the moment when that front was subjected to the most enormous strain. Haig and Robertson may have had their faults but they did work as a team and, rightly or wrongly – I would say rightly – shared the view that the Western Front was where the war would be won or lost. Lloyd George's achievement – in disposing of Robertson and, in his wake, other key members of Haig's team – was to leave the Commander-in-Chief exposed and working with a new CIGS, Henry Wilson, who would never support him as Robertson had done, even if he would not abandon him as Haig expected him to do.

The nub of Robertson's constitutional objection to the SWC was that its Executive War Board was to have power over British forces without responsibility for their safety, thus depriving the Army Council, of which the CIGS was the first military member, of its statutory duty. On 9 February, Haig told Derby, the Secretary of State for War, that, in his view, only the Army Council or a Field Marshal senior to him could give him orders – the orders of the Executive War Board might not be lawful. He maintained, as Robertson had done, that the CIGS should be the source of orders. His position was correct and was mirrored by France's practice – Foch was not only France's PMR but also Robertson's counterpart as Chief of Staff. Lloyd George would have none of this – he wanted Robertson's powers limited.

He countered by agreeing with Haig that the CIGS and he alone should be the source of orders; the twist was however that the CIGS should be Henry Wilson and Robertson would be shunted off to Versailles as Permanent Military Representative. This was unacceptable to Haig. He immediately said that Wilson wasn't to be trusted and wouldn't do at all. Lloyd George played Haig like a fish. He made a second suggestion which would be equally unacceptable – Haig should be in charge of everything but from London, not from France.

When Haig had vetoed that, the two men agreed on a formula which Lloyd George knew and Haig should have known would be unacceptable to Robertson. Wilson was to be 'absolutely free and unfettered in the advice he gives' from Versailles, the concession to Robertson's constitutional objections being that Wilson's advice would be relayed to the Cabinet by the CIGS. The implication was spelt out in a document which Lloyd George sent to both Wilson and Robertson. The CIGS would no longer be responsible for issuing orders. He would continue to be the Supreme Military Adviser of the government but only in the role of a postbox – the Military Representative would be a Member of the Army Council and would be given the power to make orders.

Robertson, correctly, took the constitutional hierarchy seriously. If it were not taken seriously, the clarity of the chain of command was obscured. Immediately he had been appointed CIGS, he stipulated with Lord Kitchener, the Secretary of State and for a man risen from the ranks not an easy person to whom to dictate terms, that Kitchener should cease meddling in staff matters. Now he declined, as a matter of principle, to agree to any arrangement, which meant that the Army Council and not the CIGS had control of the Reserves. He said the scheme was 'unworkable and dangerous' and he was informed that he had resigned. On 18 February, Wilson was appointed CIGS and Robertson was detailed to take over Eastern Command. Sir Henry Rawlinson replaced Wilson at Versailles. Immediately Wilson took office, he ruled that the PMR should not have the powers he had proposed for post. The position of the CIGS remained as Wully had wanted it to be. Lloyd George was to find Wilson less compliant than he had expected. By July 1918, he was saying that Wilson was 'Wully *redivivus*'[16] – Robertson brought back to life.

Hankey, the Cabinet Secretary, circling round Lloyd George like a planet drawn by a powerful magnetic force, was not surprised that his master was anxious to get rid of Robertson. He was only surprised that it had taken him so long to do so: 'On the whole Robertson was the embodiment of much which the prime minister had come into office to get rid of.' Robertson had been too popular to be disposed of immediately Lloyd George had come into office and the prime minister would not, at any rate until the end of the Third Ypres campaign, have commanded enough support in the War Cabinet or the government generally to dismiss the CIGS. To ensure the success of his coup against Asquith, Lloyd George had to make certain promises to leading Conservatives – Austen Chamberlain, Lord Robert Cecil, Walter Long and others. Amongst the commitments he was required to give was that Haig and Robertson would remain in place.[17]

And, by the stage when he had secured his base, he was faced by innumerable additional problems: the effect of the submarine blockade; the problems about introducing compulsory service for Ireland (such a real problem that Sir Edward Carson resigned from the War Cabinet in January 1918); labour problems; and so forth. Hankey described all this as 'the whirlwind which revolved round Lloyd George in the last days of 1917 and the early days of 1918'.

After Lloyd George announced Robertson's resignation to the Commons, Hankey had tea with him at the House of Commons: 'He was in great spirits and walked up and down imitating "Wully's" heavy walk. This, I hope, ends the Robertson crisis. He is gone, and Henry Wilson reigns in his stead.'[18] Hankey was blinded by his admiration for Lloyd George and told Esher that 'the incompatibility of temper between the two men and the ever-recurring quarrels depreciate LG's vitality and governing power'.

The incompatibility of Robertson and Lloyd George had indeed worried Hankey for some time. He had initiated a daily breakfast meeting between them, in the hope that they would come to understand each other. Lloyd George liked to sit and talk at length after the meal. Alas, breakfast had imperative influences on Robertson's digestion, which required his prompt withdrawal. Thus, the conduct of the war was directly affected by Wully Robertson's gastro-colic reflexes.

10

After Wully

WULLY HAD GONE. Lloyd George would have loved Haig to go too but that was an unattainable dream. Haig had powerful support from the Conservatives in the coalition government and from the Palace. Moreover, there was no one to replace him with. In his savage post-war *Memoirs*, even Lloyd George had to admit that Haig was the best man to be Commander-in-Chief.

Haig's closest associates, those on whom he relied, could however be struck down. Robertson was only the most prominent of those. John Charteris had been close to Haig for many years and was now his Intelligence Chief. He was untidy, smelly, according to Lady Haig[1] and ebullient – a licensed joker at Haig's court, 'the Principal Boy'. He began the day with a brandy bracer for breakfast. His rise had been rapid and he was not popular, though Haig liked him. As an intelligence adviser, Charteris had done Haig no service by feeding him extravagantly misleading accounts of poor German morale and imminent collapse. Haig liked to hear this and Charteris seems to have thought that it was good for Haig to be supplied with what he wanted even if it were inaccurate. In truth, encouraging Haig repeatedly to promise imminent German collapse undermined his credibility with the politicians.

Charteris went in December 1917. Haig didn't strain to save him. He was aware that, in Whitehall, the C.-in-C. was regarded with grudging and hostile respect as the best available general but one surrounded by incompetents.[2] He concluded that the loyal if smelly Charteris would have to go since he had 'put those who ought to work in friendliness with him against him'.[3]

The art of interpreting intelligence information was in its infancy but his replacements, first of all General Sir Herbert Lawrence and then Brigadier-General Edgar Cox, were distinct improvements on Charteris. In January 1918, Lawrence moved on from Head of Intelligence to become Haig's Chief of Staff in place of Lieutenant-General Sir Launcelot Kiggell, another victim of Lloyd George's purge. Kiggell had been working very long hours and finally broke down towards the end of Third Ypres. It is said that, in the course of the battle, when he was driven towards the front, he broke down in tears saying that he had no idea of what his men were having to endure. That story is almost certainly untrue and history has been unkind to Kiggell, who was an effective, hardworking officer, even if he was an uninspiring personality. Major-General J.F.C. Fuller, a student when Kiggell was Commandant of the Staff College at Camberley, said, '[H]e possessed knowledge, but little vision, and at the staff college he appeared to me to be a dyspeptic, gloomy and doleful man.' Haig found a comfortable post for Kiggell as Governor of Guernsey.

Lloyd George had found Haig's appointment of Lawrence as Chief of Staff surprising – dictated, he thought, by Haig's desire to have sympathetic minds around him. He marvelled at:

the advancement of a divisional General, inconspicuous for achievement and not endowed with any exceptional ability, to the all-important post of Chief of the General Staff. The CGS was the principal adviser of the Commander-in-Chief on all questions affecting strategy and tactics. With an army of over two million men holding a line of over 100 miles against the most formidable warriors in the world, it was essential that the Commander-in-Chief should have at his elbow the best strategist in the army, in training, in experience and in intellect. There were men in the British Army who possessed these attributes in a high degree. Sir Douglas Haig overlooked them all, and appointed Sir Herbert Lawrence ... He came to France only in 1917. He was given a divisional command, and did his duty without distinction.[4]

Some of the dismissals were sensible and some inevitable but the combination in such a short period, the removal of so many of Haig's closest associates, hardly served to reassure him about his own longevity. Unable to displace Haig himself, Lloyd George did his best to knock away all his support.

Another of Haig's favourites, Hubert Gough, was also to be dumped, although he went after the start of the *Kaiserschlacht*, rather than in the series of putsches that preceded it. He commanded Fifth Army, which collapsed in the face of the attack. In the aftermath, 'Goughie' was pretty well bound to go. Since his dismissal was part of the clear-out of Haig's circle, it may be dealt with here, rather than in its proper chronological place.

Gough, alone of the Army Commanders, had not been present at the Doullens meeting when Foch's appointment was made. He had not even known that it had taken place or that a generalissimo had been appointed. He was, by now, not in command in the line but subject to Fayolle's orders. He was told to stay in his headquarters as Foch would visit them in the afternoon of that day. When Gough recorded details of his meeting with Foch, thirteen years later, he was still a very angry man. He had not liked being roared at in French.

> Foch was peremptory, rude, and excited in his manner. He began at once by asking 'why I was at my Headquarters and not with my troops in the fighting line?' He then said, 'why could I not fight as we had fought in the first battle of Ypres in 1914?' 'Why did the Army retire?' 'What were my orders to the army?'
>
> He waited for no replies to any of these questions, and he did not expect one, except possibly the last. This was just as well, for any explanations would have probably led to an altercation.
>
> The impression that Foch made on me was naturally not a favourable one. Excitable and evidently apt to jump to conclusions, he did not inspire me with respect or confidence.[5]

Gough went on at some length in an attack on Foch He blamed his behaviour on what he had heard of Fifth Army at Doullens from 'British Ministers, British Generals and Staff Officers'.

Was he ever really up to the job? Haig had been very affected when Gough's brother, John, his Chief of Staff, had been killed by a sniper's bullet in 1915. He may, in consequence, have promoted the survivor beyond his merits. In any event, he admired a thrusting fellow-cavalryman. Derby, the Secretary of State for War, had been clear by the beginning of April 1918 that Hubert Gough should be sent home. He wrote to Haig, 'I will do my best to see that the man you send home is not left on the rocks.' Haig's initial reaction was to conclude that Gough was doing the best he could, given the shortage of troops, to defend a front inherited from the French and, without proper defences. Soon he had to give way to pressure from London. Gough was unhappy and felt he had been unfairly treated. Haig told him not to make a fuss: 'You will have every chance to defend yourself, Hubert. There will be a Court of Enquiry.' There was not. In June, Haig wrote to his wife: 'As regards Gough, I am sorry that he is talking stupidly . . . I am doing all I can to help him, but, as a matter of fact, some orders he issued and some things he did were stupid.'

Even if Haig had always rather liked 'Goughie', he was never prepared to sacrifice his own career to defend his subordinates. When Robertson was dismissed, the Secretary of State, Derby, felt that *he* had to resign and the king assured him that he had no alternative. Derby brought himself to the point of resignation four times in the course of 24 hours. On three occasions, he changed his mind after talking to different colleagues. Haig was one of them. On the fourth he didn't. Having resigned, Derby revoked his resignation. Haig did not even consider resignation. Max Aitken, Lord Beaverbrook, always malicious, specu- lated that Haig's decision might have been influenced by the king '[b]ut whatever may have been the influences prompting Haig, it is sufficient to record that he bowed at once to the civilian authority. He deserted his friends without an excuse or apology. He refused Lloyd George's sugges- tion that Robertson should be given command of an army in France. Lord Derby he left stranded like a whale on a sandbank.'[6]

Haig described Derby as being 'like the feather pillow. [He] bears the mark of the last person who has sat on him.' Beaverbrook, as we have just seen, likened him to a beached whale. And, when he was appointed Secretary of State, Northcliffe called him '[t]hat great jellyfish . . . at the War Office'. There seems to have been a degree of consistency in how Derby was regarded by his peers. Northcliffe continued, 'One good thing is that he will do everything Sir Douglas Haig tells him to do.'[7]

11

The SWC and the General Reserve

THE SUPREME WAR Council, intended to improve control on the Western Front, in practice caused confusion. From the outset, Lloyd George had seen the Council as a way of controlling Robertson and Haig. In the event, it controlled Robertson very effectively by taking him right out of the equation. When Lloyd George showed Wilson his draft plan as far back as 31 October 1917, Wilson saw that the Military Member had 'the power to alter, or even make fresh plans without reference to the CIGS'. Indeed, he saw that this had been written 'in a pencil note in Maurice [Hankey]'s handwriting at the dictation of LG!'[1]

The Council was essentially a political means by which Lloyd George sought to repatriate control of the war and the primary means of doing so was to have been by emasculating Haig and Robertson by taking away their management of reserves – the defenestration of Robertson was more than Lloyd George had hoped for, an added bonus.

The French, on the other hand, tended to see the Council not so much as a negative influence, a drag on the military, but rather as a driving force, an impetus towards the united command which they perceived as essential if France were to avoid another 1871. Clemenceau desired Foch as the generalissimo, which he was ultimately to become, and wanted the politicians off the War Council.[2] This was Lloyd George back to front.

Foch was 63 when war broke out. He was a devout Catholic who had started his career as an artillery officer. He was known best for his uncompromising advocacy of the offensive, which he promoted in books and lectures, and for his application of the offensive doctrine when he was in command. After 1915, at least, he did not however pursue the offensive unthinkingly and was critical of those who did – for instance, of Haig at Third Ypres. His forthright style and bluntness were exacerbated after he suffered head injuries in a car crash.

The contribution of the Supreme War Council to the debate and strategy ahead of the Spring Offensive was first to ignore the strong intelligence reports which had correctly identified where the offensive would take place and then to post-date its timing. The SWC also thought that it was highly unlikely that the war would end in 1918. Joint Note number 12, dated 21 January, said there would be no decision in 1918 and that 1919 would be the decisive year when America was at something like full strength. The Permanent Military Representatives recommended, in the interim, a major offensive against Turkey to put the Ottomans out of the war – a recommendation which appealed to Lloyd George, determined that the war should be fought anywhere other than Flanders and France.

The Permanent Military Representatives advocated the formation of a General Reserve for the Western and Italian fronts. Since they did not envisage a decisive engagement on the Western Front in 1918, they concluded that the Allies could hold the line if they maintained their forces at full strength and if two American divisions came over every month.

The key element, then, in Joint Note 12 was the conclusion that, on a number of assumptions, 'the enemy cannot in 1918 gain a definite military position in the main theatres which would enable him to break finally the resistance of any of the Allied Powers'. Some of the assumptions were fairly uncontentious but, in relation to the Western Front, they were important. One was the maintenance of present strengths and the arrival of American divisions at the requisite rate. Secondly it was assumed:

(c) that every possible measure be taken for strengthening and co-ordinating the Allied System of the Defences, more particularly in the sectors most liable to a heavy attack . . .

(e) that the whole Allied Front in France be treated as a single strategic field of action, and that the disposition of the reserves, the periodic rearrangement of the point of junction between the various allied forces on the actual front, and all other arrangements should be dominated by this consideration.

These assumptions amounted to the establishment of a unified command in control of a General Reserve. Troops surplus to requirements on the Western Front would be transferred to this Reserve, which could transfer units back as need arose.

The achievement of the SWC grand plan was defeated – or, at least, postponed – by the coordinated efforts of Pétain and Haig. It has been seen that they negotiated directly with each other in regard to mutual support and ignored the SWC. The Council, for its part, was too weak to impose its control on the mutinous generals. The essential contribution of the Supreme War Council to the confusion of March 1918 lay not in its attempt to take away the control of the reserves from the generals but in the failure of that policy.

Apologists of the generals criticise the SWC because they find the imposition of political control on career soldiers unappealing. The same critics usually recognise the necessity for and success of institutionalised political control in the Allied conduct of the Second World War. Churchill and others who devised the system of control in that war did so with explicit reference to events a generation earlier, when the military men hardly distinguished themselves. Similarly, those critics are quick to note how, after Doullens, the SWC withered away. Doullens did indeed kill Versailles. Yet Doullens resulted in the creation of a superior level of command which controlled the reserves. The difference seems to be the absence from the post-Doullens system of Lloyd George, the bête noire of the soldiers' friends.

Wilson was not the only man to lean towards Lloyd George's wishes. Hankey too sympathised with Lloyd George's reaction to what he saw as the failure of Third Ypres. He wrote that Lloyd George:

> had begun to feel that victory could not be won before 1919. His conviction that the war could not be won on the lines hitherto adopted was only too strongly confirmed. Yet his professional advisers [the generals] could suggest nothing better. Every alternative he had proposed had been rejected. The obvious remedy was to find new advisers. But where? The General Staff trained at Camberley nearly all shared the view of their superiors and they held together, a veritable band of brothers. Their opinion might be right or wrong, but their unanimity was remarkable. Lloyd George had as yet met no British General of distinction who shared his convictions; in France, however, there were signs of disillusionment and of a tendency to take a broader view.[3]

The Supreme War Council had to advise not just on the numbers to be deployed on the Western Front; in its groping towards unified command, it also sought to determine which sections of the line should be held by the British and the French respectively.

The Council was faced with three possibilities: an extension of the British line by 30 miles, approved by Pétain and opposed by Haig; no change, supported by Haig and opposed by Pétain; and their own preference that the British line be extended by 12 miles. Haig of course opposed this. He said that he had often extended his line voluntarily to help the French but that he was not now in a position to take on an extra 12 miles. He calculated that the expected German attack might cost him 500,000 casualties so that, by October, the British army could be reduced from 57 to 35 divisions. Lloyd George for once supported Haig, referring to the damage to the British army and their defences over the last few months and the fact that it would be a dangerous matter to overrule Haig when he said that he could not be responsible for holding the extended line. France, of course, took an entirely different view. Finally, Lloyd George announced that Haig was prepared to accept in principle the extension of 12 miles to the River Ailette,[*] provided he and Pétain could agree on the way of giving effect to the extension. They did agree and fixed on a junction at Barisis.

On 2 March, Haig told the War Cabinet that he refused to earmark any divisions for the General Reserve. He said that an enemy offensive was imminent and that he had already disposed of all the troops under his command. It was impossible to earmark six or seven divisions from these troops for the General Reserve.[4] Sir Henry Wilson wrote to the Secretary of State for War on 6 March in strong terms:

S. of S.

I very much regret the attitude taken up by the Field Marshal Commanding-in-Chief [Haig].

He admits, indeed he claims, that an enemy offensive is imminent on both the British and French Fronts, and yet . . . he declines to comply with the suggestion made to him by the Executive Committee at Versailles on the orders received from the Supreme Council.

Field Marshal Sir Douglas Haig is taking a grave responsibility in so acting, for both the other Commanders-in-Chief (Generals Pétain

---

[*] As prescribed by the SWC on 10 January 1918 – see p. 65.

and Diaz) have agreed to allot divisions. But apart from this, the Field Marshal is taking a grave responsibility, because if he is heavily engaged and unable single-handed to withstand the attack, he will find himself living on the charity of the French Commander-in-Chief who may be unwilling or unable to help . . .

At the same time, I am strongly of opinion that no pressure should be put on the Field Marshal Commanding-in-Chief at the present moment to make him conform to the action of our Allies [italics in the original].

HENRY WILSON,
C.I.G.S.
6 March 1918[5]

According to General Tasker H. Bliss, Chief of Staff in the US army,* when the Supreme War Council met in London on 14 March 1918, Lloyd George accepted that there would not be a contribution to the General Reserve. '[It] would be very difficult for Field Marshal Haig to spare the necessary reserves.'[6] Foch attempted to contradict Haig on the matter but he was interrupted by Clemenceau: 'Be quiet. I speak in the name of the French Government and I accept Sir Douglas Haig's reply.'[7]

While Haig made his concession to Pétain, he made no concession to the Supreme War Council. On 13 March 1918, Hankey had lunch with Henry Wilson. Haig wouldn't give up his quota of two divisions to the General Reserve and Wilson thought the whole scheme would have to be abandoned. The orderly Hankey was upset by this flouting of the Supreme War Council, which he regarded as unnecessary – even if Haig gave up his two divisions to the General Reserve in principle, *in practice* they would remain with him as they would be needed in the attack that was expected at any moment. On 14 March, Hankey had another lunch, this time with Lloyd George as well as Henry Wilson and they agreed to transfer the whole of the Anglo-French forces in Italy into General Reserve:

thus maintaining the principle – and by sending a special committee from Versailles to the Italian front to investigate how many of these

---

* Later Permanent Military Representative at the SWC and then Plenipotentiary at the Peace Conference.

divisions could be spared for the Western Front . . . I did a masterly draft on this (although I say it who shouldn't). Orlando [the Italian prime minister] said to Lloyd George: 'That is very ingenious indeed', and Clemenceau added: 'And if an Italian says that you may know it is.'[8]

But this ingenious scheme was never implemented. Meetings between the staffs of Haig and Pétain had taken place on 21 and 22 February and a private mutual assistance scheme had been established, which avoided having to put troops into the Supreme War Council's General Reserve. Six French divisions were to be available by the fourth day of an attack and, if France were the main victim, six to eight British divisions would support her. The detail of these meetings is surprising, extending to matters dealing with water pipes and veterinary services.[9] Haig and Pétain approved these arrangements on 7 March.

It has been said that Wilson 'came very close to predicting the date, place, and direction of the first German attack. One thing he was not able fully and confidently to predict, however, was whether it could be contained.'[10] The conditions he required for containment were never achieved. And there was a remarkable divergence of opinion about the scale of the approaching attack. The War Office was clear that there would be an *all-out* attack directed at the juncture of the British and French fronts.[11] The politicians were not so sure. There was a good deal of wishful thinking and vague hope that America would arrive in time. Haig too was reluctant to accept the War Office line because he was still talking about resuming the offensive – the best defence was 'to continue our offensive in Flanders'.[12]

The German offensive dislocated what Wilson and the SWC – especially Amery – had envisaged as grand strategy for 1918–1919. Their plan was that little would happen in the west until the Americans arrived. In the east, the war was to be prosecuted vigorously to knock Turkey out. For Amery this eastern vision was critical as part of his forward imperial policy, which envisaged a link through the Middle East to imperial possessions on the other side of the world. If Britain could control the East, she would have safeguarded her world-girdling destiny. If, on the other hand, Germany seized this prize, she would be 'in a geographic-strategic position between Asia and Africa, which would make her in fact Mistress of both of these continents'.[13] That was certainly not what

Amery wanted. What he was seeking was to create a barrier to German advance – 'this barrier to include the whole Arab region, including the railway from Cairo to Mosul and the whole of Persia and, of course, if possible Transcaucasia as well'.[14]

12

Haig's Plans and Prejudices

A DICTATORIAL MILITARY regime was prepared for a desperate, final, all-or-nothing onslaught that would deploy every tactical lesson that the war had taught. On the other side, two democratic nations, hardly less exhausted than their enemies, had constructed an isosceles trapezoid of command in which the line at the top consisted of the London–Paris axis and the line at the bottom the even weaker Pétain–Haig axis. The attempt by London to construct an X-form model with Paris and London at the top of the two strokes, Pétain and Haig at the bottom, and the Supreme War Council at the intersection, had failed. It had not truly been designed for better command but to frustrate Haig and Robertson; the French did not much like it; and Pétain and Haig would not cooperate. Indeed, the direct link between them at the bottom of the trapezoid, so far as it existed at all, did so only because of their common rejection of the SWC.

All intelligence suggested that the brunt of the attack would focus on the British front. At the Supreme War Council, Wilson had come to conclude that there would be a small attack in the north, against La Bassée, but that the heaviest onslaught would be against the French and, in particular, Paris. Leo Amery, who conveyed the new information to Haig on 29 January 1918, reported that the Commander-in-Chief 'said many stupid things: that the French were no use; that he was able to hold the line against the Germans; that he was not going to divert troops to help the French'.[1] Although one becomes inured to this sort of silly, xenophobic prejudice and although he did not allow it totally to blind him to reality, the existence and uttering of such stupid views is an indictment of the British leadership. Even when provoked by de Gaulle's most irritating behaviour in the Second World War, neither Churchill nor his generals ever behaved remotely in this way.

Haig was instructed to attend a formal briefing by Wilson and his team at the Supreme War Council. The Commander-in-Chief made a point of showing his lack of interest but appears to have accepted what he was told, which was that the main attack would be on the Cambrai-St Quentin Sector. He told his Army Commanders, two weeks later, to expect an attack between Lens and the Oise in March with a further blow against Ypres in April. Later, he refined his views, saying, correctly, that the attack would be on the Third and Fifth Army fronts with the object of cutting off the Cambrai salient.

Haig took the view that, as ground could be conceded in the south but not in the north, Byng's* Third Army in the north should be stronger than Gough's Fifth Army in the south. Gough had 42 miles to hold with 12 divisions against 43 German divisions. Byng had 28 miles and 14 divisions against 19 German divisions. Overall, the Germans had 2,508 heavy guns and the British only 976.[2] Haig's position was set out well at a conference held at French *GQG*, Compiègne, on 24 January, attended by senior French and British officers, and General Pershing and Colonel Boyd from the American army. Pershing's contribution was the usual negative one:

> General Pershing stated that an American offensive must be under-taken by an American Army under an American Commander. He deprecated any amalgamation except as purely a provisional and temporary measure. He was definitely opposed to amalgamation with the French; it was too difficult a matter on account of language. [Pétain queried the validity of the last point.][3]

The record of the conference stresses the need for considering one over-all plan for one united front, rather than considering the British and French parts separately. As for Haig:

---

* Sir Julian Byng, Viscount Byng of Vimy, is an intensely sympathetic character, different from the other Great War Army Commanders and very, very different from their caricature image. He made his way through the army from an impecunious background, if an aristocratic one – his great-great-great uncle was the Admiral Byng who was court-martialled and executed '*pour encourager les autres*' as Voltaire put it. The company he enjoyed was that of writers and intellectuals. But he had an instinctive concern for his men and his ability to reach out to them, along with his military ability, endeared him to them in a relationship that few senior officers enjoyed. In the *Kaiserschlacht* he commanded Third Army, facing slightly less of the onslaught than Fifth Army. Before that, he had commanded the Canadian Corps, where his men loved their tall, slightly scruffy chief. After the war, he was again immensely popular as Governor-General of Canada. His entry in the *Oxford Dictionary of National Biography* ends: 'Byng's greatest weakness was a guileless belief in the integrity of mankind, of which some less scrupulous occasionally took advantage. But coupled with his massive integrity, it was the basis of the trust and devotion of his soldiers and the root of his reputation as a battlefield leader.'

Field Marshal Sir Douglas Haig stated that it must be admitted by everybody that the best form of defence is to attack. If and when the German reserves are used up we must pass to the [the French text adds 'counter-'] offensive, but in order to do so we must have the troops. He questioned whether the Germans were in a state to go on persevering with an attack, or whether they had the necessary reinforcements to enable them to do so. [The French text omits this sentence.]

He pointed out that on the British front we could not afford to give up ground owing to the shallow depth between our front line and the sea, the necessity for covering our communications to the Channel Ports, and the necessity for protecting important localities, such as the Béthune Collieries.[4]

He was still saying what he had said to the War Cabinet on 7 January – that he did not expect a sustained attack. Both GHQ and French *GQG*, although expecting the attack, severely underestimated its scale. Because of this, although they expected to withdraw, they thought the withdrawal would be fairly leisurely, allowing time for reserves to be brought forward.

Interpretation of intelligence in a defensive situation is tricky but, all the same, Haig's failure to apprehend the nature of the attack must be criticised. He had seen detailed German orders for the battle of Riga in September 1917, involving the sort of tactics that were to be deployed in March on the Western Front. At Riga, the assault troops had detrained well back from the front and moved forward under cover of night. Similarly, the artillery had been placed without detection and the guns set by pre-calibration so that there was no preliminary ranging. There had been a short bombardment followed by infiltration by storm troops. These were certainly newish tactics but not totally novel. Similar tactics had been used against the French in the summer of 1917.[5]

German concealment and deception played some part in blinding the Allies to what was about to happen (but, after Riga, concealment and deception should have been expected). In any event, the tone of Haig's diaries and, in particular, his letters to his wife at this time clearly reveal that he expected defence to be much easier than the offensive operations in which he had been involved for the last two years. On 2 March, after inspecting the defences on the front of three armies, he was pleased by what he found. Knowing what we do of the poverty of Fifth Army's defences in particular,* it is difficult to know why he was. But, not only did he not fear attack; he positively looked forward to it. He wrote in his diary on 2 March, after his inspection and after he had addressed the Army Commanders: 'Plans were sound and thorough, and very much work had already been done. I was only afraid that the enemy would find our front so very strong that he will hesitate to commit his Army to the attack with the almost certainty of losing very heavily.' Again, on the day before MICHAEL began, he wrote to his wife, who had just produced his first son, saying that – on balance – he should delay seeing her for a week. If the enemy attacked when he was in England, 'it might lead to "talk"'.

At a conference on 16 February, he had given an appreciation of the situation. He said that he thought the main effort would be against the French and that there were no signs of an imminent attack on the British front. Gough, in retrospect, found it difficult to know how Haig had reached his conclusions. In the days that followed, Haig did come to accept that there was a possibility that the attack would concentrate on the British front, although he clung to the notion that the German command was promoting this idea as a deceptive ruse.

If there were an attack on the British sector, it was obviously crucial to know whether it would concentrate on the north or the south. Haig's judgement on this issue is critical. The view of many, with which this book agrees, is that Haig was unreasonably fixed in his conviction that the north would be the final and main target; that the attack would threaten the Channel ports; that these ports were essential for a number of reasons, including preserving the existence of the British army; and that his response to Ludendorff's offensive was flawed by his adherence to these views, an adherence which might well have led to withdrawal of his army as in 1940 or, more plausibly, its defeat on the coast.

The first foundation of the argument – the proposition that retention of the north, Flanders, sector was more important than defence of the south – was unarguably correct. The charge against Haig is that he failed to adapt as circumstances showed that the Germans were concentrating on the south. So, at the outset, Gough agreed entirely with Haig that defeat in the north and loss of the ports would be far more serious than defeat in the south. 'Haig was, therefore,' Gough later conceded in relation to Haig's *initial* dispositions, 'absolutely sound in his judgement to keep his reserves in the north, and to leave the Fifth Army to do the

---

* See Chapter 15.

best it could with its few divisions to hold up and perhaps exhaust the German forces.'[6]

While Gough recognised the importance of the north, that did not mean that he didn't think it likely that the attack would fall on him. In fact, his view was that, owing to the state of the ground in the Flanders area, it was likely that the Germans would attack him in the south in the hope of a swift conclusion. Correspondence between Gough and GHQ acknowledged that the ground Gough's Fifth Army held was devastated by operations earlier in the war and that the state of communications made any prolonged defence of the battle and rear zones difficult. The main question was how far the army should fall back.

On 3 February 1918, Gough had told his corps commanders that the main attack was expected to be against both Third and Fifth Armies, with Amiens as its objective. Two days earlier, he had asked GHQ to amplify his instructions. In response, on 9 February, Haig's Chief of the General Staff, Lawrence, told Gough that he was, at all costs, to protect Péronne and the River Somme to the south of Péronne, counter-attacking from there with the possible assistance of French Third Army.[7] Forward and Battle Zones* were not thought to be important enough or communications to them good enough to warrant reinforcements and could be abandoned if need be, falling back to link up with British Third Army to the north and preparing for a counter-attack.[8]

According to the Official History, GHQ, which means Haig, perceived the main objective to be Paris and considered that the French army could withdraw behind the Loire and still be available to help Haig if he were attacked. On the other hand, if the Channel ports were attacked, that would be critical for a variety of reasons that are discussed below. The Channel ports were only 50 miles from the Germans and could be destroyed by artillery and aerial bombing from a much shorter distance. Britain had little room in which to manoeuvre in the face of a German attack whose flanks would be protected – the right by the sea and the left by rivers which would hold back French aid. Haig's conclusion was therefore that, if the *British* front were attacked, Germany would devote her main efforts to Flanders with only a limited assault in the south. In February and early March, he did move divisions from the north, around Ypres, to the south, but his main preoccupation remained Flanders and the Channel ports. Although he progressively edged his

---

* See Chapter 15.

predicted area of attack southwards, he did so slowly and inadequately, the objective evidence of German intentions taking second place to fear of the consequences of an attack in the north.

As well as getting the location wrong, Haig continued to under-estimate the strength of the attack, as is clear from his diary and his statement to the king, reported by Henry Wilson on 18 March, that he could smash any German attack. These two factors contributed to the retention of reserves in the north. Lloyd George referred to this as Haig's 'Passchendaele obsession' and could not refrain from saying that there would have been no shortage of troops if Haig (and Pétain) had gone along with the General Reserve.[9]

Haig and the Official History subsequently rationalised the danger in which Fifth Army had been placed by saying that the extent of the area behind the army was so great that a German advance there would not do much harm. This argument was only communicated to Gough once, in the back of a motorcar.[10]

Haig's plan – 'such as it was', as Gough put it – was to allow Fifth Army to retire in the face of the German advance. Fifth Army would then launch counter-attacks with the help of Third Army and possibly France. The logic for the withdrawal on the Fifth Army front was to keep the Flanders front safe. The risk, which Haig did not appreciate, was that withdrawal would become a rout and lead to breakthrough. He failed to acknowledge the significance of the fact that, while the BEF had been trained in offence and in the defence of trenches, it had not been trained in the very special techniques of retirement.

Haig repeatedly told his wife how much his men were looking forward to meeting the German offensive. His confidence was absurdly misplaced and rested on a strange failure to appreciate how powerful the attack would be or how fast things would move. Ahead of the known start of the offensive, 88,000 troops were sent on leave. Less than two weeks before the offensive, Haig told the French that the Germans were unlikely to attack because the British defences were very strong – 'a pity that they wouldn't attack because they would be severely defeated if they did'.[11]

'Why,' Gough asked afterwards:

GHQ entirely neglected the Fifth Army even in the very early stages – why they reinforced the Third Army with all those air squad-rons and nearly every infantry division they could – why they never took any steps to get in touch with us by coming to see me personally and thus understand the desperate nature of the problem and the task they had set the Fifth Army – why they did, or did not do these things beats me – I consider it was because neither Lawrence nor any of his underlings had the faintest conception of how to command in battle.

Gough complained particularly about GHQ's lack of contact with Fifth Army: 'If I, in the midst of that terrific storm, could have gone round my four Corps commanders and covered 60 miles – surely to heaven, Lawrence or his deputy, or even Haig, should have come to me, even if it had been in the middle of the night?'[12]

We have seen that Gough was sent home in the aftermath of MICHAEL. He probably deserved it. His army was destroyed. There was, in truth, not a lot to be said for him. He had played a questionable political role in relation to the Curragh Mutiny. He was unpopular. He was a 'thruster', which is why Haig had given him a forward role at Third Ypres – which he had not discharged with distinction – and he was careless – not least with the lives of his men. The Secretary of State, Derby, was aware of this and warned Haig in early March that Gough did not enjoy the confidence of his army. Lloyd George told Haig that he could fire Gough whenever he wanted.[13] Lloyd George had thought of having Gough removed in December 1917, on the pretext of his involvement in the carnage at Third Ypres but truly probably as part of an attritional attack on Haig. On 5 March 1918, Derby wrote to Haig:

It looks now as if an attack might come within a very short time on your front, and on that part of the front on which Gough is in command. You know my feelings with regard to that particular officer. While personally I have no knowledge of his fighting capacity, still, it has been borne in upon me from all sides, civil and military, that he does not have the confidence of the troops he commands and that is a very serious feeling to exist with regard to a Commander at such a critical time as the present. I believe the Prime Minister has also spoken to you on the subject.'[14]

But, to an extent, Gough was a scapegoat. Given the weight of the German attack and the flimsy defences that had been constructed against impossible time constraints, Fifth Army could only have been saved if Haig had been prepared to weaken the north sector. As time went by, Gough increasingly felt that his army had been treated shabbily:

> It may come ineffectively from me [because I was their commander and not an objective observer] to make heartfelt acknowledgements to my officers and men. Some words or really adequate recognition from the Commander-in-Chief would be valued very much more by survivors, and by those who lost relatives and friends in the battle. Neither in the Dispatches, nor in the book, *Sir Douglas Haig's Command** is there any really adequate recognition of the particularly stern and arduous task which he laid on the Fifth Army.[15]

Gough felt that he and his army had been let down. He had been aware of the weaknesses in Fifth Army's defences ahead of the attack and he knew that Haig had been too. He did not blame Haig for starting by concentrating his strength on the north of the front but he considered that, as events developed, he should have been given more support. Some of his anger was directed against the French. He thought that, when 'Mr Lloyd George forced Haig' to take over part of the French front, the corollary was that the French were to be available for help. But his main grievance, certainly later but probably at the time too, was with Haig and GHQ generally. During the eight days of the battle, he complained, the only member of GHQ who came to see things for himself was Haig – and he only came once. 'All he said to me was, "Well, Hubert, one can't fight without men.", a fact which I could well appreciate.'[16]

Gough felt that his army had done exactly what it had been asked to do – execute *une manœuvre en retraite*:

> [U]ntil he knew definitely that the attack on the Fifth Army was to be the main attack, Sir Douglas Haig felt compelled to keep reserves in the north. To the Fifth Army, therefore, fell the role of sacrificing itself for the common good . . . This is an operation of war which has been carried out before, and is often one of the most brilliant combinations of strategy.[17]

---

*   Haig's post-war *Despatches* and Dewar and Boraston's fulsome *Haig's Command* are dealt with later in regard to the moulding of the history of 1918.

Gough's point was that Haig felt compelled to keep his reserves in the north for too long. That is a fair point. It is also a fair point that the collapse of Fifth Army and its rout was no brilliant combination of strategy.

Part Three

Five Days

A PERSPECTIVE

No one on the Western Front in January or February 1918 thought that the war was a phoney one. The army was shaken by the prolonged haemorrhage of Third Ypres, which had, indeed, horrified civilian opinion as the Somme had not done. The casualty lists in the papers were not as long as they had been in the autumn of 1917 but they were still unconscionable. Vera Brittain wrote of the start of the New Year, 'The War had gone on for such centuries; its end seemed as distant as ever, and the chances of still being young enough, when it did finish, to start life all over again, grew more and more improbable'.[1]

But, however bad the start of the year may have seemed, the change in March was seismic. The scale of what happened is illustrated by the following figures. For the month of February 1918, the total British casualties on the Western Front amounted to 9,809 men. For the month of March, it was 173,721. Having absorbed these figures, reflect further. The German attack did not begin until 21 March and, consequently, this almost 14-fold increase in the casualty rate was concentrated into just ten days.

13

21 March

'One of the decisive moments of the world's history'

THE 21ST OF March was the anniversary of the opening of the first Reichstag of the German Empire in 1871 and the same date Hitler would choose to open the first Reichstag of the Third Reich. This was the day on which Ludendorff opened his offensive.

Casualties on 21 March are estimated at 39,929 for Germany, of which 10,851 were killed, 28,778 were wounded and 300 were taken prisoner. For Britain, the figure was 38,512, of which 7,512 were killed, 10,000 wounded and 21,000 were taken prisoner. These were the heaviest casualties for a day in the whole war although not the largest number of killed – that was the distinction of 1 July 1916. The British army, being the smaller, suffered disproportionately and her prisoners, unlike Germany's wounded, did not fight again.

Despite all the Allies' speculation about precisely what was afoot (and there was no doubt that something major *was* afoot – the interrogation of German prisoners taken in raids, the reports of Royal Flying Corps reconnaissance and the intelligence reports from each army front and those of Edgar Cox* made it impossible for commanders to believe that no attack was pending), the surprise element of the attack was superbly effective. There was no artillery preregistration. The bombardment

---

* When Cox replaced Lawrence as Haig's intelligence chief, at 35, he was the youngest brigadier in the army. He performed well but never established the sort of relationship his predecessor had enjoyed with the C.-in-C. – his realism conflicted with Haig's often unfounded optimism. He burned himself out in the course of his travails in 1918 and suffered from two bouts of influenza. He went for a swim to re-energise himself and drowned, either because of his reduced physical condition or as the result of suicide. 'Strong, straight, clean, keen, selfless, humble-minded, loyal, true,' his former headmaster wrote, 'he leaves a bright example of a character always prized as a moral asset in English life.' (*The Times*, 14 Sept. 1918).

began at 04.40 and was precisely targeted on positions identified in advance by aerial photography. High explosive was complemented by gas – phosgene mixed with a lachrymatory gas against which British gas masks were ineffective. Soldiers would remove their masks to relieve the irritation to their eyes and then inhale phosgene. At 05.30, the barrage was shifted from occupied targets to the ground that was to be attacked. This lasted for ten minutes and was followed by a series of further defined barrages, all concentrated on specific targets. By the time the infantry attack began at 09.40, 6,608 guns had fired 3.2 million rounds on the target front.[1]

Perhaps, however, some of the surprise was because of the blindness of those who would not see. Eighteen years later, Lloyd George was to write, 'As the battle approached, there was nothing that struck me more at the time, as even now when looking back upon it, than the kind of composure, amounting almost to supineness, which reigned amongst those who would have the most direct and terrible responsibility for the lives of myriads and the fate of nations when the struggle commenced.'[2]

But GHQ were not the only people to fail to recognise what was happening. Wilson got it wrong too, according to Major General Sir Frederick Maurice, the Director of Military Operations at the War Office:

> GHQ reports heavy bombardment on whole front between the Scarpe and the Oise. Rang up and asked if infantry had attacked, was told yes. Told Wilson the battle had started. He still doubtful; cannot get rid of his conviction that attack would be further north. He told Cabinet that this might be nothing more than a big raid. He hasn't got our manpower position into his head and in spite of his Versailles war game wants the Boche to put in a heavy attack on us. So would I if we had the men but we haven't.[3]

German High Command had set out, as far back as 10 March, what was to happen in an order that purported to come from the Kaiser himself:

> His Majesty commands
> 1. The MICHAEL attack will take place on the 21st March. Break into the first hostile position at 09.40am.

2. The first great tactical object of Crown Prince Rupprecht's Group
   of Armies will be to cut off the British in the Cambrai Salient and
   gain, north of the junction of the Omignon stream with the Somme,
   the line Croisilles – Bapaume – Péronne – mouth of the Omignon.[4]

Not only had Gough reported on 1 February that there was evidence
of preparation for an attack on this, his front, it was known also that
General von Hutier, a star of the offensive, the man who had used storm-
troop tactics at Riga in September 1917, was on the front.

Why did Haig hold so strongly to the view – even when events pointed
so clearly in the other direction – that the north had to be defended?
Partly because Germany had taken quite some time in deciding where
she would concentrate her thrust. Deceptive ruses also helped and
infantry and artillery activity was maintained on the length of the front.
In the days running up to the start of the battle, the weather had made
early morning air reconnaissance impossible and the Germans cleverly
concealed signs of activity. But a number of prisoners had been taken on
19 March and, as a result of the intelligence obtained from them, the
Intelligence Officers of Fifth and Third Armies agreed that the main
attack would come in the south, with no more than minor operations in
the north. It was expected that operations would begin on 20 or 21
March. Gough thought the blow would be on his Fifth Army. The Fifth
Army Intelligence Summary for 19 March concluded: 'Indications of a
more than usually definite nature point to the fact that the enemy's
preparations are practically complete.' Gough wrote, 'I expect a bombardment will begin tomorrow night, last six or eight hours, and then will
come the German infantry on Thursday 21.'[5]

According to Lloyd George, the reason for Haig's fixation on the
north, the reason that most of his reserves were in the north, was pique
because the Commander-in-Chief resented the fact that he had been
obliged to extend his line.[6] Gough took the same view as Lloyd George.
According to Gough, Haig was 'in such a temper by being forced by
Lloyd George to extend his front southwards that he abandoned the
Fifth Army in order to let the consequences fall on Lloyd George and
the French'.[7] He said that Haig misjudged the direction of the German
attack and had concentrated his defence on Third Army, despite the fact
that Fifth Army had evidence that the attack would come south of the
Bapaume-Cambrai road and not north of it. I do not find the pique and
temper argument convincing.

Haig as he wanted history to remember him, collected and in control. Here in his headquarters train, with his secretary, Philip Sassoon, at his elbow. (© IWM, Q23633)

Haig's adversaries, Hindenburg (left) and Ludendorff, photographed at the end of the Spring Offensive. Hindenburg would be president of Germany. He opposed Hitler but was obliged to appoint him Chancellor. Ludendorff felt the Nazis did not go far enough. (© IWM, Q23979)

Ferdinand Foch: The man who emerged from Doullens as generalissimo. (© Hulton Deutsch/Getty Images)

Crown Prince Rupprecht of Bavaria: An able and realistic soldier, and a strong and brave opponent of Nazism. (© IWM, Q45320)

Henry Wilson: A wily manipulator who found life fun. Some of his colleagues warmed to him; others regarded him as shallow and unreliable. (© National Portrait Gallery, London)

Willy ('Wully') Robertson: A thoroughly decent and very able soldier, though uninspired. Haig never gave him his unqualified backing. (© IWM, Q69626)

ST. GEORGE OUT-DRAGONS THE DRAGON.

[With Mr. Punch's jubilant compliments to Sir Douglas Haig and his Tanks.]

Left. It must be remembered that Haig enjoyed the admiration of much of the populace if not that of many of the Cabinet; Lloyd George was particularly hostile. This image appeared in *Punch* after the Battle of Cambrai.
(© Punch Limited)

Below. 'I can call spirits from the vasty deep,' boasted Glendower, fellow countryman of Lloyd George. Here the Welsh wizard practises water divining. He would have welcomed a spell that could have rid him of Haig.
(© Popperfoto/Getty images)

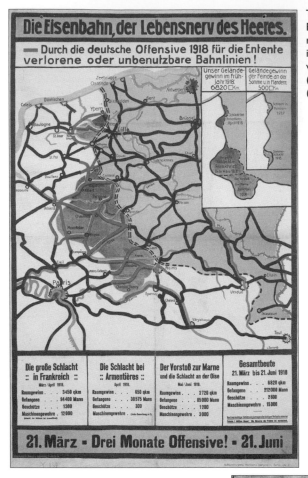

The title of this poster translates as 'The Railway, the Living Nerve of the Army'. It reflects the importance of logistical imperatives. By 1918 Germany's rail links with the Western Front were in bad shape. (Reproduced with permission of IWM (Art.IWM PST 12950))

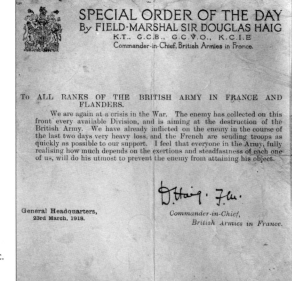

Haig's Special Order of the Day of 23 March 1918 is thought by some to show signs of panic. That is questionable, but he acknowledges Britain's vulnerability and – as he would not later – the importance of the French. (© IWM, Q56794)

Human history: (*Left*) A captured British soldier. A pitiful reminder of what defeat meant. He at least survived. (© IWM, Q24047). (*Below*) Some of the huge numbers of British captured by the Germans in the early stages of the offensive. (© IWM, Q24050)

In recent years the *mairie* at Doullens, described in 1918 by the French Minister of Munitions as architecturally mediocre, has become a tourist attraction. (Author's image)

These portrait panels hanging on the exterior of Doullens' town hall are slightly airbrushed images of the two marshals. Foch, who was always notably whiskery, has been sent to the barber. Unlike Haig, he has been allowed to display his marshal's baton. (Author's images)

The room in which the conference took place has been untouched since 1918. Haig's chair is nearest the camera. The small size of the room and the number of people in it contributed to confusion and the doubt about who said what. (Author's image)

Another gathering at Doullens: Haig and Prime Minister Clemenceau, the latter now effectively directing the war, at the station three weeks after the conference. Clemenceau's hat is wonderfully uncompromising. (© IWM, Q364)

Above. The outcome of five days: Clemenceau's manuscript minute, recording the appointment of Foch as Allied Commander-in-Chief. The scribble, the alterations and the illegibility all reflect the confusion and improvisation that characterised this passage of history. (© IWM, Q60790)

Right. The outcome of a war: Just one of the almost countless memorials that populate French villages and towns. This one commemorates the sons of Monchy-le-Preux who died as soldiers. But the village itself and its inhabitants also suffered, as was so often the case in the north of France, as Monchy repeatedly changed hands in the course of the war. (Author's image)

At any rate, Gough had accurately predicted what would happen. He was wakened on the morning of 21 March by the noise of a bombardment 'so sustained and steady that it at once gave [him] the impression of some crushing, smashing power'. 'I jumped out of bed and walked about the passage to the telephone in my office and called up the General Staff. On what part of our front was the bombardment falling? The answer came back almost immediately: "All four corps report heavy bombardment along their front".'[8] Gough said he was wakened at 05.10 but the bombardment had started at 04.40 – he must have been a heavy sleeper. While Gough had read the critical direction of the attack correctly, his response to it and his conduct of the battle are to be criticised. Gough's orders to his core commanders on 21 March, repeated on the following day, caused confusion – the commanders were told to use their own discretion as to whether they should retire. Different corps commanders interpreted this order differently, some seeing it as an instruction to retire in the face of strong attacks.

It is very strange that Haig expected a light attack. When he spoke to his Army Commanders on 16 February, he had said that the Germans would 'follow sound principles. They will try to wear us down before the main attack.' He was confident that the German forces would be dispersed. As late as 20 March, he thought that there would be plenty of time to bring up French support after the attack began. He was, thus, in a relaxed mood when he wrote to his wife just a day before the expected attack: 'The cook is making some soup for you and I'm arranging to send it by King's Messenger on Friday . . . My actual presence in France at the moment of the attack is not necessary . . . But, on general principles, I ought to be with the Army when the battle is active.'[9]

On the morning of 21 March, he was still dismissive of the German effort and had time to write as usual to his wife:

Thursday morning, 21 Mar, 18

My darling Doris,

Your letter written on Tuesday [19th] came last night. I was much amused at your account of your battle with our son over the feeding. Little monkey! he is starting early in the starvation tack of his Aunt Violet [Doris's twin sister]! I return the children's letters. They are most amusing; and those to their brother are so important.

It is as well that I y'day decided not to cross over to see you on Friday because the enemy started his attack this morning by bombarding from Arras in the north all the way southwards to beyond Rheims in the French area on our right.

I am glad that the attack has begun at last, because our men are eager for it, and have been expecting it for some time. I was beginning to be afraid if the attack did not come till later that our men might have become stale from expecting and preparing for so long. But they are in the best spirits now, and I have every confidence that the enemy will get more than he anticipates when his infantry does attack.

The enemy's attacks seem to be coming in exactly the points on our front which we expected, and where we are prepared to meet him. Our information, thanks to our numerous successful raids, has been very good.

Fondest love, my Darling,
Always your very loving husband Douglas[10]

That was his reaction in the morning and, when he wrote up his diary in the evening, his mood was still extraordinarily sanguine:

Glass rising. Frost last night. Foggy morning with sun trying to come through.

About 8 am Gen Lawrence came to my room while I was dressing to tell me that the German attack had begun.

Having regard to the great strength of the attack (<u>over</u> 30 extra Divns having reinforced those holding the original German front line for the battle) and the determined manner in which the attack was everywhere pressed, I consider that the result of the day is highly creditable to the British troops: I therefore sent a message of congratulations to the Third and Fifth Armies for communication to all ranks . . .

German evening communiqué is short and only says 'Between Cambrai and La Fère we have forced our way into portions of the British positions'. So evidently the enemy is not quite satisfied with the result so far of his great effort![11]

The scale of the attack, judged by the build-up for it, had been understood and expected by the British armies, if not fully by Haig himself. They had also known pretty well where and when the attack would take place. The consequences of the attack were exacerbated in particular by Haig's focus on the north and more generally by over-extension of the British line: 'Never before,' said the Official History, 'had the British line been held with so few men and so few guns to the mile; and the reserves were wholly insignificant.'[12] The Official History puts as good a gloss as it can on British performance, referring to the fact that Haig had been compelled to take over frontage from the French and that the losses of 1917 had not been made good. Looking back at 1915, 1916 and 1917, the History says that there was ample evidence that attacking troops, if in sufficient force, could always penetrate into the front system of defence. The difference now, as opposed to these earlier years, was that lost ground was not regained or, if regained, was not held. That was what was special about the Spring Offensive. Even the official historian concedes that the British troops were untrained in defence and in the techniques of fighting a retreat. He saw the events of 21–26 March not as a coordinated rear guard action but 'just a series of retirements and unnecessary retreats'.

What of the French on 21 March? There was no formal machinery for collaboration between Pétain and Haig. The only thing that they had spent much time working on together was making sure that Foch was not in a position of superiority with the overall control which putting their troops in the General Reserve would have implied. They had seen off the Supreme War Council but had not elaborated plans for meeting the German attack in concert and had taken care not to communicate to the Supreme War Council such plans as there were.

Later, on 3 April, Amery met Brigadier Sir Hereward Wake, a British Staff Officer attached to the Supreme War Council, and another officer. 'Both agree that there is no one at GHQ who has any brains or approves of brains in anyone else. Hereward in a moment of bitterness summed it up by asking what was to be expected with a fool like Haig and a liar like Pétain, or as Sackville-West* put it "if Haig and Pétain had only spent half the energy they spent in defeating Versailles [over the Reserve] in preparing against the Boche, the line would never have been broken".'[13]

The French line from Barisis, the point of junction with Britain, southeast as far as Verdun, was held by the Sixth, Fifth and Fourth French Armies known as the *Groupe d'armées du Nord* under General Franchet d'Esperey. The remainder of the line was held by French Second, First, Eighth and Seventh Armies. The second group of four

---

* Charles John Sackville-West, later Baron Sackville of Knole, British Military Representative on the Supreme War Council.

armies were the *Groupe d'armées de l'Est* under General de Castelnau. Both groups were under the command of Pétain.

Pétain was not a defeatist but a realist. He was aware of how much France had already suffered and was determined to achieve victory at the cost of as little blood as possible. He recognised that Britain, though she had left the initial burden of the fighting to France, was now seriously weakened by her own efforts. He looked rather to the Americans to take up the burden: 'I await the tanks and the Americans!'[14]

But he too got the direction of the German assault wrong. Generals think of their own concerns before their allies'. As the attack grew closer, he was convinced – and, even after it began, continued to be convinced – that its weight would not be directed against the British line but against his own Fourth Army in the Champagne area or even through Switzerland. Because there was ample room for him to withdraw, he tended to defend his line less heavily than Britain could afford to and to keep a larger proportion of his troops in reserve. Of the 99 divisions under his command, 60 were in the line, with 15 behind the Vosges front, 20 behind the Central front and four available to support Haig.

Pétain and Haig were not the only people to fail to perceive what was happening. Shuttling between Versailles and London, Amery, still mesmerised by his brainwashing by Henry Wilson and the war games, '[a]ttended a meeting of the War Cabinet where the CIGS gave us his news of the German attack on a 50 mile front. I don't yet feel convinced that this is the real thing and more than a gigantic raid to be followed by similar attacks on the French before Italy and Salonika are seriously attacked. An interminable discussion on Japanese intervention in Siberia followed.'[15]

Gough expected aid from his designated French support, commanded by General Georges Louis Humbert. 'Humbert came in to see me, and when I said something to the effect that it was a desperate struggle and that I was glad to see him with his Army, he replied, "*Mais je n'ai que mon fanion*", saying that he had no more than the little pennant on his car with the Army colours. This, however, was not exactly the aid that we were looking for at that moment.'[16]

Though the fact only became clear by degrees, this was a black day in British history. There were mass surrenders and the loss of 500 guns. Gary Sheffield has compared 21 March to 1 July 1916, the first day on the Somme.[17] In London, Maurice Hankey managed to have a planned lunch with Lloyd George and Robert Donald of the *Daily Chronicle*, sustained by the belief that '[o]ur fellows will hold [the Germans] up'. All the same, he didn't misunderstand the momentous nature of what was happening: '*March 21st*: Today the long awaited Hun attack began on the very front where we had expected it, and on the ground which I had been over with Smuts some seven weeks ago. It is one of the decisive moments of the world's history.'[18]

Haig's ordered day was little disturbed by the events of this momentous day. At 11 in the morning, he met representatives from the Siamese army, whose contribution to the Allied cause was plucky but hardly critical. Later, he gave dinner to a potentially more significant ally – the American Secretary of War, Newton D. Baker.[19] Even a day later, he was scarcely taking in the reality of what was happening. He wrote, 'We had a great battle yesterday and have done very well. Reports this morning state that our men are in great heart, and had very good targets y'day. It was a case of "Kill, kill, all day long." So the enemy must have lost very severely.'[20] Even allowing for Haig's optimism, it is difficult to understand how he could have so misinterpreted intelligence reports.

His reaction seems, indeed, to have been a very *personal* one, divorced from the objective facts reported in two GHQ cipher telegrams to the War Office. The first was sent early in the day on 21 March:

At about 8.0 am this morning, after an intense bombardment of both high explosive and gas shell on forward positions and back areas, a powerful infantry attack was launched by the enemy on a front of over 50 miles, extending from the River Oise in the neighbourhood of La Fère to the Sensée River about Croisilles. Hostile artillery demonstrations have taken place on a wide front north of the La Bassée Canal and in the Ypres sector. The attack which for some time was known to be in course of preparation has been pressed with the greatest vigour and determination throughout the day.

In the course of the fighting the enemy broke through our outpost positions and succeeded in penetrating into our battle positions in certain parts of the front. The attacks were delivered in large masses and have been extremely costly to the hostile troops engaged, whose losses have been exceptionally heavy. Severe fighting continues along the whole front.

Large numbers of hostile reinforcing troops have been observed during the day moving forward behind the enemy's lines. Several enemy divisions, which have been specially trained for this great attack, have already been identified, including units of the Guard. Captured maps depicting the enemy's intentions show that on no part of the long front of attack has he attained his objectives.[21]

Later in the day:

Throughout the afternoon enemy continued his attacks with great determination. Situation as follows: Fighting is taking place on front portion of three battle zone [*sic*] from Doignies to Croisilles . . . The exact situation of our own troops and those of the enemy cannot be given as the situation is necessarily confused, and this has been accentuated by a thick mist.* There has been exceptionally severe fighting and the enemy's losses very heavy. Our reserve divisions have been moved forward in the Third and Fifth Army areas. Repeated to Brig-Gen Spears and Versailles.[22]

---

*   The front line reported thick fog.

14

22 March

'The British must really have run like rabbits'

BRITISH BATTLEFIELD CONTROL had been shattered by the power of the onslaught. On 22 March, as a result of the successes of the previous day, the Kaiser recognised what had been achieved by bestowing the Iron Cross with Golden Rays on Hindenburg, the first man to receive the honour since Prince Blücher 104 years earlier. He also ordered victory salutes to celebrate the triumphs at Monchy, Cambrai, Saint Quentin and La Fère.

To be fair to Haig, the speed of the German attack and the confusion in which the British defenders fell back were such that there was little time to get reports back to GHQ. All the same, the disturbing disjunction between Haig's personal judgement and the formal assessments by GHQ persisted on the second day of the attack. In his diary, Haig summarised the Morning Reports:

[A]ll reports show that our men are in great spirits – all speak of the wonderful targets they had to fire at y'day. Enemy came on in great masses. Our 16th (Irish) Divn which was on right of VII Corps and lost Ronssoy village, is said not to be as full of fight as the others.

Our Flying Corps did wonders y'day. They crashed 16 enemy machines and we only lost one. They too had marvellous targets, masses of Infantry on roads, horses, guns etc. Into these they fired with m-guns and spread consternation and disorder.

10.15 am. Third Army reports situation generally quiet. Withdrawal successfully carried out on V Corps front . . .

129

The GHQ cipher telegram to the War Office was much more sombre:

> This morning the enemy renewed his attacks in great strength along practically the whole battle front. Fierce fighting has taken place in our battle positions, and is still continuing. The enemy has made some progress at certain points. At others his troops have been thrown back by our counter-attacks. Our losses have inevitably been considerable, but not out of proportion to the magnitude of the battle. From reports received from all parts of the battle front, the enemy's losses continue to be very heavy and his advance every-where has been made at a great sacrifice. Our troops are fighting with the greatest gallantry ... Further fighting of the most severe nature is anticipated.[1]

Before dawn on 22 March, seven out of eight reserve divisions had been ordered forwards. At least two of them, however, were obliged to move *across* the line of battle and supply.

As usual, Hankey summarised what was an enormously fluid situation very succinctly but it is clear that he and the War Cabinet, like Haig, had not yet come to terms with what had happened:

> *March 22nd*: War Cabinet 11.30. Although terrific fighting is going on on the Western Front and some bulges have been made in our battle zone, especially on Fifth Army front, there appeared to be no cause for alarm. During the day, however, the news became worse. Fifth Army (Gough) was obviously giving way, and the situation was menacing. The Third Army (Byng) was holding splendidly.[2]

The 'bulges' to which Hankey referred arose because British troops, not experienced or properly trained in the art of defence, failed to form up to create a new defence line when they fell back. Units diverged incoherently and independently in what has been described as a fragmented and centrifugal retreat, which caused ever-widening gaps in the British line.[3]

Haig's personal detachment from Intelligence reports and the general GHQ line is to be noted again in relation to the northern fixation. At 22.00 on 22 March, his Director of Military Operations, General Sir

John Davidson,* phoned General Clive, the British liaison officer at French HQ, Compiègne, saying that Haig expected a strong attack at Arras and could not 'denude his troops any further in that direction because it would be most serious for us . . . It is therefore essential as the battle is developing for the French to send up considerable forces and take over as far as Péronne . . . The situation to the north is critical and we therefore cannot send any more reserves down south.'[4]

In the course of this telephone call, Clive confirmed that France would respond to the request for more men. She had already done so and would now send two more divisions immediately. Haig thanked him: 'I feel sure that the close and cordial co-operation of the French and British troops in the great battle which has developed will have a decisive influence on the course of the operations and lead to the defeat of the enemy.'[5] At GHQ, it was estimated that the losses of the previous day had absorbed all available reinforcements in France[6] and Wilson noted in his diary that 'DH is asking the French to take over up to St Simon and they must take over much more. They must take at least half of this immense battlefront if the Boches continue to attack on it. I am afraid we must have lost a good many guns today as we have given up so much ground. A lovely summer's day.'[7]

Haig wrote his diary in instalments. As the day went on, he mentioned that Fifth Army had been penetrated as far as the Reserve Line and that Gough had been authorised to fall back on the Somme and to hold Péronne. 'I at once sent to tell Gen Pétain and asked his support to hold line of Somme and Péronne Bridgehead. [*Inserted*: I expect big attack to develop towards Arras.] He had already agreed to send 3 Divns to the Crozat canal and hold that portion of our front.'[8]

So, contrary to Haig's complaints then and later, Britain fought with the benefit of assistance from her ally. While Haig was always more concerned about the Flanders Front and protecting the Channel ports than for Gough's Fifth Army, faced as it was by von Hutier, a most effective offensive commander, Pétain had considered, as early as 20 January 1918, sending as many as forty divisions, almost half the strength of the whole BEF, to provide support in the Fifth Army area within fifteen days of a German attack.[9] Foch was equally concerned about the

---

* 'Tavish' Davidson, though the most loyal of Haig's supporters, both at the time and afterwards, in his 1953 book, *Haig: Master of the Field*, was an original military thinker, who made his own contribution to advances in tactical doctrine.

lack of reserves on this front and persuaded the Cabinet to transfer two
infantry divisions and a squadron of aircraft from Italy to France.

Pétain acted speedily to support Haig – even before he was formally
requested to by GHQ. At 02.00 on 22 March, he had already committed
three divisions of French Fifth Army Corps which moved in the course
of the afternoon. Later in the day, a French reserve division from French
Sixth Army came into action beside British Third Corps. On the following day, French Third Army took responsibility for the area south of the
Somme, including what was left of Fifth Army. Between 22 and 26
March, 21 French units were moved to the front in addition to a further
48 artillery regiments. This was done despite the Intelligence reports
being received at *GQG* to the effect that a German attack was about to
take place in the Champagne sector.[10]

In terms of the British–French agreement of February 1918, six
French divisions were to be available within four days but, in fact, they
arrived within two. Between 21 and 31 March, France suffered 37,278
wounded and 20,175 killed or missing. The French Air Force was also
committed. On 23 March, there were more than 125 fighter patrols plus
120 reconnaissance missions.[11]

The Germans recognised the role of the French in what was osten-
sibly a British battle, referring admiringly to the sophisticated French
logistics of moving men rapidly by road and rail – a factor which ultimately thwarted the German attempt to separate the Allies. A German
artillery officer wrote, 'The British must really have run like rabbits. It
appears that the French who were thrown in to support the British
were brought up from Paris at top speed in motor cars.'[12] The only
British reinforcements on the scene, Eighth Division, were just beginning to appear when one French division was in place and two others
were en route.[13]

Because of the re-entrant which had been created by the German
incursion on the previous day, the total front held by Fifth Army was
four miles longer than it had been, at over 40 miles in length, and, by
close of play on 22 March, Fifth Army had been forced from its battle
zone and most of the Green Line which lay behind it was held by only
one corps.

The Germans thought that the British were running like rabbits. What
did the French allies think? Colonel Émile Herbillon was the liaison
officer between French Headquarters, *GQG* and the French government. 'In the morning,' he recorded in his diary:

I meet Challe [Commandant Challe, his assistant] on the road: he should have started at an earlier hour for General Pétain sent him to warn the government that the British Fifth Army (General Gough) isn't holding and is yielding under the Boche's violent pressure, the latter being numerically superior. They [the British] give ground slowly and in good order, but they give ground nonetheless. They definitely have to bear the full shock. It seems clear that Germany wishes to separate the British armies from the French, for they have made their main effort on the point of junction, as being the weakest point . . . But General Pétain has told Challe to say to Paris that there is no need to be unduly worried for the necessary measures have been taken: it will be sufficient if the British hold the Somme – and that river seems easy to defend – and with the forces he is assembling he will take the enemy in the flank. That will be a battle undertaken in favourable conditions. The essential thing is that the English hold on this front. Douglas Haig has promised this. I let Challe continue to Paris . . .[14]

Challe reached Paris and the narrative moves to the diary of Raymond Poincaré, president of France from 1913 to 1920:

Commandant Challe, one of the liaison officers, says that the British don't seem worried by the German attack in front of Amiens, despite the ground they have been forced to abandon. He finds them far too calm for they are not reacting sufficiently. The Germans seem to be marching towards Péronne and, above all, Arras and Doullens so as to cut the British army in two and to separate it from its bases . . . Clemenceau [prime minister] came to see me about 7 pm: 'Well,' he said, 'it is not going too badly. The British perhaps have needlessly given up too much ground, but they are holding . . .'

Something has already been said about the nature of Fifth Army's defences but we shall leave strict chronology for a moment to consider the nature of these defences.

15

Fifth Army's Defensive Failures

*'The British Army fights in line and won't
do any good in these bird cages'*

THE BRITISH DEFENSIVE system in the area occupied by Fifth Army in
March 1918 was based, to a large extent, on what had been learned from
German practice – 'defence in depth'. There were three zones. The first,
the Forward Zone, was lightly defended and was intended to be fairly
readily yielded, the troops falling back on the second line, the Battle
Zone, 2,000 to 3,000 yards behind the Forward Zone and of about the
same depth. It, too, in theory at least, could be abandoned in favour of
yet a third line, the Corps Line. In practice, the Corps Line was not
established so that only the two forward lines were functional. Although
neither of the two lines was heavily manned, troops would, in theory,
move speedily to reinforce as needed. In addition, further reserve troops
were meant to be available.

All this was pretty theoretical. The Official History is remarkably
frank about that and the poor state of the defences on the British Front.
The emphasis in the last two years or more had been on offence and not
defence. On the parts of the line which had not been jumping off points:

> the garrisons . . . had been reduced to the strength necessary to deal
> with local operations [and were] usually too weak in numbers to do
> more than keep and repair those defences which were actually in occu-
> pation. On the offensive fronts, the entrenchments, thrown up
> hurriedly, or adapted from the enemy lines as troops gained ground
> under fire, were necessarily of an elementary nature and rarely sited to
> the best advantage; as a rule they marked the high-water mark of an
> advance, not the best tactical position. The gun and placements on

such fronts were extemporised; the wire was slight; there were no deep dugouts; and no deeply buried signal systems. Little, if any, labour had been available for the upkeep of such "back lines" as had been developed in the early years as insurance against a setback, and they had fallen into decay . . .

Nor were the British troops trained to meet [a major] attack. Of hard fighting all, except recently joined drafts had gained considerable experience, and under the most desperate conditions they had given proof of bravery, endurance and determination unsurpassed. But the men who had fought the defensive battles of 1914–15 had mostly disappeared, and the instruction and training of officers and other ranks of the New Army had been severely limited.[1]

In places, the Battle Zone consisted of no more than wire without trenches behind it or, alternatively, unconnected stretches of trench without wire. In theory, continuous trench systems were to have been replaced by wired-in redoubts. This was the 'blob' system, as it was contemptuously referred to by traditionalists, but even this required 300 miles of trench with wire protection and it would take 500 men two to three months to bury the telephone wires alone. Gough subsequently wrote, 'No amount of labour – nothing short of a fairy wand – could have prepared all these defences in a few weeks.'[2]

The idea of blobs was not new – it was a theory that had been advocated before the war. In general, it was a notion that experienced men viewed very critically and regarded as suicidal. If the scheme were to work, there had to be strong reserves available to counter-attack and to save the redoubts from annihilation. In 1918, there were, of course, no adequate reserves and isolated posts were defended to the death repeatedly in the course of 21 March and the days that followed. A 1914 non-commissioned officer famously described the new system: 'It don't suit us. The British Army fights in line and won't do any good in these bird cages.' The Official History was of the opinion that '[t]he majority of experienced fighters, in view of the inadequate number of men available and lack of strong counter-attacking forces, would have preferred a definite line of resistance in each zone, with posts, machine gun nests, and switches arranged in depth behind it to limit any enemy entry into the line'.[3] But, if there was not time or labour even to provide properly for blobs, there certainly was not time to construct the sort of defences which this majority of experienced fighters would have liked.

So in the event the Rear Zone was never established and the defensive feature of the Fifth and Third Armies consisted simply of a Forward Zone and a Battle Zone. In contemporary accounts, the non-existent Corps Line or Rear Zone was normally referred to simply as the Green Line.

James Edmonds was sent out by the engineer-in-chief on 14 March, along with Brigadier-General Biddulph, to report on Fifth Army defences. He found that, as far as the Rear Zone was concerned, it 'was marked out by a continuous ribbon of trench, seven feet wide and a foot deep, with occasional small belts of wire (tactical wire sited for sweeping by machine guns; protective wire was to follow later). Sites for machine guns and strong points were marked by notice boards. A report of the Fifth Army dated 10 March stated that on that date work was organised and proceeding on all sectors except the Rear Zone . . .'[4]

In those circumstances, the nature of the retreat was about as far removed from the prescriptions contained in the *Field Service Regulations*, which Haig had been involved in drawing up before the war and to which he attributed victory after it, as could be the case:

> [B]y selecting rallying positions, organising a covering force, and arranging for the early withdrawal of all transport, a defeated army may to some extent be saved the demoralizations which usually accompanies a retreat. **It is of great importance to clear the roads chosen for the withdrawal of all vehicles which are not essential to the fighting troops** [original emphasis], therefore in order to restore the *moral* [i.e. morale] and efficiency of the fighting troops supplies of ammunition and food should be deposited alongside these roads.
>
> When retreat appears inevitable the routes to the rallying position should be communicated confidentially to commanders.[5]

All of this explains Pétain's interruption of Haig's reference to Fifth Army at the Doullens conference: 'Very little of it remains, and in strict truth we may say that this army no longer exists.'[6]

16

23 March

'A crisis in the War'

'Douglas Haig is fleeing from Pétain'

BY 23 MARCH, the Germans had advanced about 22 kilometres along an 80-kilometre breach in the British line. Haig appended a postscript to his upbeat letter to Lady Haig of the previous day. Its tone was more sombre although designed not to worry her: 'Saty morning, 23 Mar. Situation is serious – but keep cheerful, as you always have done. The enemy has brought his whole strength agst us. DH.'

Later, he wrote an Order of the Day to be read out on 24 March which showed that he had, indeed, now grasped the seriousness of the situation:

For All Ranks of the British Army in France and Flanders.
We are again at a crisis in the War.
The enemy has collected on this front every available division and is aiming at the destruction of the British Army.
We have already inflicted on the enemy in the course of the last two days very heavy loss, and the French are sending troops as quickly as possible to our support.
I feel that everyone in the Army, fully realising how much depends on the exertions and steadfastness of each one of us, will do his utmost to prevent the enemy from attaining his object.[1]

It was only on this date or perhaps the following day that Haig and the general staff realised how serious the situation was. This was, in part, directly the result of the doctrines set out in *Field Service Regulations* of

137

1912 and 1914. Part II provided how British armies would be organised and administered in the field. The staff were split into sections: G Branch (with an Intelligence Sub-Branch, I), responsible for planning and conduct of military operations and intelligence; A Branch, dealing with administration generally; and Q Branch, under the Quarter Master General, dealing with supply. G and (G) (I) intermeshed only very poorly with (A). Immediately the March Offensive began, A Branch became aware that serious problems were developing. G Branch appears not to have taken on board the concerns of their colleagues.[2]

In London, Amery's diary reveals that the news got worse as the day went on. He thought that Lloyd George's government was at risk and that there might be a return of 'Squiff and Wullie' – Asquith and Robertson. In Paris, Britain's stock was falling. Edward Spears, the chief British liaison officer with the French, met Foch. Foch asked him why the British didn't put machine guns behind their fleeing troops 'to shoot them if they move. Such measures have to be taken.'[3]* Spears was one of the growing number who wanted to see Foch given command of the British and French armies. He wrote to Rawlinson on 23 March to recommend this.

Haig's staff had prepared an advanced HQ at the château of Dury, about six kilometres south of Amiens. It was the setting for a controversial meeting with Pétain the following day, which will be discussed later. A less critical, but still important, meeting took place there between the two Cs-in-C. on 23 March. Pétain arrived at 16.00, having kept Haig waiting for three-quarters of an hour. He said that he had put two armies, 11 divisions plus two cavalry divisions, one mounted and one dismounted, under General Fayolle. The only principle on which they would act would be to keep the Allied forces in touch.[4] Haig's response was to ask for more, about 20 divisions, to be placed near Amiens. The request for 20 divisions – in fact, '*at least* twenty divisions' – was repeated in writing on 25 March. It was an extraordinary demand. The full

---

*   By the following day, Spears' fiancée, Mary Borden, reported that the French in Paris were being sarcastic about the British collapse. She and Spears married on 30 March in Paris, which was then being shelled. Mary spent the morning lying flat out in her bath – not because she was afraid of being killed, but because she didn't want to be disfigured on her wedding day. This remarkable woman came to France at the outset of the First World War from America, via India and a disastrous first marriage, and London where she was the muse of Wyndham Lewis. In France, she ran a mobile hospital for the French army, receiving medals for her bravery under fire, so the shells in Paris were nothing new for her. Between the wars, she enjoyed considerable literary success. In the Second World War, she again ran mobile hospitals, this time in both France and the Middle East.

strength of the BEF at the beginning of the year had been 62 divisions – he was asking for an increase on that of almost a third. Twenty divisions on top of the 15 already committed by France would mean a total of 35 French divisions in the British sector, against 62 British divisions. Moreover, in a letter to Weygand, Haig explicitly said that the divisions were 'to operate on the flank of the German movement against the English Army *which must fight its way slowly back covering the channel ports* [author's emphasis]'.[5]

Pétain said he could not do this, as he was expecting a German attack in Champagne, but he stressed that what he would do was to keep in touch with the British. He said that, if the Allies were separated, the British would be driven back into the sea. His prescription was that the British northern wing should be brought back, even if that meant abandoning the Channel ports. He said that Fayolle's two armies had already been placed in support on the British right in the Somme valley. He was very emphatic about the need to keep the French and British armies in touch.[6] To maintain cohesion, he recommended that Fayolle should take over all troops, British and French, between the Oise and Péronne. Haig agreed and Gough was told that, with effect from 11 p.m. on 24 March, the Fifth Army south of Péronne would come under French command.

Haig's diary record of the meeting is unusually warm and its tone should be contrasted with all he said of Pétain and his plans after the next meeting, just 30 hours later. 'P is most anxious to do all he can to support me. The basic principle of cooperation is to keep the 2 armies in touch. If this is lost and enemy comes in between us, then probably the British will be rounded up and driven into the sea! This must be prevented even at the cost of abandoning the North flank.' This emphasis on keeping in touch – *and* at the cost even of abandoning the north flank – was something entirely new for Haig but was not sustained. Pétain had injected him only briefly with a *communitaire* spirit.

That is certainly what Paris thought Pétain was trying to do. Poincaré said in his diary that the British were giving ground too fast and that Gough seemed to have lost his head. 'Pétain is having to visit Haig this afternoon, to ask him to hold up his army and bring reserves from the north.' Herbillon was equally critical when he wrote up his diary:

The situation is becoming grave. The British retreat continues and Douglas Haig, while asking for help from General Pétain, is not trying to help him, since he is continually thinking of moving northwards to cover his bases and not of trying to rally to us; it is we who have to stretch out our hand to him, and we are stretching out too wide, we are stretching too wide. It is dangerous: one may say that Douglas Haig is fleeing from Pétain, and there isn't that unity of action which had been suggested to us.

Haig's *communitaire* approach did not survive the day. The outstretched hands very soon threatened to part. The midnight meeting between the two commanders on 24 March provoked a crisis whose implications were addressed at the Conference at Doullens on 26 March.

LUDENDORFF'S CHANGE OF PLAN

The Doullens meeting contributed to averting defeat but no less important was something the Germans did. On 23 March, Ludendorff, whose plans had always been fluid and opportunistic, chose to amend his original aim of hitting the British between Arras and St Quentin.

Ludendorff reported on the battle to the Kaiser and Hindenburg at a conference at the advanced headquarters of German Supreme Command – *Oberste Heeresleitung* (*OHL*) – at Avesnes. He said that the British had been decisively defeated and that France had been obliged to go to her ally's aid and would therefore not be able to mount an offensive. He now changed the original MICHAEL plan which had been to head north-west to the Channel with a view to forcing Britain back to the sea. He decided, instead, that Britain and France were to be separated by an attack in a south-westerly direction.

Ludendorff has been much criticised for this radical change in his line of attack. These criticisms are evaluated in Chapter 24, but here it can be said that his mistake was not so much in abandoning the north-westerly swing for a drive westwards as in retaining elements of the north-westerly drive and adding to that a surge against the French in a south-westerly direction. The combined exercise was over-ambitious and unjustified by any benefits it could have garnered. He would have done better to have concentrated his attack on the more vulnerable element of the opposition – the retreating British armies. To that end, he had requested the High Seas Fleet to be ready to counter evacuation attempts by the Royal Navy at Dunkirk.

The change was, in part, determined by his success – while his main objective had been British forces north of the Somme, in the event, this attack, under German Seventeenth Army, was less successful than the attack in the south by German Eighteenth Army. The swing to the north-west was, therefore, not developed and, instead, the main thrust was moved to the south, which had the appealing, but strategically barren, promise of separating Britain and France. Moreover, logistical arrangements for transport and communication had been laid down to support a north-westerly movement and not a southerly movement. Ludendorff sacrificed that and the sort of lightning attack which he had launched and to which the Allies, without a strong general reserve and overall command, had been vulnerable.

The change of plan was confirmed in orders issued by German *OHL* on 26 March, directing the main effort south towards Amiens. In his memoirs, Ludendorff claimed that the original strategic aims had not been achieved by 23 March and that taking Amiens instead would disrupt his enemies' communications arrangements. This retrospective assertion has not impressed historians.[7] All the same, on 18 April, Rawlinson wrote to Henry Wilson saying that, in the Amiens area, and in that area alone, a German success could result in defeat of the Allies.[8]

So now the aim was specifically to separate the British and French by advancing on both sides of the Somme. This was made all the easier because a gap was already opening up between the British and French troops. Although French reserves were coming into place, it was difficult to deploy them effectively as they met broken and often panicking British troops which retreated through them. Helped by fog and their storm-troop tactics, the Germans had moved far faster than Haig had expected. The British right flank had swung back so fast that the last elements of the French Sixth division to arrive had to leave their artillery behind and move forward with only the ammunition each man could carry. Pétain responded by bringing up another six divisions to close the gap but Gough's army was falling back so fast that it could not be supported. The Germans had correctly apprehended that Britain could not strengthen Fifth Army because of the time involved in bringing troops down from the north.[9]

As always, Ludendorff faced opposition from within. The essential element in Germany's push so far had been General von Hutier's success against Fifth Army. Crown Prince Rupprecht and Hutier wished to continue this advance. Rupprecht believed that the British were in 'a highly critical condition and should not be allowed a moment's rest'.[10] He was overruled. Rupprecht was not the only one to object. Hermann von Kuhl, Ludendorff's Chief of Staff, complained. He too was concerned that the objective had been extended from a limited and attainable undertaking on the north of the Somme.[11] Von Kuhl wrote:

> *The earlier plan was abandoned.* Previously the *Schwerpunkt*, the centre of gravity of the attack, was to be north of the Somme, where the English were to be attacked. The 18th Army was to provide cover for the flank of this attack from the French. Now, *the French were to be attacked*, while at the same time the 17th Army was to beat the English as before. In the centre, the second army was to advance on Amiens to separate the French and the English. The goals of the attack were extended considerably on the left without limiting those on the right. [The emphases are von Kuhl's.][12]

In the course of the afternoon, Ludendorff conferred with von Kuhl and Schulenberg, the Chief of the General Staff of the other army Group involved. He declared that the German High Command view was that:

> A considerable part of the British Army is beaten. The British may still be estimated to have 50 divisions. It is no longer likely that the French are still in a position to make an offensive to relieve the pressure. They will be forced to come to the MICHAEL front. They have about 40 divisions available.
>
> The object is now to separate the French and British by a rapid advance on both sides of the Somme. The *17th* and *6th Armies* and later the *4th Army* will conduct the attack against the British north of the Somme in order to drive them into the sea. They will keep on attacking at new places . . . in order to bring the whole British front to ruin.[13]

Simultaneously, other units would conduct operations against the French by a wheel to the line Amiens–Montdidier–Noyon and then an advance south-westwards on both sides of the Somme.

Ludendorff's change of plan was an example of the exploitative approach that he favoured. It was mistaken and that is evident in retrospect but this was very far from the perception of the British or French at the time. They saw Britain, in the shape of Fifth Army, annihilated, the Allies about to be separated, one to be swept back to the coast and defeated in detail, another to lose its capital and to be forced back to defeat as in 1871.

Haig's defensive moves on 23 March were confused. He sent orders to Third and Fifth Armies at 12.30, telling them to fall back to positions occupied by the Allies prior to the 1916 Battle of the Somme. This was followed within a few hours by a further order saying that the line of the river Somme was to be held at all costs. 'There must be no withdrawal from this line. It is of greatest importance that the Fifth Army should effect a junction with the French on their right without delay.'[14] It was envisaged that Péronne would be a pivot which would allow Third Army to swing against the right wing of the German attack. These orders demonstrate how out of touch GHQ was – the Somme had already been crossed before the order was received. GHQ also failed to give Byng, commanding Third Army, a definite order to abandon the Cambrai salient, and withdrawal was late and confused. The result was that Germany was able to separate Third and Fifth Armies.[15] There was now no continuous line on the fronts of the two armies and communications had broken down completely.

In the course of the day, Pétain began to worry that Haig was falling back too fast and that his intention was to withdraw to the Channel ports. He sent his liaison officer to notify the president, Poincaré, and Prime Minister Clemenceau. When Clemenceau visited Pétain's head-quarters on the evening of that day, he found the atmosphere so depressed that he concluded that Poincaré should leave Paris. He sent a senior officer to Paris to tell the president. Poincaré was more resolute at this stage than 'the tiger', Clemenceau.

Pétain said that he was being forced to hold his hand out further and further to keep contact with an ally that was continuously falling back.[16] The stretching out of the hand metaphor was one which appealed to Pétain. A month later he recalled that he had told Haig 'that I was stretching out my hand to him, that I could not go on indefinitely stretching it further and further; that if he were to cut off from me, I should be all right, because I have all France to fall back on; but he would be in a "*trés mauvaise posture*", a very uncomfortable position'.[17]

He returned to the metaphor again in 1931 when he was admitted to the Académie française. He said that, at his 11 p.m. meeting with Haig on 24 March, to which we shall turn shortly, he warned Haig that there would be irreparable consequences of any split between the armies, 'if he refused the hand [he, Pétain] was holding out to him'. He said that, at the end of the meeting, he was clear that he failed to convince Haig but was determined, all the same, to speed up the provision of reserves.[18] Already, on 23 March, he acceded to a request by Haig for support, repeated at the late night meeting the following day. Pétain's response was all the more generous as, on 23 March, German shells started to hit Paris.

It would be wrong to exaggerate the privations or panic in Paris. On 31 March 1918, Leo Amery wrote to his wife. He reported that it was said that 'many people have left Paris but the Boulevards and Parks look full enough of Easter Sunday crowds. The shelling has been going on steadily and shells fell yesterday in the Place Vendôme and the Rue de Rivoli . . . From what I see in the papers I believe the Yanks are just waking up to the fact that there is a war on, and that they may miss the last call for the dining car.' Nonetheless, he had managed to have 'a fat lunch with Winston and Bendor [Duke of Westminster] – A dozen huge blue Marennes oysters, a fried sole, roast chicken, Barsac, and all round hundreds of people were eating the same and more.'[19]

By close of play on 23 March, Hankey wrote in his diary:

March 23rd: News kept coming in all day of the increasing seriousness of the position on Fifth Army front. In fact Fifth Army is retreating to the line of the Somme, and one could not but fear a *débâcle*. Third Army is still holding well, but a hole is said to have been made at Mory, whither I walked some seven weeks ago from St. Leger with Smuts and Byng. The War Cabinet met at 4pm. They . . . decided to send the 18 and a half to 19-year-old men to France. I am rather uncomfortable about the effect of this on home defence.[20]

17

Channel Ports

*'The occupation of the channel ports
cannot decide the issue of the war'*

IN CHAPTER 16, there was reference to Haig's letter to Weygand in
which the Commander-in-Chief said that supporting French divisions
were 'to operate on the flank of the German movement against the
English Army which must fight its way slowly back covering the channel
ports'.[1] In following sections of this narrative, there will be repeated
references to the Channel ports. Their significance is important.

To the French, Britain was demoralised and shaken, ready to pull
out of the line and fall back to the coast, hoping to be able to withdraw
to England. Haig was more circumspect, talking of 'covering' the
Channel ports, a defensive manoeuvre rather than retreat. The distinction between the two interpretations is the difference between a Haig
properly planning for all eventualities and a Haig whose nerve was
badly shaken. In his own subsequent accounts and in all the writings
by others which he was able to influence,* Haig took enormous trouble
to try to dispose of the latter image and to represent himself as the
strong man, the man of decision, the great captain who pulled the
waverers together.

There is little room for doubt that his position was far less marmoreal
than that. I am far from saying that he was *committed* to withdrawal
beyond the ports, if that were possible, but he was certainly preparing to
pull back to them to defend them or for a last stand, and neither he nor
anyone else knew what would follow from that. General Gort, who
commanded the BEF in the Second World War, started falling back

---

* Which is dealt with in Chapter 18 and elsewhere.

towards Dunkirk in 1940, several days before evacuation plans were formulated.

When, in 1961, Hankey published the extract from his diary quoted at the end of the last chapter that concluded with a reference to his fears about home defence, he added in a footnote: 'What I had in mind was the kind of situation that developed in the summer of 1940 when our army in France was driven into the sea, and the danger of invasion became very real, especially as we had no army adequate to deal with any large-scale attack.'[2] The possibility of a last stand on the coast was in his mind. It was also, as I shall narrate, very much in the mind of an increasingly panicking War Cabinet. It would have been strange, indeed remiss, if it had not been in Haig's mind too and it is implicit in much that he said and did in these critical days. Haig's supporters who emphasise the 'covering' of the Channel ports have to face what Hankey said, the panicking War Cabinet and the fact that the CIGS shortly commissioned an evacuation plan.

Haig was not the first British commander in the First World War whose thoughts turned to the Channel. From the start, the War Office line on the Channel ports and the Instructions given to the Commander-in-Chief were distinctly ambiguous. Back in 1914, Sir John French, badly rattled at Mons, had hankered after retreating to the coast and having a long rest there. He may well have wanted to be able to pull back to England. After consultations, the Secretary of State for War, Kitchener, told French what the BEF should do in an emergency. There should be no retreat to the Channel ports, since that would involve breaking with the French. On the face of it, Kitchener's instructions were explicit and unambiguous – he rejected 'the idea of the British forces in any circumstances withdrawing from joint operations with the French Army owing to any ulterior object of defence of the channel', despite the fact that Germany would attack England from the ports.[3] The same view was contained in the Instructions which Kitchener gave to Haig when he succeeded French.

Again, in 1915, when Sir John French had expected an attack that would separate him from the French Army, he said that he intended to fight his way back to the Channel ports. Wully Robertson, his Chief of Staff, disagreed and the prime minister, Asquith, asked for the comments of the Army Commanders. Haig was one of them. His analysis reached the conclusion that, at the end of the day, it was more important to hold the coast than to maintain contact with the French, whose role, in the event of a split, should be to attack the southern flank of the advancing German army. His position had not changed three years later.

Kitchener was inclined to have his cake and eat it, at the cost of confusing the Commander-in-Chief. His Instructions to French and also to Haig, on the matter of support to the French, were difficult to follow. On the one hand, the British armies were to do everything they could to assist the French; on the other, their equally primary duty was not to risk destruction. Thus Haig's Instructions from Kitchener:

> If unforeseen circumstances should arise such as to compel our Expeditionary Force to retire, such a retirement should never be contemplated as an independent move to secure the defence of the ports facing the Straits of Dover, although their security is a matter of great importance demanding that every effort should be made to prevent the line which the Allied Forces now hold in Flanders being broken by the enemy. The safety of the channel will be decided by the overthrow of the German Armies rather than by the occupation by our troops of some defensive position with their backs to the sea. In the event, therefore, of a retirement, the direction of the retreat should be decided, in conjunction with our Allies with reference solely to the eventual defeat of the enemy and not to the security of the channel.

That seems clear enough but, without even moving into a new paragraph, Kitchener went on:

> Notwithstanding the above, our Expeditionary Force may be compelled to fall back upon the channel ports, or the circumstances may be such that it will be strategically advantageous that while acting in cooperation with the French Army, it should carry out such a retirement. Requisite steps required to meet this contingency should therefore receive due attention.[4]

This permission to head for the Channel and possibly home was supported by the overriding instruction that the Commander-in-Chief must preserve the armies under his command.

Haig's own inclinations were equally contradictory. When Sir John French was wobbling, Haig told him that '[b]y joining the French and defeating the enemy Britain would cover the channel ports more effectively than if our troops acted on the defensive!' On the other hand, the

defensive line in front of the ports 'ought not to be voluntarily abandoned. It was a kind of bridgehead to England at all costs.'[5] Not, it should
be noted, a bridgehead *from* England.

At the beginning of 1918, according to Denis Winter, Haig adopted
the analysis that he had made for the government earlier in the war and
based his planning on the assumption that it was more important to
hold the coast than to maintain contact with the French. He elaborated
his plan and advised his Army Commanders accordingly.[6] Charles
Bean, Australia's official war correspondent and official historian,
summarised a press briefing by Gough: 'If the Germans break through,
even to Calais, our routes of retirement right back to the sea are already
laid down and our plans prepared.' If the Germans had reached Calais,
it's not clear how much room for retirement would have been left to
Britain. Winter's position seems overstated when he says that the crux
of a plan devised by Haig and Pétain was that, if Britain were attacked,
her armies would fall back on the Channel ports and, if France were
attacked, they would retreat south-westwards. Far from endorsing this
approach, by 24 March, Pétain was criticising Haig strongly for threatening to fall back on the Channel and Haig was even more immoderately
attacking Pétain, alleging, without foundation, that he was about to
retreat south-westwards.

Haig's plans in 1918, in regard to the Channel ports, were not formulated in a vacuum. Hankey was not alone in thinking of evacuation.
General Frederick Maurice, the Director of Military Operations at the
War Office, said that the Cabinet started to panic on 23 March and
began to talk 'of arrangements for falling back on the channel ports and
evacuating our troops to England'.[7] That is what was being thought in
England and it would be foolish to imagine that such thoughts had not
travelled to France.

Churchill's position, as Minister of Munitions, is interesting, given
that he would have to deal with a similar predicament in 1940. He wrote
a memorandum in which he concluded that, despite the dangers involved
in losing the ports, if France and Britain continued to hold hands, the
Germans would still have an enemy to fight – and an enemy which
would be reinforced by the Americans. On the other hand, if Britain fell
back on the ports, the armies would be contained there and would be
defeated. This view was the official War Office view and was set out
explicitly by the incoming Secretary of State for War, Milner, when he
updated Haig's Instructions in June 1918.[8] The Instructions badly

needed updating, as they were still framed on the pre-Doullens model. The background to the new Instructions lay in the fact that, in April 1918, the British Government insisted on a declaration on strategic priorities on the Western Front. Foch declared that the first priority was unity of the Anglo-French front. Only subordinate to that was the defence of the Channel ports.[9] Haig became unhappy about this and contemplated appealing to his government.[10] As a result of his chivvying, on 21 June 1918, his Instructions were altered – effectively, the British Commander-in-Chief was no longer responsible for his own troops. It was a humiliating acknowledgement of subsidiarity.

The Channel ports were important for a number of reasons. Control of these ports allowed Britain to move her troops to and from France and supply them there; to defend herself from invasion; and to interdict the free movement of the German Fleets, the better to enforce the blockade. The ports were also important to Britain's allies. For them, coal supplies were critical. By January 1916, France and Italy were seriously deficient in coal. On 4 January 1916, the French government asked for a special shipment of a million tonnes.[11] A year later, there was a system of daily convoys to supply coal from Southend for Boulogne and Calais and from other British ports for the southern French ports.[12] By July of that year, the reorganised systems put in place by Sir Eric Geddes had much improved the cross-Channel supply.[13]

France's principal need from overseas was very much coal, steel and munitions but she needed food supplies too. 'Thanks,' said the Official History, 'to the success with which the sea routes were kept open, and to the immense assistance given by British shipping and by mutual shipping under British control, these essential needs were fulfilled in sufficient quantities to avert famine or military disaster.'[14]

Conversely, while control of the Channel enabled Britain to supply France, the blockade which flowed from control of the Channel also enabled Britain to deny Germany's supplies. The winter of 1916–17 was the worst of the war. The 1916 German harvest was very poor and principal cereal crops harvested were 25 per cent below their usual levels.[15] Before the war, the average consumption of calories in Germany was 3,215 per day. The Germans were possibly eating too much as, in Britain, at the same time, the average consumption was 2,772 calories. At any rate, by 1917–18, German consumption was reduced to 1,510.[16]

So, for these various reasons, the ports mattered and that must be acknowledged. But they were not as important as Haig claimed. While

the northern Channel ports (Boulogne, Calais and Dunkirk) were significant and particularly vulnerable because they lay so close to the British
front, the more important base ports for the BEF were Le Havre,
Cherbourg and Rouen.[17] In terms of supply, the northern ports did not
represent a critical bridgehead and, therefore, did not require to be
protected at all costs. In February 1917, 56.2 per cent of the supply flow
came in through the northern ports and as much as 43.7 per cent via
the southern ports and, if the fairly insignificant percentage coming
through the four *small* northern ports, Étaples, St Valéry, Tréport and
Fécamp, is discounted, the balance is almost equal.[18] By 1918, equality
had been achieved – half of supplies came through the southern ports,
Rouen, Le Havre and Dieppe. The French argued that the railhead of
Amiens, which was to be threatened when the British and French line
risked breaking, was a more important supply point than the northern
ports. The French Head of Supply, Colonel Charles Payot, offered to
'guarantee to feed the British Army from our southern bases and the
other French ports'. The attitude of the French was slightly ambivalent.
First Joffre then Foch underlined the critical importance of Dunkirk,
Calais and Boulogne and the necessity of covering them. Indeed
Dunkirk was so important that the French insisted it was defended by
their own people. But certainly in 1918 they thought that holding the
line unbroken was even more critical. If both objects were equally
important, one was more equal than the other.

What was Haig's thinking about the Channel ports in 1918? Was
he planning simply to cover them, as his supporters claim, or was he
ready to evacuate through them? There is no direct evidence one way
or the other but he would have been negligent if he had not at least
been keeping the latter option open. The defence of the ports, covering them, was not an absolute necessity but there was nothing
inherently wrong about thinking of retreating to them and, perhaps,
further. Despite the ambiguities, there was little doubt that the truly
primary duty imposed on Haig by his instructions was to keep his
army intact. In 1940, Churchill was vastly relieved that the bulk of the
BEF could be withdrawn from Dunkirk to fight another day. Eventual
success in the Second World War, as in the Napoleonic Wars, involved
Britain in standing back for a time until conditions for an aggressive
stance were propitious. In March 1918, Haig and the bulk of the
Cabinet would have preferred withdrawal, however undignified, to
defeat in the field.

Everyone else was talking about evacuation. We have seen what Hankey thought. We have seen what General Maurice said. We have seen that the Cabinet were running around talking of evacuation. And such talk did not even end when the *Kaiserschlacht* was checked. On 29 May 1918, Sir Henry Wilson ordered that detailed planning for the evacuation of the BEF from the continent was to begin.[19] Two days later, Haig and Lloyd George discussed evacuation – indeed, via Dunkirk – with Sir Eric Geddes and Sir Rosslyn Wemyss, the First Sea Lord.[20]

So there would be nothing surprising about the fact that the man whose instructions, above all else, were to keep the army with which he was charged intact, was perfectly ready to do what Churchill did in 1940. But, when the war ended in circumstances that could not have been imagined eight months earlier and following a victorious advance led by British armies under his command, Haig, this man of unvarying self-regard, wished to be remembered as the man of strength and resolution – which were, indeed, his dominant characteristics – rather than as the man who had contemplated scuttle. Extensive differences between the manuscript and the typescript diaries are always an indication that Haig felt vulnerable. In 1915, he wrote in his diary, 'It is obvious that the occupation of the channel ports cannot decide the issue of the war. On the other hand, if the enemy inflicts a decisive defeat on the French, it only remains for us to get what terms we can from Germany!' In the typescript edition of the diaries, he inserted, after narrating that occupation of the ports could not decide the issue of the war: 'Without them our operations would be greatly hampered.' Lord Blake, the editor of the first published edition of Haig's diaries, was of the view that, while Haig did not deign to intervene personally and controversially during his lifetime, the amended diaries were intended to be his posthumous and authoritative vindication.[21]

It is, therefore, time to look, as we shall do in the next chapter, at the role and nature of Haig's diaries and how he shaped the Official History of the war.

18

The Diaries and the Official History

'The whole truth cannot of course be told'

IT HAS BEEN seen that Haig altered his account of his actions at the Council of War on 5–6 August 1914. Something similar arises in relation to his account of the five days in March. In particular, his narrative of his night-time meeting with Pétain on 24 March is significantly altered between the manuscript and the typescript account.

It was the typescript diaries which formed the basis of the published diaries which Lord Blake edited in 1952. When he read them, Lord Geddes (formerly Sir Auckland Geddes), who had been on Sir John French's staff and later worked with the War Cabinet, said, 'Many of the important men and episodes were known to me personally but I do not recognise the picture presented.' He had known Haig well and was asked to review Blake's edition of the diaries. He said, 'At the core of Haig's being there was a sense of the existence of powers opposing him. He had a persecution diathesis,* not a persecution mania, and was always suspicious that someone was plotting against him.'[1]

Lady Haig accepted everything her husband communicated to her. Indeed, after his death, it went further than that – this kind, loving and totally supportive wife was distraught and swept into blind hero-worship which saw conspiracies everywhere containing evidence of attacks on his memory. At a Foyle's Literary Luncheon in 1936, she said, 'Two years before my husband passed away, he told me that he had heard that Mr Lloyd George was going to bring out some terrible reminiscences of the war and that Douglas felt that it was his duty to the army – not for himself – to get together a story from his diaries in order to be ready to

---

* *Concise Oxford Dictionary*: a constitutional predisposition.

neutralise any harm that might ensue. He did not live to accomplish this. The work on his diaries and letters after Douglas's death took me three years to accomplish.'[2] The Haig version had thus a polemical purpose.

After the war, it was decided that an Official History should be written. Haig did not directly contribute to it but he hugely influenced it. In the lack of other records during the chaotic days of March 1918, when there was little time for units in the field to write up their war diaries, it was Haig who was asked to supply accounts of what happened at critical conferences. This was the first way in which Haig was about to influence the record.

Secondly, in 1922, George Dewar and Lieutenant-Colonel J.H. Boraston wrote an absurdly fulsome tribute to Haig, *Haig's Command*, which, even at the time, was recognised as being inaccurate and uncritical. Haig himself had taken a vow not to seek to justify his conduct during the war publicly – he did, however, speak through proxies. Dewar and Boraston were the first.

Haig's Command, for all its imperfections, was published and in the public realm long before the Official History and, if the latter had taken a markedly different line, there would have been precisely the sort of controversy that the War Office wanted to avoid. Thus Haig, via Dewar and Boraston, had formed the mould for the Official History before it was written.

Thirdly, when work began on the Official History, he was sent drafts for his approval or comment. The editor tended to accept Haig's emendations, even when he privately disagreed and criticised Haig.

In other ways too, Haig was able to influence the public record. During the war, his despatches had been published in the official *London Gazette*. Their content was, for propaganda reasons, unashamedly upbeat. After the war, he republished them in their entirety. Lord Birkenhead, then Lord Chancellor, was intrigued by the fact that the Commander-in-Chief was thought to have retained the copyright of his communications to the Cabinet. While the slanted nature of the despatches had been appropriate during the tensions of the war, that bias was inappropriate for what were now appearing as documents of record. Haig said the despatches were 'at the moment the only available account of a most splendid and most critical period in our national existence' – a period in which he had directed military events and in which he wished a heroic role.

He then moved on to a *Memorandum on Operations on the Western Front 1916–18* which he deposited in the British Museum in 1920. It was to remain embargoed until 1940, not least because it was heavily critical of the French, but, in fact, Haig distributed copies to moulders of public opinion – Arthur Conan Doyle, John Charteris, John Buchan, Hubert Gough, General Sir John Davidson and John Spender of the *Westminster Gazette.**

The senior editor of the Official History was Sir James Edmonds. Edmonds had been a contemporary of Haig at Staff College. He was highly intelligent and his memory was formidable but he was not really any rival to Haig, who always referred to him with heavy-handed joviality as 'my dear Archimedes'. During the retreat from Mons, he broke down as a result of physical and mental strain and thereafter remained at GHQ, latterly as Deputy Engineer-in-Chief.

Edmonds was determined not to use his role as historian to provide provocative material for the public or to criticise those in senior office. Soon after Haig died, Lady Haig wrote to Edmonds, concerned about what the Official History would say. Edmonds' reply was: 'You may be quite sure that I shall endeavour to write the history of his command as he would have wished.'[3] That he did.

The volumes relating to 1918 were published between 1935 and 1937. In relation to the 1918 material, Edmonds told Basil Liddell Hart[†] that he 'had the views of [his] comrades to consider'. One was Gough and Haig was another. Later, more generally, he said, 'the whole truth cannot of course be told'.[4]

The fact that the Official History was intended to be something less than objective truth is reflected in an intervention by the Foreign Office in 1927 regarding Gallipoli and General Sir Ian Hamilton's reputation. At Gallipoli, Hamilton had French and dominion troops under his command. The Secretary of the Historical Branch of the Foreign Office referred, therefore, to there being '[a] public side as well as a private one ... Is it not therefore politic that the official history, so far as it is compatible with historical truth, endeavour to present [Sir Ian Hamilton] in a favourable light?'[5] History was malleable.

---

* Spender was the editor of the *Westminster Gazette* from 1893 to 1922. Under him, the *Gazette* enjoyed enormous prestige without ever making a profit. At Oxford, Spender had been advised by Benjamin Jowett, the Master of Balliol, not to have anything to do with journalism, 'an impossible profession ... foolishly partisan ... fatal to good manners and honest thought'. He ignored the advice and became possibly the most sensitive and authoritative journalist of his time.
† Liddell Hart was a controversial but generally respected military historian. Before occupying that *métier*, he was the tennis correspondent for *American Lawn Tennis* and published his collected writings in 1926 under the title *The Lawn Tennis Masters Unveiled.*

The work of the official historians was partly a propaganda exercise rather than a commitment to historical truth. It was an exercise which was fairly easily controlled since Edmonds had only one higher clerical officer and three clerks.[6] When the documents were being assembled for his team, there were precise restrictions on who was allowed to access different materials. Civilians, for instance, were not allowed to read anything produced above divisional level. And Edmonds enjoyed very considerable discretion, dividing the documents between those for burning, for retention under lock and key and, a smaller quantity, for passing to the Public Record Office where they would reveal no inconsistencies between their contents and those of the Official History itself.

Edmonds was aware of Haig's problems with Lloyd George and Henry Wilson and that Charteris's intelligence had been unreliable. He acknowledged that the Dewar and Boraston book had been 'silly' but ruled that Haig's errors should not be discussed in public.[7] His own philosophy in relation to the history is reflected a little in what he wrote to Churchill when he read a draft of the latter's *The World Crisis*: 'In view of your high and esteemed position in the hearts of your countrymen I think you might cut out some of the sarcasms about the military leaders.'[8]

One of the central elements in Haig's diary was his insensate prejudice against the French. Attempts have been made to provide an explanation for his bias. He certainly didn't like the fact that Britain was the junior partner. From the start and long before Doullens, the British Commander-in-Chief, while not under the orders of the French C.-in-C., was expected, generally, to conform to his wishes. Foch was given authority to coordinate the Somme offensive, and English politicians, particularly Lloyd George, kept saying that the British lost their battles while the French won theirs. But these factors did not cause Haig's hysteria, though they did exacerbate it. The fact was that he simply disliked the ungentlemanly French in contrast to the professional German soldiers, whom he had known well and never criticised.

Professor William Philpott has well said that the diary 'fundamentally misconstrues the coalition nature of the war Haig is fighting at the operational level, and has skewed the Anglophone history of the western front as a consequence'[9]. And that skewed view of the French was imported into *Haig's Command* and the Official History. It is from this source that the narrative derives of a French army broken by Verdun and never to be relied on thereafter. Thus Dewar and Boraston: 'The fighting *capacity* of the French armies remained high and even improved . . . But from Verdun onwards the fighting *spirit* of the French troops declined, and the decline showed itself on many occasions and in many ways.'[10] This is wildly inaccurate but wholly consistent with what Haig said to the Reverend George Duncan after the failure of Nivelle's 1917 offensive: '[T]he French are a decadent race' and the offensive 'just failed because they are French'.[11]

There was discussion about who should edit the volumes for 1918 which, of course, covered the critical events of March of that year. The War Office had wanted Sir Frederick Maurice, who had written a controversial pamphlet in 1922, *Intrigues of the War: Startling Revelations Hidden until 1922, Important Secrets now Disclosed*. The Committee of Imperial Defence wanted General Aylmer Haldane,* a close friend of Edmonds, but, in the end, in a wonderful disregard of objectivity, both sides agreed to let Haig make the choice. Haig's choice was Launcelot Kiggell, who had been his Chief of Staff in 1916 until 1917, when he was dismissed at the government's insistence.† He was not a forceful personality, never held command in the field and was only in France between January 1916 and his dismissal. He was no more effective as an editor than as a chief of staff and, after some years of inactivity, Edmonds himself took over.[12]

Denis Winter's perhaps extreme judgement is that: 'The end product of Edmonds's work was . . . an Official History which presented a fraudulent account of the Western Front, supported by documents mischievously selected and leaks maliciously planted in the path of writers pressing too hard on the truth.' However, Winter mitigates his judgement by saying that Edmonds was doing what he had been told to do. Even thus mitigated, Winter's verdict is too harsh. When the Chief of the Imperial General Staff accused Edmonds of being too gentle to the commanders, Edmonds said that he preferred to hint at things rather than to state them boldly: 'We do not want everybody to see the troubles we had and the mistakes we made.'

It is unfair to criticise the Official History for being the product of its times, when it was thought important not to criticise authority or the institutions of a society threatened by world events. There was a desire,

---

* Haldane was a very able soldier, technically advanced, who commanded his corps with distinction in March 1918, averting serious consequences.
† See p. 97.

which would last for another generation, to find heroes and rejoice in strong leaders. Edmonds and his History need not be criticised for giving the public something to celebrate about the war and for portraying that war, in which so many had died, as a worthwhile and well-prosecuted endeavour. If we are today, however, seeking to establish the truth of what happened in 1918, we have to look behind the veil.

In the view of one historian, Elizabeth Greenhalgh, the British Official History is less comprehensive and 'arguably more flawed' than the exhaustive French one.[13] On the other hand, the French Official History, exhaustive though it may be, is unreadable and largely unread. Cyril Falls said of the French History that the general public 'neither could nor would read it . . . [I]t is one of the most inhuman documents that one can imagine.'[14]

The British Official History is readable and is all the better for containing elements from the German records as well as the British. But the fact that it is readable must not obscure that it should be read with great caution. Bearing in mind Edmonds's desire not to upset accepted judgements, it can be argued that, in the emphasis on the first day of the Somme, on Third Ypres and on the March 1918 breakthrough, the implicit if not explicit judgement on Haig is unfavourable.[15] Edmonds gently hints, for instance, that Gough was unfairly treated for his role in March 1918.

19

24 March

The Great Retreat Begins

THE MIDNIGHT MEETING

The 24th of March was a Sunday and Haig attended church that morning, as always. The Reverend G.S. Duncan, who was Haig's chaplain for much of the war and who wrote a very perceptive study of his chief, was struck by his calm, confident demeanour. Haig quoted from Chronicles II: 'Be not afraid nor dismayed by reason of this great multitude; for the battle is not yours but Gods.'[1] Although we may find evidence of cracks in Haig's resolve, what is more surprising is how rare they were and how steady he was in appalling times and under the weight of burdens imposed by a command structure that had not adapted to the needs of modern, industrial warfare.

The situation which Haig faced on 24 March was more alarming than it had been at any time since the German advance began. Fifth Army was still crumbling away but now Third Army was also in retreat and French Third Army, which had taken control of part of the battlefield, was beginning to come under more pressure than it could cope with. Thus began the most critical of these five days, which was to end with a meeting between Haig and Pétain at Haig's advanced headquarters at Dury at 23.00. The controversy over what happened at that meeting has persisted for a hundred years.

But much was to happen before the meeting took place. The situation of Fifth Army as dawn broke on 24 March was that the line was on average four to six miles further back than it had been a day earlier, with an exception just on the left of XVIII Corps. There were not adequate troops to hold the line of 18 miles behind the Somme. Gough's position was precarious and he was reliant on French reserves. Throughout Saturday, 23 March, Fifth Army had disintegrated and, at 07.00 on 24 March, six battalion commanders of the Royal Naval Division concluded that their position was indefensible. They decided to withdraw. Thus began the Great Retreat of 1918.

Men were moving about in bodies composed of personnel from different units. It was impossible to say where the front was. Sometimes German troops simply moved through the British. The chaos and demoralisation was never publicised. In the Official History, the break-down in command is evident only to sophisticated readers who could draw inferences from what Edmonds did describe.

Haig met Byng, commanding Third Army, on 24 March before the late night meeting with Pétain. Byng wrote, 'Haig made it quite clear that the BEF had now to safeguard itself and no help could be expected from the south. Further withdrawal must now be to the north-west with the Third Army safeguarding the right flank of the BEF by swinging back its own right. Haig took for granted that no help was to be expected from Gough.'[2]

Hankey's diary for the day had started with domestic items but, by the evening, reflected the enormous gravity of the situation – a reality of which only senior commanders and politicians were aware:

> *March 24th*: At 6.30pm, while I was singing part-songs with the chil-dren in the garden, I received an imperative call from Downing Street that the Prime Minister wanted me. [In London he caught up with Lloyd George who was having dinner with Churchill. Henry Wilson was also there.] The news was about as bad as it could be, for the right of Third Army had been stoved in and a breach made between it and Fifth Army. Haig's message concluded: 'The situation is seri-ous'. There was nothing to be done but Churchill, supported by Wilson, was bombarding the Prime Minister with demands for a *levée en masse*.

Churchill, just back from France, recalled the meal. He said, 'I never remember in the whole course of the war a more anxious evening.'

Foch did not panic. On 24 March, he made two important sugges-tions. He told Clemenceau that '[a] French mass held in reserve' should be established both for defensive function and counter attack. He also said that 'a directing organ of the war' was required. This and certainly not anything Haig proposed was the nucleus of the proposal for the appointment of a generalissimo two days later.[3]

What was emerging was a conviction on the French side that the war would be lost unless France controlled it – and not only in a military sense. Men such as Foch and Clemenceau were despairing of the lack of cohesion between the Allies and the lack of overall, dynamic direction. This weakness, for Foch, was exemplified in the way in which, as he saw it, Pétain was not forceful enough with a wobbling Haig. He said that Pétain did not impose his will sufficiently on Haig – he wanted the French 'to deal with Haig as he [Foch] did with [Sir John] French at First Ypres'.[4]

The tension lay in clear but contrasting views. The clarity and strength of French logic said, 'We are fighting in France and for French territory. You are here to help but we are in control.' The British position was not logical, only emotional – it was unthinkable that the British Empire should be subordinate to France.

This was the background to the critical and contested meeting between the two Commanders-in-Chief. At 11 p.m., Haig and Pétain met at Dury. The controversy about this midnight rendezvous fascinates us still for two reasons. First, very few people were involved. The only witnesses to Haig's meeting with Pétain at Dury were Haig's Chief of Staff, General Lawrence, and the Head of the British Mission at French army headquarters, General Clive. There was no official French record of the meeting and the French Official History dismisses it in just a line and a half.[5]

Secondly, Haig was peculiarly able to make his version of events the official one. Almost a month later, on 19 April, Haig wrote to his wife, asking her to type out a copy of the notes he had made of various meetings with Pétain after 21 March. Haig thanked her on 23 April: 'I am very grateful to you for typing the notes of my meetings with Pétain etc. they are very well done, my Darling, and put things so clearly & in a business like way. You are indeed a very valuable private secy!!' In the confusion of the German attack, record keeping by the British staff was minimal. Haig told his wife that he had been asked by GHQ for notes about these meetings because they had none. Haig was, therefore, able to inject his own preferred account of events into the official record. The account of the late night meeting with Pétain is only one of many episodes in the course of these five days where Haig was able to turn his interpretation of events into the official record.

THE MEETING

The debate about the meeting is whether, as Haig alleged, Pétain was in a funk and had ordered his army to fall back to defend Paris, leaving Britain to fend for herself, or whether, as Pétain alleged, Haig had decided to let go of France's hand and fall back on the coast.

Louis Loucheur, the French Minister of Munitions, kept a secret diary. In it, he recorded that he met Pétain at *GQG* at 16.30 on 24 March. According to his account, Pétain was not in an optimistic frame of mind and envisaged that his left might be overwhelmed and forced to retreat to the Seine, involving the abandonment of Paris and the departure of the government. Loucheur described Pétain's mood as calm but black. There is, however, no mention of an order to his Montdidier divisions to pull back, which was to be Haig's key charge. Instead, Pétain did not dissent from Loucheur's instructions that, while he must cover Paris, he must, even more importantly, maintain contact with the British '*à tout prix*' – at any cost.[6]

The president's liaison officer, Émile Herbillon, had seen Pétain earlier in the day. He found the C.-in-C. concerned but certainly not panicking – rather quietly confident, aware of the risk of losing contact with the British but planning to make sure it did not occur:

> He will do everything possible to avoid this and is bringing up divisions at top speed; and this is going all the better since he had prepared against this and the transport plan is all prepared; we are implementing it with the greatest possible speed, but the persistent way in which the British retreat, Douglas Haig's obstinacy in always leaning to the north makes him [Pétain] fear that he will not be able to maintain the link; in any case he will cover Paris at all costs and, to do that, he will give battle with the troops he will bring up to his left; he asks the Government immediately to put pressure on the English to make them lean towards him and not to force him endlessly to reach out towards them; unless that happens it means a separation and in that case Douglas Haig will find himself in an impossible situation, far beyond his resources . . . [Later he reports to President Poincaré, who declares,] 'I don't and never will admit that we should let ourselves be cut off from the British; let us use our reserves; let us not be cut off.'[7]

The meeting was to be of critical importance to Haig's version of events – a turning point. For the French, it was treated as pretty low-key. On their side, only Pétain was present. He completely ignored the meeting in his 1919 official Report on operations and there is no French record of it other than Pétain's assertions over the years.* It is noteworthy, however, that these assertions are supported in places by Clive and Lawrence. The only account with which they are inconsistent is Haig's.

Haig's own record does not hold together. He later claimed in redactions to his diary to have sent a telegram asking for the Secretary of State, 'Milner'. I deal with this later and point out that Derby, not Milner, was Secretary of State until 20 April. The telegram is not in the records. He did send a telegram at 18.00 which did not ask for the Secretary of State and only contained the vague hope that the CIGS, Wilson, might come out to confer.[8]

There is a brief British Note of the Conference, compiled by Lawrence. It recorded none of what Haig attributed to Pétain – there is no narrative that he had ordered a fall back to cover Paris which would leave the British line hanging in the air. Moreover, there is no hint of the jumpiness of which Haig accused Pétain. On the contrary, Pétain was very positive. He agreed with much of what Haig said, gently pointing out how difficult the situation would be for the British army if it were cut from the French. *His* army would have all France to retire back into but

---

* Pétain repeatedly insisted (first on 18 April 1918 and several times up to 1933) that he had warned Haig about the danger of letting their hands part. There is the following evidence:

  a. His statement about the *très mauvaise posture* in which Haig would find himself if he were cut off from Pétain with nowhere to fall back on has already been quoted above. (Source: Clive notebook, 18 April 1918, CAB.45/201.)
  b. 'At our 11 pm meeting at Dury on 23 March [should be 24th] I said to you "not to let go of the hand which I am tending to you".' (Source: Pétain's letter to Haig of 15 December 1920, NLS Acc 3155/216a.)
  c. 'I insisted on the irremediable character of any breakdown between our armies, if he refused the hand I was holding out to him.' (Source: 'Discourse' on admission to the *Académie française* on 22 January 1931.)
  d. 'General Pétain pressed the Marshal to halt or at least slow down the retreat of the British divisions: "If you refuse the hand I am proffering," he said, "my forces cannot maintain the link with yours and there will be an open breach between our two armies."' (Source: Pétain's personal communication to the authors Carpentier and Rudet cited at p. 33 of their *La conférence de Doullens* (1933).)

This is borne out to some extent by Lawrence's record of the meeting, which says:

'General Pétain . . . pointed out how difficult the situation would be for the British Army if it were cut from the French. His Army would have all France to retire back into, but the British would be very unfortunately situated.'

the British would be very unfortunately situated. While he maintained that there were definite signs that he was about to be attacked in Champagne and mentioned that air reconnaissance had found evidence to support this, he was, however, giving Fayolle, who was supporting Britain south of the Somme, all the troops he could.

The only part of the record which supported the Haig version was not in Lawrence's own account but was added by Haig:

> General Pétain also stated that his divisions in the Montdidier area had been given orders to fall back (in case of necessity) south-westwards!
>
> NB. On this the C-in-C wired to CIGS, War Office, requesting him to come to France.[9]

There is no record of 'orders' that the Montdidier force should move. The exclamation mark is odd. The post-meeting telegram referred to in Haig's 'NB' postscript (see above) does not exist.

The next flaw in the Haig version is to be found in his alterations to the later part of his diary for 24 March. These alterations, shown here in bold – the underlinings were also added – were made to his retained carbon copy and not to the top copy which was sent to Lady Haig. We do not know how much later he made these changes, which were essential to support the idea that he had been revolted by what he was faced with at Dury:

> I went on from Beauquesne to Dury – Gen Pétain met me there at 11 pm. I explained my plans as above and asked him to concentrate as large a force ['near' deleted] **between Amiens and** Abbeville astride the Somme to co-operate on my right.
>
> <u>He said he expected to be attacked in Champagne</u>, but would give Fayolle all his available troops. **At same time he told me that he had issued an order directing French troops which are collecting near Montdidier to fall back SW to cover Paris if Germans continue their advance westward**s.
>
> I get back to Beaurepaire about 3 am (Monday). **Lawrence went on at once to office and telegraphed to CIGS asking him to come to France at once along with Sec of State.**
>
> Situation seems better, but we must expect these great attacks to continue. **Unless, then, Pétain's order to his reinforcements at Montdidier can be cancelled or modified, the British and French**

armies will be driven apart! I propose to recommend that Foch be given command on this front in order to bring up French Reserves to the decisive point, i.e. before Amiens. We must be supported <u>at once</u> in order to keep our two Allied Armies united! Time is of vital importance.

The *typewritten* diary was further amended.

The orders which Pétain did give to his reserve army group on 24 March did not direct a withdrawal or a falling back towards Beauvais. Indeed, Pétain had ruled out abandoning Amiens, north of Paris, because of its importance as a rail junction. Elizabeth Greenhalgh wonders whether Haig and Lawrence had understood what Pétain was saying.[10] Clive, who was the only interpreter, left Dury with Pétain, and Haig and Lawrence, less able French speakers, returned to GHQ together with their own recollection of what had happened. It has been suggested that they may have misunderstood a warning by Pétain about what would happen if Haig continued to fall back.

Haig's edited typescript diary is the only source for the claim that Pétain intended to or had been ordered to withdraw to cover Paris. No such instruction is to be found in the French Official History. The claim is rejected by Professor Pedroncini in both his biographies of Pétain.[11] Paris had come under gunfire on 23 March and, on the morning of 24 March, the Ministerial Council discussed the evacuation of Paris but there was no panic. Although Tours was identified as the place to which the government would move *if* that became necessary, no decision to evacuate was taken.

But, thanks to Haig, accounts of Pétain's behaviour on 24 March generally follow his line. Foch later verified what Haig told him and some other French officers also acquiesced. For instance, one French general even inserted in his account the detail that Haig had sent a telegram to Wilson asking him to come to France. The telegram only existed in Haig's false memory so the source is clear.

On the other hand, General Émile Laure, who was Pétain's liaison officer during the war, defended him strongly against what he called 'the legend of the French pulling back on Paris'.[12] Laure is supported by General Mordacq, Clemenceau's Chef de Cabinet at the War Ministry, who also used the word 'legend'. French politics, particularly after Pétain had become associated with collaboration, have confused matters further. The most authoritative study of Pétain is by Professor Guy Pedroncini.

He sought to 'disentangle' Pétain from the legend although, in doing so, he 'may have overstated his case'.[13]

After the war, in 1920, Haig made a statement to the press in which he said he had told Poincaré about having 'received notification of Pétain's orders to pull back'. This referred to a meeting he had had with Poincaré when he was saying his farewells on giving up his command. Poincaré had expressed surprise when Haig referred to these 'orders'. Haig's reaction was of amazement that the president, whom he described, not inaccurately, as 'a very conceited little man', was evidently unaware that Pétain had given orders to withdraw to cover Paris from the German advance. Poincaré's records, like Haig's original diary, contain no mention of these orders and Haig's acknowledgement of the president's ignorance of the matter weakens his case.

Pétain reacted to Haig's statement by writing to him asking what orders he was referring to since no such order had been given. Haig's response to that was very weak. He said that his discussion with Pétain at the midnight meeting on 24 March had 'led him to conclude' that the French Commander's 'primary care' was for Paris. Haig's Chief of Staff, Lawrence, was said to support this but all Lawrence did was to refer to the accuracy of the 'general impression'.[14]

Brigadier-General John Charteris was close to Haig for much of the war, finally as his Intelligence Chief until Lloyd George secured his dismissal. Charteris went on to write his own biography of Haig – not perfect but better than *Haig's Command*. In it, he described the noble calm and detachment which Haig affected to maintain after the war, standing above petty controversy:

> He never publicly gave expression to any extenuation or defence of his policy, nor did he ever authorise one word to be written in contradiction of accusations and criticisms levelled against him in the post-war flood of controversial literature. He appeared to watch with complete calm the gradual drawing aside of the curtain which had hidden and still partially hides many of the episodes of the war.[15]

Haig may have avoided public propaganda but he manipulated public relations behind the scenes, and Dewar and Boraston were used to propagate the withdrawal story. In *Haig's Command*, they said that it was interesting that the story of Pétain's withdrawal on Paris 'has remained a profound secret [which] must be emphasised and emphasised again'.[16]

The tone is suspiciously shrill – 'a profound secret' which 'must be emphasised again and again' in view of the 'indisputable evidence' and lack of 'the faintest doubt'.[17] Sir Archibald Montgomery* told Edmonds: 'A great many things have been claimed for DH, some true, some quite untrue (*vide* "Douglas Haig's Command").'

Dewar, journalist and former war correspondent, had been savaged by the pro-Lloyd George press during the war and wanted his revenge. He admitted that the book was not a balanced account of events. Boraston was an active Conservative and Unionist and the book was intended to influence opinion at the time of the November 1922 general election which, in fact, ended Lloyd George's period in power.[18] Emphasis on the story about withdrawing on Pairs was intended to expose the way in which Lloyd George had, as was argued, suppressed the truth about Haig and the army. Haig was quite clear about what was going on. He wrote to Boraston, 'I am very glad that you are working with Dewar. He is v. ignorant of military matters but is a fine fellow & keen to enlighten the public. There is great need for enlightenment. Indeed the current estimate of the part played by the British Army in 1916–18 is very incorrect & I hope your book will completely change it.'[19]

Despite Haig's claim to stand back from debate about his conduct in the war and letting the facts speak for themselves, he was very much involved in the Dewar and Boraston book.[20] There was, indeed, a number of his supporters involved in it too. Some chapters were written by Lord Esher, always favourable to Haig, and some by Sir Herbert Lawrence, his Chief of Staff. General Maxse told Liddell Hart that it was common knowledge that Dewar and Boraston 'actually was really by Haig'. The Australian official historian Charles Bean referred to the book as 'Haig and Boraston'. Haig visited Dewar and Boraston and corrected their drafts. He wrote a letter to Lawrence about Pétain and what had happened at the late night meeting at Dury. He addressed Lawrence in jocular mode. 'Dear Lorenzo, I still maintain – and in this I'm supported by a note in my diary – that Pétain *warned* the French divisions collecting about Montdidier that their lines of retreat would be southwest in the event of a German advance on Amiens continuing. So

---

* Later Montgomery-Massingberd, he was Rawlinson's Chief of Staff in Fourth Army, which played a very important role in the advances of the Hundred Days and very much Rawlinson's protégé. Liddell Hart detested him but he was a very able CIGS in the inter-war years, who played a key role in preparing the BEF for the Second World War. His comment on Dewar and Boraston's book is the more telling because of his notable discretion.

I have struck out your last two lines and added in their place about the line of retreat given to the French divisions on our right.'[21] The use of the word 'warned' is something of a retreat from 'ordered' and confirms that Haig knew he was on thin ice. We do not know what was said in the lines he excised.

A review of *Haig's Command* in *Truth* said, 'While this is the most fascinating of war books that has yet appeared in England, it is about as safe as a mills bomb with the pin out. Explosions must follow.' The review said that 'Lord Haig stands behind the writers', which was perceptive, but went on to say more controversially, 'That at once raises the book to the first rank of importance.' The more appropriate conclusion is that it destroys the book's claim to objectivity. The reaction of the military historian Cyril Falls was more scholarly: 'The writers' aim and object is the glorification of the British Commander-in-Chief and they continually overreach themselves in attempting to prove too much. As a consequence, their references to the French are frequently unfair and sometimes almost ludicrous.' Even a reader who was outspokenly hostile to Lloyd George and a defender of the generals, particularly Gough, could say that 'unsound arguments from Colonel Boraston are a frequent occurrence'.[22]

Haig, being the man he was, could not afford to acknowledge, even to himself, that he had wobbled at Dury or that he had thought of retreating on or perhaps through the Channel ports. Pétain had to be the wobbler. Haig told Clive, on 21 April 1918, that he had felt less confidence in Pétain ever since the Dury Conference when Petain had said 'that he would retire S.W.'.[23]

In his typescript diary but not the manuscript, Haig was at pains to add credibility to his account of events by his description of Pétain as '[v]ery much upset, almost unbalanced and most anxious'. This was not the way Haig had always described the French Commander. Pétain had been appointed in May 1917 in the face of some opposition by Henry Wilson, who did not think him sufficiently aggressive. When Haig met him, however, he thought he was 'clear-headed and easy to discuss things with'. On 18 May 1917, Haig said he was 'business-like, knowledgeable, and brief of speech. The latter a rare quality in Frenchmen!'[24] This meant quite a lot coming from Haig, who considered the French 'a decadent race ... bound to fail in an offensive ... I never thought much of them and I have had a great deal to do with them since the beginning of the war.'[25]

Haig found Pétain particularly endearing when he visited his head-quarters on 20 January 1918. He reported to his wife on:

> a successful and most friendly visit. Pétain has certainly surrounded himself with a much more practical set of officers than either Joffre or Nivelle had. I also think Pétain means to be straightforward and co-operate wholeheartedly with me. We thus discuss the situation of our respective armies in a frank and open way. This is a great advantage for the allied cause.
>
> I left at 10 pm last night after dining with him. We motored to the station together as he was going off to Nancy. I took him round my train which is very simple and plain as compared with his. In my sleeping apartment he saw your photo on a table beside my bed and *greatly admired* it, saying that he had heard on all sides how charming you are, and what fine work you had done during the war, etc, etc. He is thought to be rather vulgar and coarse in his language and stories. Certainly to me he has always been most gentlemanly and on occasions like last night when seeing your photo and saying goodbye, he gave expression to the most kindly and indeed lofty feelings. The truth is I think that he is very shy, and often talks to cover his shyness! With me he is quite natural . . .

It wasn't unusual for Haig's opinion of the French generals to veer dramatically. He liked them when they agreed with him and despised them when they didn't. But the starting point for the pendulum's swing was at a position of almost violent, pathological antipathy towards the French nation. Even allowing for attitudes of the times, it was puerile and indefensible. Some of his colleagues had thought that he should not have been appointed Commander-in-Chief because of his difficulty in getting on with the French.[26]

Joffre was French C.-in-C. at the start of the war, a wonderfully phlegmatic and unshakable countryman, in some ways a little like Haig himself, although more genial. Haig referred to him as 'old' Joffre and regarded him as lethargic. He claimed that he couldn't even read a map. Nivelle, Joffre's successor, was an urbane, polished man who spoke excellent English and whose mother was indeed an English woman. He was a popular figure in London society and Haig got on well with him until Lloyd George, in a shameful subterfuge, tried to place Haig under Nivelle's command at the Calais Conference in 1917. Haig claimed to like Pétain best of all three although it is suggested that this was simply because they saw so little of each other.[27] But, when Haig decided that the narrative of March 1918 had to be corrected to show his own dominant part in it, he had to portray Pétain as craven, unbalanced and unreliable. Foch he seemed to regard as almost his equal, which was necessary if the alliance between them was to be shown as the factor that delivered victory.

Nothing that anyone else recorded about Pétain's conduct at the midnight meeting suggests that he was unduly rattled. Indeed Clive, Head of the British Mission at French HQ, said that, as he was leaving, Pétain remarked, 'I shall sleep better tonight than I have done for many nights.'[28]

Pétain's standing amongst his military colleagues was not as high as it was amongst the French population generally. He was widely regarded as a plodder and a pessimist. He lacked the aggressive fighting spirit of Foch and that is why Foch, and not he, was entrusted with the Supreme Command at the Doullens Conference. But he was not defeatist – at least, not until 1940 – and the general criticisms of him were such as could have been made of Haig – that he was cold, controlled, impassive. While Haig described Pétain on 24 March as 'unstable', a few weeks earlier, according to Barry Pitt, 'Haig got along with him very well, appreciating his cold manner, his dignity, his firmness, his lucidity.'[29]

Of the two men, Haig was personally more vulnerable on 24 March. He was well aware that Lloyd George wanted to be rid of him. He was presiding over a major reverse which might lead to defeat in detail. If he lost the Channel ports, he would, no doubt, have been sacked as French had been in 1915 or as Gough was about to be. The lack of commitment to a joint cause and his particular concern for the British element in the alliance are reflected in the remarkably shaky Order of the Day quoted above which Haig had written on the previous day for reading to all ranks on 24 March: 'We are again at a crisis in the War. The enemy . . . is aiming at the destruction of the British Army . . . [T]he French are sending troops as quickly as possible . . . I feel that everyone in the army, fully realising how much depends on the exertions and steadfastness of each one of us, will do his utmost to prevent the enemy from attaining his object.' It is interesting that Haig saw the purpose of the attack specifically as the destruction of the British army and revealing that he saw salvation as consisting in French assistance. The order is not repeated in the Official History, which is unusual.

The Official History uncritically accepted the interpretation of Pétain's order which Haig chose to give it and which its terms do not support. In relation to 25 March:

> Sir Douglas Haig did not relinquish his plan of operations . . . in consequence of the visit to General Pétain, when the latter expressed the intention of directing Colonel Fayolle,* in command of the GAR [French Reserve Army] on the British right, to fall back south-westwards on Beauvais in order to cover Paris. The Field Marshal still assumed that the French Commander-in-Chief would, under orders of his government, even if not of his own free will, send strong forces to the vicinity of Amiens to ensure the continued junction of the Allied Armies.[30]

The Official History records Pétain at Dury as 'being evidently upset and very anxious'. The impression could only have been communicated by Haig. The tone of the account is of a decisive Haig outlining his plans for British troops south of the Somme operating under General Fayolle, with a request for a concentration of a large force about Amiens astride the Somme to cooperate with the British right. Pétain, in the course of his reported reply, goes on to say that he had directed Fayolle, in the event of the German advance being pressed further, to fall back south westwards in order to cover Paris.[31] That again must come from Haig. A copy of Pétain's order was handed to Haig and is contained in the Official History in translation. It conflicts with Haig's impressions. Section II, 'Intentions of the General Commanding in Chief', consists of the following:

> Before everything to keep the French Armies together as one solid whole; in particular, not to allow the GAR [Group of Armies of the Reserves] to be cut off from the rest of our forces. Secondly, if it is possible, to maintain a liaison with the British forces.
>   To conduct the battle on these lines.

Section III, 'Mission of the GAR', directs that the French First Army will 'a) either prolong the left of the Third Army in order to connect it to the

---

* The lower levels of general in the French army do not equate to the same rank in the British army but, in 1918, he was a general by any standard. He commanded the reserve, the GAR, and had already commanded First and Fourth Armies. He was to be a marshal of France.

right of the British, *if the latter continued to hold*; b) or reinforce and support the Third Army . . . [author's emphasis]'

It is not logical that the Official History immediately goes on to say that:

> It was clear to Sir Douglas Haig that the effect of this order must be to separate the French from the British and allow the enemy to penetrate between the two national forces. He at once asked General Pétain if he meant to abandon the British right flank. The French General did not speak but nodded his head, and then said, 'It is the only thing possible if the enemy compels the allies to fall back still further.'

As well as being illogical, the statement is inconsistent with all the records. It is even inconsistent with Haig's tweaked typescript. In any event, at its highest, the allegation rests on the hypothesis that Britain did not hold. If Britain continued to fall back either under pressure or, as Pétain believed, as a deliberate move to the Channel, it would be Haig who would effect the rupture between the Allies.

It was not Pétain who was wavering. His concern was that the British would not hold. With specific reference to Fifth Army (now under French command), the order directs that it 'will hold the enemy as long as possible on the Somme and will retire, should it become necessary, on the line of the Avre between Montdidier and Amiens'. There is some doubt about exactly when GHQ placed Fifth Army south of the Somme under the control of the French General Fayolle. Gough said that '[placing] the Fifth Army under Fayolle's group of Armies made no material difference. He issued no orders to me, and I only saw him for a few minutes.'[32]

20

25 March

'The crisis of the nation's fate'

ON THE MORNING of 25 March, the mist and fog, which had been such a feature of the fighting so far, cleared earlier than had been usual, disappearing from the river valleys soon after 07.30,[1] but, although this favoured the defence, there was substantial retirement – the right flank of Third Army by the close of the day was over four miles behind the left of Fifth Army. The Somme, as a defensive line, had been lost.

General Maurice, Director of Military Operations, considered this to be the most critical day. The 88,000 men who had begun leave on 21 March were now back in France. In addition, 106,000 recruits had been deployed and twelve French divisions were with the British. Maurice concluded that, although the situation was 'undoubtedly serious, it was still far from desperate'. It would only become desperate if Britain was pushed across the Ancre. This happened within 24 hours.[2]

Third Army was increasingly feeling the pressure to which Fifth Army had succumbed and General Byng telephoned orders which the Official History described in an unusually censorious tone as 'somewhat ill-arranged' and only 'in the main' following those from GHQ, directing a general retirement with a view to a stand on a fresh front on the following day.[3] One German General wrote, 'The sun of Germany's victory was high on the zenith on 25 March.'

Haig had got back to GHQ about 03.00 on 25 March, following his 23.00 meeting with Pétain. An important part of projecting the image of his being in control of events is the telegram which he claimed to have sent to London immediately after his meeting,*

---

* Not to be confused with the telegram sent at 18.00 on 24 March, *before* the meeting.

asking that 'Foch or some other determined General who would fight' should be in supreme command. This was an essential element in his retrospective mission to emphasise that it was he who had taken the initiative in having Foch appointed. As has been seen, there is no record of such a telegram[4] and the first official record of the meeting with Pétain did not mention the telegram. It was added as a postscript. Similarly, the first version of the manuscript diary makes no mention of a telegram. In edited versions, Haig says that he asked for Lord Milner and Henry Wilson, the CIGS, to come out to France. The reference to Milner is a giveaway because, as has been noted, Milner was not at the time the Secretary of State for War. Derby was. Haig didn't think much of Derby, the 'feather pillow'. Lord Milner was the British Minister at the Supreme War Council. He didn't become Secretary of State for War until late April 1918 – the fact that Haig refers to him shows that the emendation was made long after 25 March.

Milner was, however, in France and did attend the conference at Doullens. But he did not come at the invitation of any telegram of Haig. He had left for France 15 hours before the telegram is alleged to have been despatched. Milner himself said that '[t]he Prime Minister . . . asked me to run over to France in order to report to the Cabinet personally on the position of affairs there'.[5] Lloyd George confirmed this, going on to say, 'I authorised Milner to do what he could to restore the broken Versailles Front by conferring on Foch the necessary authority to organise a reserve and control its disposition.'[6] That detailed claim is very doubtful, though it may be reflective of a notion that was gaining currency, but Milner can always be relied on and he was particularly clear that his Memorandum to the War Cabinet on his Mission to France[7] was specially sound: 'As far as it goes, my memorandum, which you saw, is minutely accurate. I wrote it all down the very next day, when every detail was fresh in my memory, though with no intention of making public use of it.'[8]

He went immediately to GHQ on 24 March. There, he missed Haig and saw General Davidson, his Director of Operations. Although there is no suggestion that Davidson saw Haig before he went to Dury, Haig did dine with General Byng, his Third Army Commander, that evening and it has been suggested, as a matter of speculation, that Haig would have learned that Milner was around.[9] There is no evidence to support that – all we know is that Milner and Haig did not meet. Whether or not

Haig knew Milner was in France has nothing to do with the fact that the alleged telegram was never sent.

In any event, Milner then went on to Versailles and the Supreme War Council. The Official History concedes that when Milner was at Doullens for the historic conference on 26 March, he had not seen any message from Haig suggesting that the Supreme Command should be given to Foch, an assertion which, as we shall see, Haig was anxious to promote. Prime Minister Clemenceau, like Prime Minister Lloyd George, also wanted Milner, '*l'homme d'action par excellence du cabinet anglais*' ('the outstanding man of drive in the British cabinet'), to be sent over, a request which was relayed by General Spears, the Head of the British Mission to the French government. According to Lloyd George, Milner's despatch was the initiative of the War Cabinet – or, at least, of some of its members. There had been a suggestion that Lloyd George himself should go to the conference but it was thought that it was better that he should remain in London to be able to despatch further reinforcements if that were necessary.[10]

Similarly, no telegram was needed to get *Wilson*. Foch had asked him to come over when he telephoned him at 17.30 on 24 March and GHQ repeated the request an hour later, when Wilson decided to come across on 25 March. Haig's spurious telegram was superfluous so far as both Milner and Wilson were concerned and the only reason that it was invented, as it appears to have been, was to show him as the pivotal man of decision.

The flavour of this critical day, the eve of the Doullens Conference, can be recreated from some of the events. Wilson started from London by a 'Special' train from Victoria at 06.50 and was conveyed across the Channel by the destroyer *Morris*, arriving at Haig's headquarters at Montreuil at 11.30.

Henry Wilson's entertaining diary has always to be read with caution. He claimed that, when he arrived at Haig's headquarters on 25 March, he found the usually imperturbable Commander-in-Chief 'cowed', saying that 'unless the "whole French Army" came up we were beaten & it would be better to make peace on any terms we could'. Although Wilson may have enjoyed exaggerating, he was presumably building on what he did see and not entirely fabricating what Haig had said.

> I pointed out that in his present flush of success the Boche would only consent to make peace if we laid down our arms which was out of the

question, and he agreed. After much talk I told him that in my opinion we must get greater unity of action and I suggested that Foch should coordinate the action of both C-in-Cs. DH said he would prefer Pétain but I simply brushed this to one side. Pétain is a very inferior person and is now proving all I have said against him. In the end DH agreed. I arranged that at our meeting at Dury tomorrow I would suggest that he (Foch) should be commissioned by both Governments to co-ordinate the military action of the 2 C-in-Cs. I got back to Versailles at midnight.[*]

Wilson's claim[11] that Haig would have preferred Pétain to Foch is interesting and does not suggest that Haig had found his French colleague unbalanced just a few hours ago, as the revised diary was to suggest. If Wilson is to be believed, the comment also contributes to the weakening of Haig's surely unsustainable claim to have been Foch's consistent supporter for Supreme Command.

At 16.00, Haig went to Abbeville to meet Clemenceau and Foch. They were unable to attend the meeting and he handed General Weygand[†] a note intended for them:

The intention of the enemy is evidently to push strong forces between the English and French Armies, and having effected this purpose, to detain the French Army while throwing his whole available strength on the English and force the latter back upon the sea . . .

It becomes necessary to take immediate steps to restore the situation, and this is only possible by concentrating immediately astride the SOMME west of AMIENS at least 20 French divisions to operate on the flank of the German movement against the English Army which must fight its way slowly back covering the Channel ports.[12]

Denis Winter's contention that this shows that Haig was 'running away . . . to the Channel ports'[13] has been challenged powerfully by John Hussey.[14] The words Winter used are not appropriate to a fighting retreat but a fighting retreat is what Haig was contemplating. How it would have ended will never be known.

---

[*] According to his diary, Wilson allowed himself to remind Haig that it was he, Haig, who had killed off the General Reserve and that he, Wilson, had warned Haig that, without it, he would be living on the charity of Pétain. He also said that the German onslaught was the attack he had foreseen in January, when he had, in fact, been predicting activities on other fronts.

[†] Foch's senior staff officer, French PMR at Versailles.

An hour later, there was a conference at Paris at which Poincaré, Clemenceau, Foch, Pétain, Loucheur and Milner were present. Amery was not present at the conference but, afterwards, he joined Milner and Pétain for dinner. Later, they walked together in the garden. Pétain told them that Foch was charged with coordinating operations and ensuring the liaison between Haig and himself. Amery records Pétain as saying that he had advised the meeting in Paris:

> of the gravity of the situation, the British tendency always to pull back to their bases, not seeking to keep contact with him, and consequently obliging him to extend his line in a way that is more than dangerous. He told them that the British high command is not trying to keep contact with him and continues to fight its battle alone, without taking account of his directives or what is possible. He told them that he did not have the means to make him [Haig] keep his promise to stay close to his [Pétain's] side; in these circumstances he feared that the breach could open and that with the French fighting another battle on a separate front, the English could be pinned to the sea coast and perhaps forced to capitulate in the open field. Lord Milner was very struck by all this and without further discussion accepted the designation of General Foch to ensure the link between the two Cs-in-C.

Amery ended his diary entry quoting Pétain: '"It is a step towards the unified command," says Pétain to me at the end of this conversation; "a crisis was needed to bring it about. I hope it is not too late and that the English, finding themselves in the marmalade, will obey."'[15]

Apart from the comparison between the English phrase, 'in a jam' or 'a pickle', and the French, 'in the marmalade', the interest in Pétain's speech is, first, how different is his demeanour from what Haig had described of the previous night and, second, how remote Haig was from the initiative that would place Foch in supreme command the following day.

On his way to Paris, Amery had been with Milner. Milner then went off to his meeting with Clemenceau but reappeared for the meal that has just been mentioned, in the course of which Henry Wilson also arrived, from the meeting with Haig and Weygand at Abbeville. All were impressed by Clemenceau – Amery thought he would have made a good soldier. Amery's chronology for the events of the afternoon and evening of a hectic day becomes a little confused but the consensus of the various discussions was that supreme control, sometimes short-handed to 'control of the reserve situation', should rest with Clemenceau and Foch, with Foch in the role of technical adviser. According to Amery, Foch told Wilson that this would not be acceptable to him. He wanted to be in sole control although he would accept Clemenceau's decision on what ground was to be held or ceded. It is interesting that, whatever the relationship between the two men, it was a combined political and military control of the war by the French that was envisaged. Foch wanted Milner to endorse the formula at the Doullens meeting the following day.

French control of what was preponderantly a French war was not an unreasonable concept. France was fighting in her own land to preserve her territorial integrity. Britain was not. No one, indeed, was quite sure why Britain was fighting. On 3 August 1914, Sir Edward Grey had said it was because she could not stand back and watch the unchecked aggrandisement of any one European power – a fairly nebulous war aim. France had more men in the field, had suffered more losses and would continue to do so, even if she won the war.

If the Entente powers lost, the consequences might not be too bad for Britain. If she could get her men off Continental Europe, there was little real prospect of invasion. For France, things were very different. The kind of treaty that Germany imposed on her enemies had been demonstrated at Brest-Litovsk and by her treatment of Romania after defeat in December 1917. France had been beaten before and knew what humiliations Germany was capable of. The defeat in 1871 and the Kaiser's enthronement as Emperor – in the Hall of Mirrors in Louis XIV's Versailles – was a real memory for most of the principal actors in the present war. The provinces of Alsace and Lorraine were still lost to France, the statues that symbolised them still covered in crepe in the Place de la Concorde. How unreasonable, then, that France was not in control of the battle for her existence. And particularly when her British allies, as she saw it, had not distinguished themselves in the war so far, and now in retreat were looking over their shoulders towards the Channel.

At 20.00, Loucheur wrote up his diary and recalled a serious discussion he had had with Pétain after lunch. Loucheur had suggested that the chances of defeat for the Entente were perhaps 90 per cent. Pétain said no, 96 per cent. His mood appears to have been quietly realistic and there was no question of panic. Indeed, he thought that, in the event of suing for peace, France might obtain generous terms because her armies were unbroken. (Loucheur disagreed: 'That is badly to misread the

Boche.') Pétain envisaged the eventuality of the French and British armies separating. 'The British Army would beat its way backwards on Calais and defend its bases. That would be the *quasi*-abandonment of all France. France has suffered from Russian betrayal, Italian cowardice, British feebleness, the failure of the Americans.'[16]

Hankey's diary on the night of 25 March again records starkly just how bad things were:

> *March 25th*: Slept very badly. This has been a really terrible day. Although the gap between Third and Fifth Armies has been filled in, our troops are everywhere being driven back and must be extremely exhausted. I told [Sir Eric Geddes] we were at the crisis of the nation's fate.'

21

26 March

'Everything now depended on the French'

THE FIGHTING

Rupprecht had complained that Ludendorff's opportunistic approach lacked strategic purpose. 'Ludendorff is a man of absolute determination,' said Rupprecht, 'but determination alone is not enough if it is not combined with clear-headed intelligence.'[1]

Rupprecht's sophisticated reservations were not reflected in Ludendorff's headline achievements. By 26 March, in the course of five days' fighting, Germany had taken 90,000 British and French prisoners and had advanced about 60 kilometres.[2] The Germans had gained more ground on the Western Front in just a few days than the Allies had in three years. In the course of the day, there was a further retirement of the French and British troops under Fayolle south of the Somme. North of the Somme, Third Army broadly maintained its position.

The Official History recorded that 'everything now depended on the French'. They had arrived unsupported and had initially been forced to retire. It remained to be seen how robust they would prove.[3] In reviewing the state of the battle years later, Edmonds could look back and see that the conflict was becoming stabilised: '[A]fter the 26th March the enemy, although he made desperate and despairing efforts, gained from the British no ground worth mentioning.'[4]

Edmonds applauded the optimism of the British soldiers but he does record the despondency that had been caused by 'the movement to the rear – "going out of the line", as the troops call it – often on the slightest provocation, of Corps and Divisional headquarters'. He recognised that some divisional commanders had moved their fighting headquarters forward, thus steadying subordinate commanders. 'But this was the exception.'

The German achievements had been enormous. In addition to the huge area of ground gained, munitions had been lost by the Allies and almost 250,000 casualties inflicted, 178,000 of them British. French casualties of 77,000 were substantial in what Britain thought was exclusively her battle. But the Germans had suffered about the same level of casualties and, by 26 March, their discipline was fraying. There was looting and drunkenness and morale was badly affected when the Germans found how well equipped and well fed the British troops were in comparison with their own reduced state.

A German Staff Officer, Rudolf Binding, wrote in his diary on 28 March, describing, in words that have often been quoted, how the effects of the Allied blockade brought an infantry advance to a halt near Albert:

> I jumped into a car with orders to find out what was causing the stoppage in front. As soon as I got near the town I began to see curious sights. Strange figures, which looked very little like soldiers, and certainly showed no signs of advancing, were making their way back out of town. There were men driving cows before them on a line; others who carried a hen under one arm and a box of notepaper under the other. Men carrying a bottle of wine under their arm and another one open in their hand. Men who had torn a silk drawing-room curtain from off its rod and were dragging it to the rear as a useful bit of loot. More men with writing paper and coloured notebooks. Evidently they had found it desirable to sack a stationer's shop. Men dressed up in comic disguise. Men with top hats on their heads. Men staggering. Men who could hardly walk.

Binding himself was not immune from excitement at the riches which had been so long denied to his countrymen. He smeared his boots 'with lovely English boot polish'. He was so impressed by the uniform of a captured English officer that he had 'an inward temptation to call out to him, "kindly undress at once," for a desire for English equipment, with tunic, breaches and boots had arisen in me, shameless and potent'.[5]

The first part of Hankey's diary for 26 March showed how, at one level, life went on in London remarkably undisturbed by the very real possibility of defeat in detail for the allies:

March 26th: Slept nearly ten hours at Club and woke up enormously refreshed. At the morning Cabinet I learned we had been driven back to the Ancre, but later the news got rather better and on our front there seems to be a lull ... in the evening Lloyd George and I dined with Eric Geddes. His housekeeper, Miss Shepherd, is a wonderful singer and accompanist, and he, to my surprise, a fine singer with a voice like a bull.* We had a regular sing-song. The Prime Minister and I came to the conclusion he is prouder of his singing than of his professional attainments!

But on the other side of the Channel the principal actors were participating in something more compelling than listening to the intertwined voices of Eric Geddes and Miss Shepherd.

THE CONFERENCE

On 25 March, when Milner had met Poincaré, Clemenceau and Foch at Pétain's headquarters, they arranged to meet again at 11 a.m. the following day. This 26 March meeting, which turned into the Doullens Conference, did not, therefore, take place at Haig's suggestion. Instead, it was those who were present at the 25 March meeting who decided to ask Haig to join them at French HQ the following day. The gathering, as it finally took place, was not what had been planned. When Haig received his invitation, he said that he had arranged to meet his Army Commanders at Doullens, which is just a few kilometres from his headquarters at the Château de Beaurepaire, and suggested that the separate conference that was now proposed should take place there and not at Pétain's HQ, and at midday and not at 11.00.

The politicians and French generals had been told of the change of venue but not the change of time and they arrived while Haig and his Army Commanders – 'the robber barons', as his staff referred to them – were still conferring upstairs. We have seen that one Army Commander, Gough, was not present. Maybe he was thought to be too busy looking for his dispersed army. Maybe, because he was now commanded by Fayolle, he was no longer regarded as commanding an army. Perhaps he was already yesterday's man. Not only was he not summoned to the

---

* Geddes's build, as well as his voice, was bull-like. He required the services of Miss Shepherd because his wife, to whom he was devoted, was an invalid.

conference; he was not told that it had taken place and knew nothing about it.[6] He learned that something had happened when he received the dressing-down from Foch that has been described. He was already bitter about the fact that, because he was under Fayolle's command, GHQ knew nothing about the situation and morale of Fifth Army. When, months later, he learned the nature of the conference from which he had been excluded, he was very angry. His account of what he learned of the conference may, therefore, be of doubtful accuracy. He says that, from what he was told, the atmosphere at Doullens had amounted almost to panic. But then, in his account of Fifth Army's War, he got the date of the meeting wrong.

The French Minister of Munitions, Loucheur, had left Paris with Poincaré, Clemenceau and the others at about 08.00. They reached the *mairie* of Doullens, 'architecturally a mediocre building fronted by a little square', around 10.45 and walked in the garden, waiting for Haig. Haig had to interrupt his conference with the robber barons to greet them. He came out at around 11.00 and asked for a delay while he heard the reports of the Army Commanders. As he came down the steps of the town hall, a French general nudged Clemenceau to say, 'There's a man who will be obliged to capitulate on the open field within a fortnight, and we'll be very lucky if we're not obliged to do the same.'[7] Haig was pretty much in the dock at Doullens.

The French party remained in the garden. It was very cold. Loucheur suggested that Clemenceau should take shelter but he declined. 'Along the road which bordered the narrow square of grass the British Army was passing in retreat, tired but marching in order, pulling back to the north: none of us could tell whether they were going to join the troops fighting before Arras or were going further back towards the sea.'

Foch moved around between the different groups, giving voice to heroic sentiments. 'We must stop yielding even fifty centimetres of ground . . . Hold where you stand and die there. Remember September 1914 . . . The enemy has forced open the centre of the double door, pushing Haig back and Pétain back; a new force must push them shut again. Above all, don't tell the troops of a rear line otherwise they'll want to rush back to it.'

Clemenceau turned from Foch, took Loucheur by the arm and said, '*Quel bougre!*' Loucheur said, 'I always told you, Premier, that he was a *rude bougre.*' Martin Kitchen appealingly translates this by saying that Clemenceau described Foch as a 'right bugger'[8] – a more accurate but less satisfying translation might be a 'difficult bugger' or 'tough customer'.[9]

According to Poincaré, Pétain said to Clemenceau before the conference opened that he had given orders for the retirement of the French army south and away from the British and that he expected the total defeat of the British in the open field followed by that of the French army. Clemenceau was appalled by this pessimism and reported it at once to Poincaré. The two men were persuaded by Foch that Pétain was being unduly pessimistic. This account of Pétain's panic is not supported by any other evidence and is inconsistent with the fairly upbeat remarks which he was to make at the beginning of the conference proper.[10] Clemenceau's claim that, on his arrival at Doullens, Haig said that he wanted to uncover Amiens and fall back on the Channel ports can perhaps also be dismissed in the interests of balance. Haig told Milner that this was not true and there was almost certainly a misunderstanding. Milner said that 'all [Haig] had meant to say' was that, without more support, the line might break.[11]

Milner and Henry Wilson arrived next. Milner asked for a brief discussion with Haig and the Army Commanders after which, at 12.30, the conference opened. Poincaré was in the chair. Clemenceau started with a brisk attack on Haig. Did he intend to defend Amiens or to continue to fall back, perhaps to the Channel ports? Haig said he would stand firm north of the Somme but that he could not do much south of the Somme where, in any event, Fifth Army was under French command. It was at this point that Pétain interrupted to point out that, for practical purposes, Fifth Army no longer existed. Haig finished his response to Clemenceau and querulously asked what the French were doing. Pétain said that he had moved troops from the eastern sector of his front so that he could now bring 24 divisions to the area under threat. He added, however, that these divisions would take some time to arrive, coming in at the rate of two a day.

According to Loucheur, when Pétain was talking in detail of the need to defend Amiens, Foch cried out in frustration, 'We must fight in front of Amiens. We'll fight where we are now. As we've not been able to stop the Germans on the Somme, we must not now retire a single inch.' Loucheur's published version[12] of what happened next says that there was a silence, broken only by Haig's intervention: 'If General Foch will consent to give me his advice, I shall gladly follow it.' Haig wanted the appointment to be his idea, his statesman-like initiative. I shall return to the matter but, briefly, it is pretty doubtful that Haig uttered what Loucheur calls 'these simple words' but certain rather that Haig's was the least important role in Foch's appointment. A courteous readiness to hear advice in any event amounted to much less than the nomination of a generalissimo.

Milner claimed that it was he who had pushed for the appointment of Foch and that Clemenceau and Haig had agreed.[13] That accords with what had happened at the meeting on the previous evening, accords with all the reliable accounts and is, indeed, the case. He was clear-sighted, analysed the situation and then took action. Afterwards, he said to Amery, 'I hope I was right – you and Henry [Wilson] always tell me Foch is the best man.'[14] Milner was certainly influenced by the views of others. He could scarcely have ignored the opinion of his prime minister. Lloyd George claimed in his *Memoirs* that it was he who had chosen Foch. He said that he told Milner to do what he could to restore the 'Versailles Front' (meaning direction by the SWC) by giving Foch the authority 'to organise a reserve and to control it'.[15] The outcome of these manoeuvres was, in fact, much more radical than that. Haig's wings were clipped, as were Pétain's, and the role of the SWC was enhanced to an extent but what was much more significant was that the remainder of the war was essentially run militarily by a French general in very close collaboration with a French prime minister. Lloyd George may not have objected to that but it wasn't quite what he'd intended.

Lloyd George had always seen Foch as a dynamic leader suitable for supreme command of some sort. At the meeting of the Supreme War Council that began on 30 January (to consider the Military Representatives' Note Twelve), he proposed that the president of the Executive Committee should be 'General Foch, on account of his experience, his record and his energy, his military gifts and his reputation'.[16] He was to describe Foch as 'the head and front of the "Versailles soldiers" . . . the greatest soldier of the War'.[17]

Afterwards, Lloyd George, like Haig, wanted to be the man of vision who had been responsible for Foch's appointment. His writings on the matter should be treated with as much caution as Haig's. The appointment was a collegiate decision, in which Milner had the most decisive role and Haig the least decisive. But Milner certainly had the backing of

Lloyd George and Wilson and all three are entitled to a share of the glory, if that is what it was.*

Standing back from the detail of the discussions, it is pretty clear that the outcome of Doullens was never in doubt – the appointment of a generalissimo with Foch as that man was the cumulative result of the events of the five days. At this critical moment, there was consensus on the need for unified command. Poincaré and Clemenceau wanted it. Lloyd George and Milner wanted it. The British generals could not obstruct the inevitable. Foch wanted it and behaved throughout the conference as if he already was generalissimo.†

Milner and Clemenceau went off to confer in a corner and then Clemenceau prepared a form of words which he read out. It is referred to in the War Office record[18] as 'A Resolution by M. Clemenceau'. Haig said that the brief was too narrow – Foch should be placed in control of the Allied armies 'from the Alps to the North Sea'.[19] Clemenceau went back to his draft and substituted 'on the Western Front' for 'around Amiens'. Again, Haig intervened – the forces under Foch's control should not be simply the 'British and French Armies' but, rather, every single army available, including the Belgians, the Americans and presumably the Siamese forces – 'British and French Armies' was replaced by 'Allied Armies'. While the majestic Churchillian phrase, 'from the Alps to the North Sea', is most unlikely ever to have rolled out of Haig's famously tongue-tied mouth, the two extensions in Foch's responsibilities were certainly the result of his intervention. While the War Office record could have been influenced by him, it is corroborated by Milner.[20]

It is fair to ask what the actors at Doullens thought they were doing when they adjusted Foch's grandiose job description. Two years earlier, he had been given overall responsibility (to Haig's annoyance) for coordinating the Somme battles. Did anyone think that Doullens amounted to much the same thing? Not the French – they regarded the conference as privatising the war, returning it to their ownership, and Foch and

---

* There is a pleasing, if unintentional, acknowledgement that Doullens was Milner's conference in the fact that, while two of the town's streets are named after the military men (Avenue du Maréchal Foch and Rue du Maréchal Haig), only one British civilian is so celebrated (by the Boulevard Lord Milner).

† Foch *did* want the appointment and Clemenceau knew that. At the end of the conference, the prime minister patted the generalissimo on the head, called him '*un bon garçon*' and said, 'Well, you've got the job you so much wanted.' Foch replied, 'A fine gift. You give me a lost battle and tell me to win it.' Does the Hôtel aux Bons Enfants in the Rue Jacques Mossion commemorate this little exchange?

Clemenceau were to act now on that assumption. Not the War Cabinet – Lloyd George and Milner saw that dual control had brought the Allies to within a whisker of defeat, a 96 per cent likelihood, as Pétain had said, and thought that united direction, not just coordination, was needed.

The generals' position is more ambivalent. They certainly recognised that something more than a return to the 1916 formula was involved – the gravity of the situation, the solemnity of the discussion, the importance attached to adjusting the form of words, all show that. But Haig and even Wilson may not fully have appreciated the significance of what was happening. Both of them were to have regrets in the course of the months ahead and Haig, as will be seen,[*] thought that a wrong and hasty arrangement had been reached – a reflection which sits uneasily beside his eagerness to claim ownership of that arrangement.

When the Second World War broke out, less attention was paid to the sensitivities of the War Office or the generals. A Supreme War Council was set up immediately on the outbreak of war. But, this time, the British Expeditionary Force was immediately placed under the direction of the French Commander-in-Chief.[21]

Moving slightly ahead to complete the matter, Foch's status was further enhanced a few weeks after Doullens. A conference was held at Beauvais on 3 April. Lloyd George was present this time and also the American Generals Pershing and Bliss. The formula arrived at Doullens was replaced with a fuller definition of Foch's powers:

> General Foch is charged by the British, French and American governments with the coordination of the action of the Allied Armies on the Western Front. To this end all powers necessary to secure effective realisation are conferred on him. The British, French and American governments for this purpose entrust to General Foch the strategic direction of military operations. The Commanders-in-Chief of the British, French and American Armies shall have full control of the tactical employment of their forces. Each Commander-in-Chief will have the right of appeal to his government if in his opinion the safety of his army is compromised by any order received from General Foch.

---

* See p. 203.

Haig acquiesced but he had still not recovered from the events of March. Hankey said that Haig failed to inspire confidence on this occasion. A British colonel said that he looked white and shaken.[22] On the other hand, Haig said that, at Beauvais, Lloyd George was 'thoroughly frightened, and he seemed still to be in a funk'.[23] But Haig never understood Lloyd George's natural buoyancy and resilience. He thought that he was worried about reporting to Parliament. He had no understanding of the prime minister's standing with MPs.

If Haig was still shaken at Beauvais, he quickly recovered. Wilson, on the other hand, grew increasingly pessimistic. By 12 April, he had become convinced that Dunkirk was lost and that Calais and Boulogne would soon be. The situation was 'desperately serious'.[24] He wrote to Lord Robert Cecil on 13 April, 'We shall lose the war if we go on like this. What a pity.'[25]* He told Churchill and Haig, on two occasions, that Britain would have to abandon the Channel ports and fall back with the French towards Paris.[26] Foch ruled against both: '*Ni l'un, ni l'autre.* Despite Foch's resolve, Wilson's next nightmare was a fear of invasion of the British Isles.'[27]

General Henri Mordacq, Clemenceau's Chef de Cabinet at the War Ministry, wrote a summary of the events at the Beauvais Conference in 1923, based on contemporary notes. Pétain told him that he was pleased with the way things had gone since Doullens but mentioned, at length, the difficulties he had had with the British before then:

> always promising and then not performing, though one counted upon them for it, or doing so always belatedly. Moreover, their command structure was badly organised; Marshal Haig was not kept informed. In short, it was time to put them under our orders,† for their own sake as much as ours. But what General Pétain blamed them for above all (and he proved quite closed to any discussion on this point) was in not defending the Somme. 'They did not even try,' he said, 'and yet they must have known of that obstacle's tactical and strategical importance.'

Mordacq, condescendingly to British ears, sought to excuse the British by emphasising the recent and rapid growth of the British army and that

---

* The throwaway ending is typical Wilson.
† It's appealing to imagine how Haig would have reacted had he read these words.

its consequent lack of trained skills and doctrine meant that 'one had to be indulgent towards them'.[28]

In 1919 Foch wrote an introduction to the French edition of Haig's Despatches. Haig wrote to him to thank him and went on:

> In common with others of my countrymen I have also read with much interest and genuine appreciation, the letter you lately addressed to our Prime Minister. There is one passage in it however, which I think will give rise to misapprehension, and in the interest of historical accuracy I desire at once to correct. I feel sure that you at any rate would like to know the true facts. You state in your letter that '*on the initiative* of Mr Lloyd George' you were appointed to be Generalissimo of the Allied Armies. I claim for myself that honour . . . I personally pressed for this . . . I think I can fairly claim that the *initiative* in this matter was mine! It was a privilege and a credit for which I cannot abandon to anyone.[29]

The assertion is pretty unconvincing. He had not wanted to put his troops into the General Reserve and under the control of the Supreme War Council which would have meant, as Barry Pitt put it, that they would be 'at the disposal of the French representative, General Foch, at whose command General Wilson had always leapt like a lap-dog'.[30] Putting his troops under the command of Foch, whose appointment he claimed retrospectively to have welcomed and indeed promoted, had been so intolerable to Haig a few weeks earlier that he preferred to do his private deal with Pétain. Foch made the change that Haig desired and replied generously to Haig's letter. But, although he was ready to defer to Haig as a matter of courtesy, it appears that Haig's recollection was inconsistent with his own. He had already written an article for the magazine *L'Illustration*, saying that the proposition to appoint him to Supreme Command came from the British government.

Elizabeth Greenhalgh refers to, inter alia, Robert Hanks, who considered that Haig was the 'last one on board' in regard to Foch's appointment[31] and concludes that Haig's claim to have been responsible for the appointment may be dismissed.[32] Her view is that Haig sought to demonstrate that the blame for the events of 21 March onwards lay with Pétain and not him and that Pétain's guilt was demonstrated by the need to impose superior control. That seems to me an unnecessarily elaborate explanation. Haig had palpably not been in control in the days running up to Doullens. Ideally, he would, no doubt, have wished to be appointed generalissimo himself. That was out of the question but he could at least represent himself as having directed events by having been the man who was responsible for the appointment of the generalissimo. As time went by and the British role in the last hundred days of the war became very important indeed, it was all the more desirable that he should be remembered not as the man who had faltered in March but as the man of vision who had created the conditions for victory.

Rawlinson's Chief of Staff, Montgomery* took notes at Doullens as a record, such as it was, for GHQ but, when Edmonds asked him for details after the war, he said that the language had been French, people had been talking simultaneously in different parts of the room and he had been stuck in a corner.[33] In any event, he said, Haig had personally amended the account before it went to GHQ. Again, Haig was writing his own history. Montgomery thought that the 'official' account was as suspect as his own memory. In 1934, Lloyd George's secretary found Montgomery's original draft. It is interesting, as ever, to compare an original document with the version amended by Haig. According to the contemporaneous note, Haig had been very shaky on Amiens: 'It is vitally important to hold Amiens but there must be no break between the First and Third Armies. This is more important than holding Amiens. All available reserves are therefore to be sent to the Third Army. We will cover Amiens as long as possible but will then fall back on the Arras-Doullens Line.'[34]

Lawrence also replied to the Official Historian and said that he was almost certain that Montgomery's record was drawn up on his, Lawrence's, instructions. He recalled Haig's extension of Foch's responsibilities from just defending Amiens to covering the whole front: 'After all, the whole point was that the French wouldn't fight or help in any way and Haig was prepared to make any sacrifice to force them to take a hand in the battle.'[35] Neither side had much time for the other. Montgomery confirmed that view: 'As Lawrence says, the thing was to get the French to fight and the way to do that was to put Clemenceau and Foch in charge.'[36]

The Official History adds a little to the War Office record, reflecting Haig's input. Clemenceau, it says, took Milner into a corner and

---

* See footnote, p. 166.

subsequently Pétain. Milner then went into another corner – the room seems to have had a remarkable number of corners for a straightforward rectangle – and spoke to Haig who was 'not only willing but glad to accept the control of General Foch'. This is new detail but nothing very substantial. The form of words rather implies the acceptance of someone else's proposal.

The Official History continues with the account of the adjustment of Foch's responsibilities. Clemenceau and Milner signed the agreement and Poincaré said, 'I hope, gentlemen, that we have worked well towards victory.' Haig was heard to have expressed his relief that, in future, he'd be dealing with a man and not a committee, presumably the Supreme War Council. Milner asked the Chief of the General Staff, Sir Herbert Lawrence, how he could help the generals. Lawrence replied, '[B]y leaving them alone.' Milner became Secretary of State for War a month later and, according to the Official History, 'took this advice to heart and unreservedly followed it for the rest of the war'.

When Hankey recorded the events of the day, after describing the duet by Sir Eric Geddes and Miss Shepherd, he continued:

> At 11pm we went back to Downing Street where we were joined by Milner and Henry Wilson, who have come straight from a most important conference at Doullens, not far from the Front, with Poincaré, Clemenceau, Foch, Pétain and Haig, Plumer, Byng etc. They reported that they had agreed to make Foch 'coordinating authority' over the whole Western Front, i.e. practically generalissimo . . . Milner gave a fine account of the army commanders, who, he said, were cool as cucumbers and in great heart . . . Here is a good story [which] Henry Wilson, in the midst of our troubles, tells of Clemenceau who is in great heart. 'Lloyd George,' says Clemenceau, 'goes to Beauvais. He sees plenty of "sheeps"* and plenty of "muttons", and he goes back to England and says France has plenty of "breads"!'[37]

The Army Commanders had been described in different terms in Downing Street earlier in the day. 'After the cabinet,' said Milner, 'Lloyd George asked French (who was attending regularly), and myself and

---

* Impressed by the number of sheep he had seen, Lloyd George had said to Clemenceau that France didn't seem to be short of food. The joke, such as it was, was at the expense of Lloyd George, whose French wasn't as good as Wilson's.

Winston Churchill to stay behind and discuss the situation. French was most bitter about Haig, who, he said, was no judge of men, had surrounded himself with stupid people and bad commanders.'[38]

END OF THE DAY

Herbillon had opened his diary that morning by describing the sad aspect of *GQG* at Compiègne when he awoke – the local people gathered in front of the palace, hoping for news, the evacuees on the road reminding him of the opening days of the war, the cannonade in the distance, the retreating British troops. 'In five days we have lost the gains of three years. The English retreat has been extraordinarily rapid.' At 17.00 Poincaré returns from Doullens and calls him in:

> 'Well, Colonel, General Foch is officially charged with Franco-British operations and both must obey his directives. I believe we have achieved the unified command, at least on our front. Are you content and do you think we have done good work?'
>
> I smile with satisfaction and say that it was the only solution which could save us . . . The English, finding themselves caught in the net, this time could not refuse what had long been necessary. All military circles will feel relief and confidence. 'Yes, it's good work and it was high time,' says the President.[39]

Thus France had gained her objective – control of the war that was being fought on her soil. It was a necessary arrangement. The French press did not rise to the occasion. Haig was criticised for having failed to make adequate defensive arrangements. French commanders complained about the British and Haig regretted the consequences of his concession. But a unified command delivered victory a few months later and, without it, the alliance might well have been unable to resist. Clemenceau recognised the price Britain had paid in terms of self-esteem and reported generously to Lord Bertie, the British ambassador in Paris. At Doullens, he told him the British had conducted themselves magnificently, with great dignity.[40]

22

View from the Street

WE HAVE SEEN how the events of these few days appeared to the actors on the spot – senior officers, the innermost circle of the War Cabinet and their privileged advisers – but it is important to recognise that this innermost circle was a very small one. Most Cabinet ministers were kept in the dark. The War Cabinet minutes went only to the members of that small council and to the foreign secretary and the heads of the Services. Minutes of sensitive meetings did not go that far. They were kept in manuscript by Hankey and scarcely circulated at all. Other ministers and ordinary MPs had to rely on gossip and the press for their information.[1]

So did the man and woman in the street. This was a citizens' war: what did the ordinary citizen know of just how close Britain had come to defeat, of the fact that the Allied armies had almost parted, that a British army had broken, that the French considered themselves betrayed by an ally that was not truly committed to the cause, that the solution had been to subordinate Britain to French control?

Top people took *The Times* in 1918 – as, indeed, the paper still claimed 50 years later – but we have seen that, because Lord Northcliffe uniquely controlled both quality and popular titles, he was able to influence all classes of the nation. His message was consistent across his titles and was often, but not always, followed by his brother's *Daily Mirror*. Accordingly, looking at *The Times*, the source of the fullest news coverage of his papers, gives a good flavour of what the intelligent man and woman in the street or on the Clapham omnibus knew of what was happening.

When the student of war or of political history turns from the narrow focus to the wider world, she or he is reminded sharply that there is another dimension to life. Looking at the records of municipal councils, businesses, even at parliamentary debates, one is struck not by how much the war dominates everyday life but by the extent that life goes on unaffected by the upheavals on the Western Front. On 1 January 1918,* for example, a letter-writer complains about something where the war is only indirectly involved as a tangential irritation: 'As one of those who, for medical reasons, are limited to whisky as a stimulant, I should like to place our case before the public.' Profiteering by distillers, merchants and retailers should be controlled by the government.

In the early months of the year, the Italian campaign dominated military coverage but there are several references to the threat to the French in the Champagne area. In the search for war news, we come across, on 1 March, facsimiles of the king's and queen's ration cards, 'royal meat cards', complete with signatures. On the same date, it is reported that Wully Robertson has been appointed ADC-General to the King, royal consolation for what Lloyd George had done to him. On 20 March, there are reports on precautions against the smallpox outbreak which is causing some concern.

Two days later, the day after the start of the offensive, a story about the new Fish Orders was followed by an item about an 'Invasion by Aliens', particularly Russian Jews in Maidenhead. It was very apparent because 'in the street one is jostled by these aliens at every turn'. Further into the paper, where the main news is to be found, the same issue records the fact of the offensive. The headlines were dramatic: 'Great Battle Opens' . . . 'Massed Attacks on 50-mile Front' . . . 'Advance into British Zones' . . . 'Enemy's Big Losses'. The news must have been all the more alarming because readers had not been prepared for it. Nor apparently had the leader-writers – there was no editorial comment.

By the following day, 23 March, the paper was properly prepared. The cover was extensive, intelligent and supported by very good maps. The tone was distinctly grave, although anything upbeat in GHQ communiqués – and there was quite a lot that was upbeat – was highlighted: 'Some Progress by the Enemy'. There was a leader, headed 'The Great Attack':

Half a million Germans attacked the British Army on Thursday morning on a front of sixty miles, and so began the greatest and most critical battle of the war. If Germany fails to achieve her purpose now, as we believe assuredly she will, her doom is sealed in spite of all her glittering successes in Eastern Europe. The British Army, already tried

---

* All the quotations in this chapter are from *The Times* for the day in question.

in this war in a hundred fierce conflicts, is battling today for the safety and the liberty of these islands and of Western civilization. Upon our own brave soldiers this signal and supreme struggle has been thrust, and we believe with the PRIME MINISTER, who spoke some straight and burning words to a deputation of miners on Thursday afternoon, that every nerve will be strained in this country to back them in their gallant stand.

The following day was Sunday and there was no paper. By Monday 25 March, the coverage was very full and punches were not being pulled: 'Péronne and Ham Lost . . . Back to the Somme'. A leading article adopted a suitably grave tone:

The world stands today at a special crisis in its destinies, and upon this country falls the full brunt of the struggle. In the immense conflict which is raging, the greatest and the most terrible in history, the eyes of all free peoples turn towards her as to their champion. It is hers to bear the standard of right and of liberty, their standard and hers, in the forefront of the battle. They watch eagerly to see how she will endure the test.

A further leader analysed the development of the battle:

There is no disguising the fact that the Germans have broken clean through the defensive line which we held in France when the great battle began on Thursday. SIR DOUGLAS HAIG was the first to say so, and he has indicated the place where the breach was effected. Our line was forced on a considerable front west of St. Quentin on Friday afternoon. The Germans confirm the British statement, and tell us that the army leader who broke our defences was GENERAL VON HUTIER, who pierced the Russian positions and took Riga last September.

A Special Correspondent reported that '[a]s for the fighting of our men, I have no forms of praise sufficient. The battle has seen a thousand Thermopylaes, and every officer's voice rings with pride when he speaks of the behaviour of his men.' But there was room for an advertising feature, 'Rest at Easter', which contained advertisements for 'Bath – the Spa for a Healthful Holiday' and 'Droitwich's Natural Brine Baths'. There was also concern about an imminent strike by engineers.

A leader on the following day, Tuesday, 26 March, gave a very misleading picture in terms of losses of personnel and *matériel* and, indeed, of the quality of the defending troops – 'a living wall', as the newspaper called it.

Two broad impressions emerge from an examination of the fragmentary news which is constantly arriving from the scene of the titanic struggle in France. The first is that the enemy continue to make steady progress, though their advance is noticeably uneven. The second is that our gallant troops are making the most stubborn resistance and are exacting a heavy toll from the Germans, while in the southern portion of the long battlefield French forces are rapidly moving in to their assistance. The task of explaining the exact situation, so far as it is known in this country is extremely difficult, because we are bound to describe it mainly in terms of ground. To speak of ground at the present stage of the battle is largely misleading, for the real object of the enemy is not so much to capture particular areas as to destroy our forces. In this at all events they are not succeeding, nor are they likely to do so for it is quite certain that on balance their losses have so far been considerably heavier than our own. We are still justified in saying that considering the magnitude of the battle, our losses up till now remain relatively light in proportion to the number of troops engaged. It is true that we have lost much valuable material, including guns and tanks, but the available supplies are so huge that this class of loss is not the most serious matter. Even the 'break through' the line as SIR DOUGLAS HAIG accurately and obviously described it, is liable to be misunderstood. The fact is that the enemy broke through our prepared defensive positions, but they have not broken through the living wall which still confronts them. Our armies have not been cut asunder, and, though there has been a long withdrawal, our retiring line remains intact and continuous.

Wednesday's paper said that the events of that day and the next would be critical. By that following day, Thursday, 28 March, despite the fact that the Germans had taken Albert, had pushed up the Ancre Valley to within 12 miles of Amiens and, in the south, had made a good deal of ground in the Somme Valley, a very positive spin was being given. Haig was reported as saying that 'our troops fought magnificently' and had 'thrown back the enemy all along the British front'. A reference to French reinforcements failed to indicate their scale or importance.

The following day, Friday, 29 March, was Good Friday, when the paper was not normally published. On that Good Friday, it was because of the importance of the events of the week. The paper gave a little more coverage to the French now. 'They counter-attacked with magnificent dash and retook two of the villages near Montdidier. To the south towards Noyon they have also recaptured ground.' By now, the reports tended to suggest that the great attack had been checked or had run out of steam. There was a distinct suggestion that a gamble had failed and that time was not on Germany's side.

What is interesting about the coverage in general is the perhaps inevitable lack of any advance warning of what was afoot and, secondly, the optimistic spin that ignored the possibility of defeat in detail. Most surprising of all, when the month ended, the British public had no hint that her armies were now fighting under French control. Nothing had been said about any conference or change of command. It was only on Easter Monday, 1 April, that the paper reported a very brief statement that Lloyd George had issued on Saturday, 30 March – the Saturday before the Monday Easter holiday was a good time to bury bad news. Under headlines that began 'The Southern Battles. Rush Stemmed by the French' but which made no reference to the conference, there is a paragraph of just 24 words: 'General Foch has been charged by the British, French and American Governments to coordinate the action of the Allied Armies on the Western Front'. The importance of what had happened and the heart-searching that lay behind it remained hidden.

Elsewhere in the same edition, there was a brief account of the career of this general who, from the earliest days of the war, had stood out as 'one of the most brilliant leaders on the Allied side'. There was an extract from a character sketch that had appeared on an earlier occasion and which quoted Foch when he taught strategy at l'École de Guerre: 'Battles are . . . lost morally [not materially], and it is therefore morally that they can be won.' The writer of the sketch had added, 'His grey-blue eyes give a singularly striking impression of a man whose life has been devoted to translating philosophy into terms of the casualty list.' Foch did not conform to the pattern of English generals.

Care was, indeed, taken to avoid any impression that this very French Frenchman was directly in charge of British armies. An editorial which bears the signs of official input represented Foch's appointment as nothing dramatic, the culmination of a continuous process. The nature of the appointment, too, was carefully downplayed, implying nothing more than coordination: 'We feel bound to say at once, in view of bygone discussions of the "Generalissimo" ideal, that the public will be well advised to accept the official statement as meaning precisely what it says ... GENERAL FOCH, as we understand the position, neither possesses nor desires the title of "Generalissimo". His function is properly described by the Government as that of coordinating the action of the Allied Armies.'

The truth but not the whole truth and nothing to disturb the *amour propre* of government or generals or the chauvinism of newspapers and their readers.

Part Four

After the Conference

23

The End of the *Kaiserschlacht*

IT IS SOMETIMES said that, even by 26 March, the German attack was beginning to fail. That was not evident at the time. In the 40 days of the first three waves of the *Kaiserschlacht* – MICHAEL, GEORGETTE and BLÜCHER-YORCK – British casualties were 236,000 and French 90,000. As late as 11 April, Haig issued a famous Order of the Day which ended:

> Many amongst us now are tired. To those I would say that victory will belong to the side which holds out longest. The French Army is moving rapidly and in great force to our support.
>
> There is no other course open to us but to fight it out! Every position must be held to the last man: there must be no retirement. With our backs to the wall, and believing in the justice of our cause, each one of us must fight on to the end. The safety of our homes and the freedom of mankind alike depend on the conduct of each one of us at this critical moment.
>
> D. Haig, F.M.

The 11 April Order of the Day is interesting. It is the most eloquent and most emotional Order which Haig ever issued, standing in sharp contrast to his preferred tone of imperturbability. He was still shaken. The Order is a little like Nelson's signal at Trafalgar and, just as some of Nelson's sailors resented the fact that their commander thought it necessary to remind them to do their duty, so Haig's Order was more appreciated by the civilians than by the army. Charteris regretted the Order. He thought that it was unnecessary and might give heart to the Germans.

By now, Ludendorff had turned the direction of his attack to the north, near Ypres. Horne and Plumer were attacked in an area where Britain could not afford to give ground and where First and Second

Armies had been depleted by the reinforcements that had earlier been sent south. Doullens had not brought the war to an end and Haig did not think that the German attack had run out of steam on 26 March. What Doullens had done was to create a sense of common cause and to put Foch in control of that common cause. By promoting France's role, Clemenceau's position was greatly enhanced. In this critical period, it was as much his dynamism as Foch's determination that energised the direction of the war. The two worked as a team.

In this new situation, Haig now said: 'The most important thing is to keep connection with the French ... I must also cover Calais and Boulogne.' The two requirements were not now alternatives and it is interesting to see which came first. Foch was faced by demands both from Haig and Pétain. He gave neither as many men as they wanted but he did give reserves to both.

At enormous cost, Britain withstood the onslaught but the support of the French was crucial. Between 26 March and 5 April, 45 French infantry and six cavalry divisions were moved to the area between the Somme and the Oise. And, in more than a physical sense, France and Britain were closer than they had ever been at any point in the war. The Entente shared reserves and coordinated their activities properly for the first time. Foch had the power to move armies and tell them when and where to fight. The offensives that took place after March 1918 were subject to his overall direction and the individual components to his coordination. He had an intuitive grasp of German intentions which he countered with, for the first time, a concerted strategic vision to which even the Americans submitted.

By the end of April, the German advance had been brought to a halt. Germany had made significant advances in the north in the area between Ypres and Béthune held by Second and First Armies. Further to the south, from Douai to the Somme, there had been a big push through the areas held by Third and particularly Fifth Army, with the bulge that threatened Compiègne and thus, ultimately, Paris. But after GEORGETTE, Ludendorff had not attempted to bite and hold. His infiltrating storm troops had run too far ahead of his guns and gains could not be consolidated. His casualties were immense – slightly higher than the combined losses of the Allies. It has been argued that the Germans defeated themselves in 1918.

There is debate about when the surge that began on 21 March ended. Some take the date as 5 April, when the attacks in the Montdidier area had to be broken off. The German attack could only work if it achieved an immediate success. The sort of war that was being fought could not be sustained for long. Between 21 and 26 March, the attacking divisions lost between 2,500 and 3,500 men and no more than 1,000 replacements per division were available so, between the start of MICHAEL and the date of the Doullens Conference, the German divisions were already severely under strength.

Exhaustion and supply problems were very evident on the Ypres Front in April. By 10 April, the German army had lost a fifth of its ration strength.[1] By that date, the MICHAEL armies – Seventeenth, Second and Eighteenth – had lost the equivalent of an entire army.[2] On 14 April, discipline was beginning to break down and one officer, Colonel von Lenz, reported that 'the troops are not attacking, in spite of orders'. Too much was being asked of them.

Now the force of the German attack was being directed to the French front. Foch accordingly asked for the return of the French troops which had reinforced the British line. Haig protested, copying to the War Office, and another Allied crisis of command ensued – although a minor one compared to Doullens. As has been seen, the Doullens formula had been expanded after just a week at the Beauvais Conference to give Foch authority over 'the strategic direction of military operations', with the national Commanders-in-Chief responsible for the 'tactical employment of their forces'. After just another ten days, a further twitch was needed – Foch was now appointed simply Commander-in-Chief of the Allied Forces in France.

Haig was far from entirely happy with the consequences of the change he claimed to have engineered. At a meeting on 7 June, which involved Milner, Wilson, Haig, Foch and Clemenceau, Haig said that circumstances were close which might compel him to appeal to the British Cabinet in terms of the Beauvais Agreement, as he expected to be ordered by Foch to transfer French troops from the British sector – an order which, in his view, would imperil the safety of the British Army in France. 'The effect of the Beauvais Agreement is now becoming clearer in practice. This effect I had realised from the beginning, namely that the responsibility for the safety of the British Army in France could no longer rest with me because the "Generalissimo" can do what *he* thinks right with *my* troops.' That was, of course, the direct result of the arrangement Haig claimed to have promoted.

The relationship between Haig and Foch at this time, for all the gloss Haig subsequently tried to put on it, was a pretty sulky one. All Haig got from the 7 June meeting were face-saving concessions from Clemenceau – orders from Foch moving French units in Haig's area were to go through Clemenceau's hands first. Haig and Foch were also encouraged to meet more frequently. Haig never really reconciled himself to working under the Allied Commander-in-Chief.

It was in this grudging and resentful frame of mind that Haig entered into what turned out to be the final phase of the war – the Hundred Days. The great advance started with the Battle of Amiens on 8 August 1918.

Before then, however, the tide had already turned. The change in the direction of the war was revealed in the Second Battle of the Marne, which took place three weeks before Amiens, immediately after the final German offensive in Champagne. The Allied forces were now truly allied – American, British, Italian and French. On 15 July, the first day of the battle, France captured 12,000 prisoners and 250 guns. By 3 August, they had freed over 200 French villages, captured 3,330 German machine guns and over 800 guns and mortars. They took 29,000 prisoners. The cost to the French was high – 95,000 casualties with about half of them killed – but the outcome of the battle was delivered by Doullens.

24

The Failure of Ludendorff's Offensive

LUDENDORFF'S LAST THROW had thus ended in failure. No one, least of all a child of the Entente, can feel sorry for him, megalomaniac and monstrous as he was, and the words 'poor Ludendorff' do not come easily to the lips. But historical assessments of his plans for the spring of 1918, relying on what happened and ignoring the extent to which he was constrained by circumstances, have been exceptionally dismissive.

David T. Zabecki, looking at original German documents which have largely been ignored by anglophone historians and some of which were thought to have been destroyed in the bombing of Potsdam during the Second World War, has written convincingly and critically of the flaws inherent in the *Kaiserschlacht*.[1] In particular, he analyses the lack of attention to the operational art, the level which must exist if tactical success is to crystallise into strategical success and victory. He concedes that Ludendorff was a very good battlefield tactician but it is his view that he had little strategical vision (which he regards as a widespread fault in the German army of his time). He sometimes takes a more sympathetic view of Ludendorff, conceding that he and Hindenburg 'did display some flashes of operational brilliance. These included the management of the Romania Campaign and the sequencing of operations in 1917.'[2] In relation to the 1918 campaign, Zabecki is, however, far from sympathetic, pointing out that, by the end of July 1918, 'the greatest string of tactical successes in World War One had failed to produce any significant operational advantage, much less strategic victory. Quite the contrary, Germany in August 1918 found itself in a far weaker strategic position than it had been in at the start of the year.'[3]

That seems unfair to Ludendorff. Even if the judgement is not informed by an element of hindsight, if, at 'the strategic level, Ludendorff's grand scheme was doomed from the start', what else was he to do? In March 1918, Germany's numerical superiority was minimal and, in reserves and artillery, she was, indeed, inferior to the Entente powers. Her equipment was worn out, fuel and other supplies were under pressure and the political will to continue the war was failing. His army was under-supplied and infected by defeatism. His lorries moved at no more than five miles an hour and rendered the ground over which they travelled impassable. Ludendorff's strengths lay in defence, rather than offence.

Ludendorff deserves to be criticised. In later life, at least, he lived on the margins of sanity, a reactionary Teutonic fantasist who wore horned helmets and whose only criticism of the Nazi regime was that it didn't go far enough. But what was he to do? As he said, 'The German people had no choice. Either we win in this offensive, or we go down forever.' He could not simply await the arrival of the Americans. For the military dictatorship of which he was part, a negotiated peace was not an option. Throughout the war, the Germans could not rely on attritional warfare. In 1918, this problem was intensified by the prospect of American deployment.

After the war, Lloyd George asked Hugo Stinnes* why 'the victorious German Army did not capture Amiens in March 1918. I [Lloyd George] informed him that they [the Germans] had already got through all our defences, and that we had no organised forces between the German advanced guard and that city. He said it was entirely due to the breakdown in their transport, owing to the lack of rubber. There was a sharp snowstorm, the rubberless wheelrims became clogged, and it was impossible to bring up the necessary ammunition for the troops and for the guns. The soldiers could not even be fed.'[4]

Thus Ludendorff: 'We will just blow a hole in the middle. The rest will follow of its own accord.' There was no time for strategy. He may have been far from in control of the battle as it developed but most generals are, to some extent, out of control of even those battles they win.

History has been kinder to other risk-takers: Cromwell, 'who went furthest where he did not know where he was going'; Hitler, 'the sleepwalker'; Napoleon at the end of his career; or Charles XII of Sweden, gambling on victory and hoping for a lucky throw.[5]

And it nearly came off. The German advance was very considerable – her armies moved far further than any army had moved after stabilisation of the Western Front. British Fifth Army was destroyed and Third Army badly damaged. In the later stages, France suffered great damage in

---

* German industrialist, associate of Ludendorff and enormously successful war profiteer.

casualties and morale. Britain seemed likely to lose control of the Channel ports or to exit ignominiously through them. Relations between France and Britain were damaged, Britain regarding France as about to crumble and France expecting Britain to scuttle. The rigidity of the British command system, which depended on the orders of senior commanders and gave little initiative to subordinate commanders, proved flawed when events moved fast and senior commanders knew little of what was happening. If, instead of trying to force a breach between Britain and France, Ludendorff had continued his assault, compelling the British to retreat as they were disposed to do, things might have been very different.

25

The Hundred Days

THE GREAT FINAL advance which was to end the war had its origins in a meeting between Haig and Foch on 16 May, when the generalissimo said that he wished to entrust a major project to Haig if the Germans did not attack within the next few weeks. The following day, Haig asked Rawlinson to consult with the French general Marie-Eugènie Debeney, who commanded French First Army on Rawlinson's right, and to study an attack eastwards in combination with the French.

At the 16 May meeting, Foch had in mind a preponderantly French project, in view of the state of British forces. But his proviso that the attack would only take place if the Germans held their hand for the succeeding weeks was not met. Attacks took place on the Aisne and the Matz. This increased the strain on the French. The Germans pushed on the bulge that threatened Paris. In the face of this and expecting a further attack in Champagne, Foch ordered four British divisions to move east. He did so when Haig happened to be on leave in London and, in his absence, Lawrence, his Chief of Staff, courageously took the risk of sending two, although delaying the despatch of the other two. On his return to France, Haig arranged to meet Foch but, before he could do so, he received a message from Wilson, pretty well telling him *not* to send further troops. His message said the War Cabinet would 'rely on the exercise of your judgement, under the Beauvais Agreement, as to the security of the British Front after the removal of these troops'.

Haig noted this ambivalence – he was being told 'to use [his] judgment' in relation to orders from the Supreme Commander, whereas, at the conference of 7 June, he had been directed to obey all his orders. 'This is a case of "heads you win and tails I lose". If things go well, the Government would take credit to themselves and the Generalissimo; if badly, the Field Marshal will be blamed!' The tensions between the Allies had not been removed by Doullens.

Because the French were occupied by these fresh German attacks and a counter-attack, the offensive operations envisaged at the 16 May conference were dominated by the British and Commonwealth contributions. Thus the Hundred Days is now celebrated as a great feat of British arms. It *was* indeed primarily a British achievement and it deserves to be remembered as such. Although historians are aware of it and have done their best to correct the record, it is a victory which has never registered in the public memory. Foch acknowledged the achievement: 'Never at any time in history have the British Army achieved greater results in an attack than in this unbroken offensive.'

It is a series of unbroken British successes but it was not achieved without cost. The fighting was as hard as any in the war and the losses were high. It was, however, fought in a different way from the battles of the earlier years. When Haig met his Army Commanders on 29 July, his remarks indicate clearly that he has sensed a different character to the war: 'Army commanders must do their utmost to get troops out of the influence of trench methods. We are all agreed on a need for the training of Battalion Commanders, who in their turn must train their company and platoon commanders. This is really a platoon commander's war.'

That remark shows just how far the nature of the war had changed from 1915 and 1916. The 'learning curve', this amalgam of various strands of new tactical thinking, had come together to favour the intelligent use of small, multi-skilled units, relying far less on the rifle than before, adapting their movements to the terrain in which they found themselves and exercising individual initiative. It has been said that now, in the Hundred Days, 'British tactics had effectively reached a pitch that would scarcely be surpassed for at least thirty years thereafter'.[1]

Preparation and rehearsal were meticulous and took place in full-scale training areas behind the lines. Security was strictly enforced, camouflage was used and misleading diversionary tactics took place in other areas. All of this has a flavour much more of the Second, than of the First, World War.

Amiens, the battle which opened the offensive, began on the morning of 8 August 1918 and was pretty well finished by 13.30. It was the day when 'we won the war in a morning'. It was the day which Ludendorff described as 'the black day of the German Army in the history of the war. This was the worst experience they had to go through.' At this stage, Haig was less involved in the day-to-day direction of the war than before, concentrating rather on encouraging and pressing Army Commanders who, like their armies, had now learned their craft. On 5 August, he told Rawlinson that his plans for the battle were not ambitious enough.

The battle that was fought on 8 August was different from anything since 1914. There was no preliminary bombardment. The insistence on secrecy was absolute and was enforced stringently. Information was limited in the most amazing ways. At first, only corps commanders knew what was happening. Deceptive ruses were employed. Tanks and cavalry were used to exploit the breakthrough. There had also been a massive advance in logistics that created the possibility of the huge advance from July to November 1918.[2] The reorganisation of transportation by Sir Eric Geddes deserves specific mention.[3]

The British were not the only nation to fight at Amiens. The French part of the battle, known as the Battle of Montdidier, involved not one but two armies and resulted in the capture of over 11,300 enemy personnel and 283 guns. Between 8 and 11 August, France gained more ground than British Fourth Army. As usual, Haig saw French successes back to front. In his diary for 9 August, he said that the French had met with no opposition because of the determined advance by the British on their left. Dewar and Boraston echoed their master's voice.

The French continued to fight in central and eastern France right to the end. There are various sets of statistics which compare the contribution of the British and the French in these last months of the war. They vary and the figures are not directly comparable partly because of different methodologies. In the French approach, for instance, but not the British, rifles are included under 'guns'. Subject to that caveat, according to the respective Official Histories, in the period 15 July to 11 November, British casualties were 314,206 and prisoners taken 188,700, while French casualties were 427,269, with prisoners taken 159,743.[4] Haig was blind to this. He complained that British press and politicians failed to acknowledge what he and his armies were doing and, instead, were 'cracking up the French and running down the British military methods and Generals!' The French army was 'worn out and has not really been fighting latterly'.[5]

This book is chiefly concerned with the events of March 1918 not August, September and October, and what happened in these later months is summarised very briefly. By 7 September, Haig was able to issue an Order to all ranks, very different from the 'Backs to the Wall' one:

One month has now passed since the British Armies, having successfully withstood all attacks of the enemy, once more took the offensive in their turn. In that short space of time, by a series of brilliant and skilfully executed actions, our troops have repeatedly defeated the same German Armies, whose vastly superior numbers compelled our retreat last Spring ...

Yet more has been done. Already we have passed beyond our old battle lines of 1917, and have made a wide breach in the enemy's strongest defences ...

In this glorious accomplishment all ranks of all arms and services of the British Armies in France have borne their part in the most worthy and honourable manner. The capture of 75,000 prisoners and 750 guns in the course of four weeks' fighting speaks for the magnitude of the efforts and for the magnificence of your achievement ...

We have passed many dark days together. Please God, these will never return. The enemy has now spent his effort, and I rely confidently on each one of you to turn to full advantage the opportunity which your skill, courage and resolution have created.

On 28 September, after Ludendorff had been to see Hindenburg, he wrote:

I explained to him my views as to a peace offer and a request for an armistice ... The Field Marshal [Hindenburg] listened to me with emotion. He answered that he had intended to say the same thing to me in the evening, that he had considered the whole situation carefully, and thought the step necessary ... The Field Marshal and I parted with a firm handshake, like men who had braved their dearest hopes, and who were resolved to hold together in the hardest hours of human life as they had held together in success. Our names were associated with the greatest victories of the World War. We now shared the conviction that it was our duty to sacrifice our names.

At 07.00 on 8 November, the German Armistice Commission train arrived at a siding in the forest of Compiègne. Foch's carriages stood nearby. Talks began at 09.00 in Foch's office on the train. The German delegates were asked by Foch the purpose of their visit. They replied that they had come to receive the Allies' proposals in regard to an armistice. Foch replied that he had no proposals to make. A German representative asked the Marshal in what form he desired that they should express themselves. He did not stand on form – he was ready to say that the German delegation asked the conditions for an armistice. Foch replied that he had no conditions to offer. The Germans then quoted from President Wilson's last note which said that Foch was authorised to make known the armistice conditions. To that, Foch replied that he was indeed authorised to make them known if the Germans asked for an armistice. 'Herr Erzberger and Count Oberndorff declared that they *asked* for an armistice.' After this little gavotte, Foch announced that the armistice conditions would be read. Between 19.00 and 20.00 on 10 November, the German government communicated that it accepted the conditions that had been put to it. The guns fell silent on the following morning at 11.00 French time.

But things did not go quite so smoothly as this brief narrative suggests. Until the very end of the war, Haig fought handicapped by an uneasy and jealous relationship with his allies and without the support of his political masters, who hated him as much as he despised them.

Afterwards, Haig took great pride in the fact that his insistence in pressing on throughout the Hundred Days ended the war in 1918 and not, as the politicians had expected, in 1919 or even later. After the war, he wrote to Churchill: [A]s for criticisms of what I did or did not do, no-one knows as well as I do how short of the ideal my command was . . . But I do take credit for this, that it was due to the decisions which I took in August and September 1918 that the war ended in November.'

This narrative was important to Haig. It is certainly true that scarcely anyone expected the war to end in 1918. On 9 September, Haig went to England to impress on the Secretary of State for War, Milner, the scale of the prize that was within his grasp: 'Within the last four weeks we have captured 77,000 prisoners and nearly 600 guns! There has never been such a victory in the annals of Britain, and its effects are not yet apparent.' But Milner, though generally a supporter of Haig, told Wilson on 11 September that the Commander-in-Chief was 'ridiculously optimistic'. He told Haig to be cautious – if he 'knocked the present army about, there was no other to replace it'. The War Office view was that the decisive moment would be in July 1919. As late as 7 October, Foch thought too that it would be 1919 although, in his view, April rather than July.[6]

Even the sanguine Churchill did not expect a result in 1918, although he was magnanimous about having been wrong:

When in the autumn of 1918, the government, often only too right before, doubted the possibility of early success, and endeavoured to dissuade him from what was feared would be a renewal of melancholy and prodigal slaughter; when in the most invidious manner they cast the direct responsibility upon him, he did not hesitate, and the war-worn, five times decimated troops responded to the will and impulse of their leader, and marched forward answering to the awful convulsions of victory, final and absolute.[7]

Throughout the war, partly misled by reports he received from Charteris, Haig had always told the Cabinet that the Germans were on the point of collapse. Now they truly were. Ludendorff had offered his resignation, which was refused. The Kaiser said, '[W]e have nearly reached the limit of our powers of resistance. The war must be ended.'[8] But Haig had been too optimistic too often. Churchill was talking of 1919; on 4 September, Foch was still thinking of 1919; Henry Wilson talked of 1919; and 1920. Lloyd George talked of 1922.

Haig was unmoved. When he received a War Office Memorandum from Wilson in July, envisaging a protracted war, he scribbled in the margin: 'Words! Words! Words! Lots of words and little else. Theoretical rubbish! Whoever drafted this stuff could never win any campaign.' He could afford to be bolder now than before. After Amiens, the committee of prime ministers of the Empire, meeting at Versailles, sent their congratulations to him and to the troops under his command. Hankey said, 'There was henceforward no question of replacing him, for which I myself was glad, as I have never discovered any other officer of the calibre of Haig.'

But the fact that he was not going to be sacked did not mean that the politicians trusted Haig. He continued to have to fight for troops and the Cabinet continued to withhold them. He had met the Adjutant General on 27 August and was told that the manpower shortage was such that he could expect to be short of 19 divisions.[9] On 1 September, Wilson sent Haig a telegram marked 'Personal': 'Just a word of caution in regard to incurring heavy losses in attacks on the Hindenburg Line as opposed to losses when driving the enemy back to line. I do not mean to say that you have incurred such losses but I know that the War Cabinet would become anxious if we received heavy punishment in attacking the Hindenburg Line without success.' Haig replied that same day: 'My Dear Henry, With reference to your wire re casualties in attacking the Hindenburg Line – what a wretched lot! And how well they mean to support me! What confidence! . . . I assure you I watch the drafts most carefully.' Wilson's response was pretty poor. He wrote, 'It wasn't really want of confidence in you.' His letter 'was only intended to convey a sort of distant warning and nothing more. All so easy to explain in talking, all so difficult to explain in writing.'

Haig's reaction in his diary was bitter:

It is impossible for a CIGS to send a telegram of this nature to a C in C in the Field as a 'Personal' one. The Cabinet are ready to meddle and interfere in my plans in an underhand way, but do not dare openly to say that they [do not] mean to take the responsibility for any failure though [are] ready to take credit for every success! The object of this telegram is, no doubt, to save the Prime Minister (Lloyd George) in case of any failure.* So I read it to mean that I can attack the Hindenburg Line if I think it right to do so. The CIGS and the Cabinet already know that my arrangements are being made to that end. If my attack is successful, I will remain on as C in C. If we fail, or our losses are excessive, I can hope for no mercy! I wrote to Henry Wilson in reply. What a wretched lot of weaklings we have in high places at the present time![10]

Wilson rather feebly tried to explain the Cabinet's concerns: '[P]olice strike and cognate matters make cabinet sensitive to heavy losses, especially if these are incurred against old lines of fortifications.' Haig's reaction was explosive: 'How ignorant these people are of war! In my opinion it is much less costly in lives to press the enemy after victorious battle than to give him time to recover & organise afresh his defence of a position!'

Haig certainly thought that he was presiding over a very successful advance. He therefore sought troops that the government tried to

---

* Lloyd George denied in his war memoirs having any knowledge of or responsibility for the telegram.

withhold. It was, however, only afterwards that he decided that he and he alone had perceived that the war might be ended in 1918. His diary shows that, even on 1 September 1918, he thought that the war would not end until the Americans could deliver it – something they would not be in a position to do until well into the following year.

His attitude to peace terms also revealed that he had not foreseen the imminence of German collapse, even though he recognised the parlous state of affairs within Germany. He wanted the evacuation of Belgium and occupied France. Metz, Strasbourg and Alsace-Lorraine were to be handed back and Belgian and French rolling stock were to be returned. But he did not want 'the French entering Germany to pay off old scores' and thus provoking sustained resistance, in which case Germany would be able to make use of the 1920 class of recruits. 'The democratisation of Germany was not worth a single English [*sic*] life.' He thought that the Germans were capable of retiring to their own frontier and holding it if there were any attempt to 'touch the *honour* of the German people'. On 25 October, at a conference with Foch and others, Haig repeated what he had already said to the British Cabinet. He argued that the enemy would not accept the terms that Foch proposed:

> because of military necessity alone – and it would be very costly and take a long time (two years) to enforce them unless the internal state of Germany compels the enemy to accept them. We don't know very much about the internal state of Germany* – and to try to impose such terms seems to me really a gamble which may come off or it may not ... Pétain spoke of taking a huge indemnity from Germany, so large that she will never be able to pay it – meantime French troops will hold the left bank of the Rhine as a pledge!

On 1 November, Haig wrote to his wife saying that he doubted that Germany had been laid low enough to accept the terms which Foch wanted to impose – the terms which Germany did, indeed, accept just ten days later. His vision of a 1918 victory was not quite as adamantine as he later claimed, in a minor example of his weakness for retrospectively conceived history.

He was still largely entitled to say to Churchill in the letter quoted above that the decisions he took in August and September were

---

* How very different from all he said in 1916 and 1917.

responsible for the end of the war in November and that very important
achievement is not diminished by the fact that he did not know or think
that the war would end in November. His subjective position does not
alter the fact that countless deaths and untold misery were avoided
because the war ended when it did. The irritation that his self-righteous
justification causes is irrelevant.

Foch, always immensely more generous to Haig than Haig to him, could
see what Haig was doing. At one stage in these days, he described him
with fulsome generosity as 'the greatest general in the world'. Later he
wrote to him:

> My Dear Field Marshal
>   Your affairs are going on very well; I can only applaud the resolute
> manner in which you follow them up, without giving the enemy a
> respite and always extending the breadth of your operations.

Alas, Foch's magnanimity was not reciprocated. When the Germans
requested an armistice, Haig asked Henry Wilson how far Foch, as
generalissimo, had the power to involve the British Army. 'If I do not
concur in such terms as he may wish to impose, what am I to do?'[11] On
24 October, Haig was incensed by Foch's refusal to return British
Second Army to him because it was politically desirable that the King of
the Belgians should be in command of an Allied army:

> I am disgusted at the almost underhand way in which the French are
> trying to get hold of a part of the British Army – and so ungenerous
> too, because they forget how, in the first instance, I handed over all
> the troops of my Second Army under Plumer at once to operate under
> the French staff of the King of the Belgians, without raising the small-
> est difficulty. I felt annoyed at the attitude of Foch and Weygand over
> this question. I told them a few 'home truths' for, when all is said and
> done *the British Army has defeated the Germans this year*. [The empha-
> sis is Haig's.][12]

Even Wilson, lover of France and the French, wrote in his diary on
the same date, 'The French are not fighting at all, and the Americans
don't know how, so all falls to us.'[13] Haig, like Wilson, said that the
French hadn't been fighting and that the Americans were 'ill-equipped

and half-trained'.[14] British casualties on the Western Front in 1918 totalled 852,861.[15] French casualties in 1918 totalled 235,000.[16]

In late November, Foch was invited to a formal reception in London. Lloyd George's plan was that Haig should play a subordinate part in the ceremony. Haig was infuriated. He had 'no intention of taking part in any triumphal ride with Foch, or with any pack of foreigners, through the streets of London, mainly in order to add to LG's importance and help him in his election campaign'.

He was aghast at the idea that he should be in the fifth carriage of the victory parade and he insisted he should receive more than a viscountcy – that was what had been given to Sir John French, 'who had been sent home in disgrace'. This is the attitude that lay behind the solipsism of his position at the end of the war. These were the emotional imperatives which brought him to distort the historical record.

Haig ended the war embittered and antagonistic to the British Cabinet and his French allies, who combined to threaten the place in history that he and his army wished to occupy. He had his revenge by writing that history for himself.

Notes

CHAPTER I

1 Quoted by John Charteris, *Field Marshal Earl Haig*, p. 80.
2 John Hussey, 'A Contemporary Record or post-war fabrication? The authenticity of the Haig Diaries for 1914', in *Stand To!*, no. 42, January 1995, pp. 29 *et seq*. See also John Hussey, 'Sir Douglas Haig's Diary and Despatches: Dating and Censorship', in *Stand To!*, no. 47, September 1996, pp. 19 *et seq*.
3 Denis Winter, *Haig's Command*, pbk edn, p. 235.
4 David French, 'Sir Douglas Haig's Reputation, 1918–1928: A Note', in *The Historical Journal*, 28, 4 (1985), p. 6.
5 Haig to Haldane, 4 August 1914, *Haldane Papers*, National Library of Scotland, cited by French, 'Sir Douglas Haig's Reputation, 1918–1928: A Note', in op. cit., p. 955.
6 Quoted by Charteris, *Field Marshal Earl Haig*, p. 91.
7 NLS ACC 3155/131.
8 Sir C.E. Callwell, *Field Marshal Sir Henry Wilson: His Life and Diaries*, vol. I, pp. 157–8.
9 John Charteris, *At GHQ*, p. 11.
10 Edward Spears, 2 July 1968, quoted by Max Egremont, *Under Two Flags*, pbk edn, p. 11.
11 Winston S. Churchill, *The World Crisis*, vol. II (2-vol. edn), p. 1264.
12 Liddell Hart Centre for Military Archives, Kings College London, *Kiggell* 2/1–7.
13 Maurice Hankey, *The Supreme Command*, vol. I, p. 80.
14 John Terraine, *Douglas Haig, The Educated Soldier*, pp. 60–6.

CHAPTER 2

1 Robert Asprey, *The First Battle of the Marne* (Philadelphia, Lippincourt, 1962, p. 42), cited by Michael S. Neiberg, 'Commanding through Armageddon: Allied Senior Leadership in World War One', in Matthias Strohn, *World War One Companion*, p. 21.
2 Quoted by Richard Holmes, *The Little Field Marshal*, p. 278.
3 Ibid., p. 279.
4 Ibid., p. 48.
5 Hankey, *The Supreme Command*, vol. II, pp. 161–2.
6 Jonathan Krause, 'The Evolution of French Tactics 1914–1916', quoted in Matthias Strohn (ed.), *The Battle of the Somme*, p. 214.
7 William Robertson, *Private to Field Marshal*, p. 42.
8 Philip Warner, *Field Marshal Earl Haig*, p. 154.
9 Churchill, *The World Crisis*, vol. II, p. 1261.
10 Ibid., p. 1213.
11 Hankey, *The Supreme Command*, vol. II, p. 446.
12 Georges-Henri Soutou, 'French Strategy in 1916 and the Battle of the Somme', in Strohn (ed.), *The Battle of the Somme*, p. 57.
13 William Philpott, *Bloody Victory: The Sacrifice on the Somme and the Making of the Twentieth Century*, p. 83. See also Michael S. Neiberg, 'Commanding through Armageddon: Allied Senior Leadership in World War One', in Strohn, *World War One Companion*, p. 25.
14 Michael S. Neiberg, 'French Generalship on the Somme', in Strohn (ed.), *The Battle of the Somme*, p. 134.
15 Jonathan Krause 'The Evolution of French Tactics 1914–1916', quoted in Strohn (ed.), *The Battle of the Somme*, pp. 199–200
16 French Official History. See Strohn (ed.), *The Battle of the Somme*, p. 138.
17 Alastair Horne, 'Marshal Philippe Pétain', in Michael Carver (ed.), *The War Lords*, p. 70.

CHAPTER 3

1 Paddy Griffith, 'The Extent of Tactical Reform in the British Army', in Paddy Griffith (ed.), *British Fighting Methods*, p. 2.
2 Correlli Barnett, Haig Fellow's Address, Douglas Haig Fellowship, *Records*, December 2004.

CHAPTER 4

1   Maréchal Fayolle, 'Cahiers Secrets de la Grande Guerre', Paris, Poln, 1964, p. 161, entry for 21 May 1916, cited by Greenhalgh, '1918: The Push to Victory', in Robert Tombs and Emile Chabal (eds), *Britain and France in the Two World Wars: Truth, Myth and Memory*, p. 776.
2   Esher to Haig, 28 June 1916, in Robert Blake (ed.), *The Private Papers of Douglas Haig 1914–19*, pp. 150–1.
3   Paddy Griffith, *Battle Tactics of the Western Front: The British Army's Art of Attack*, p. 11.

CHAPTER 5

1   Esher, Journal, 11 August 1916, quoted by James Lees-Milne in *The Life of Reginald 2nd Viscount Esher, The Enigmatic Edwardian*, p. 261.
2   Kenneth Clark, *Another Part of the Wood*.
3   Sassoon to Esher, 6 May 1917, quoted by Lees-Milne, *Life of Esher*, p. 281.
4   Esher to Sassoon, 5 February 1916, Esher Papers, Churchill Archive Centre, Churchill College, Cambridge, quoted by Damian Collins, in *Charmed Life: The Phenomenal World of Philip Sassoon*, p. 49.
5   Northcliffe to Sassoon, 6 October 1916, Northcliffe Papers, quoted by Collins, *Charmed Life*, p. 52.
6   Esher, War Journals, 1 December 1917, 'Esher Papers', quoted by Collins, *Charmed Life*, p. 61.
7   Hankey, *The Supreme Command*, vol. II, p. 618.
8   Churchill, *The World Crisis*, vol. II, p. 1136.
9   See a fascinating article by John M. McEwen, 'The National Press during the First World War: Ownership and Circulation', in *Journal of Contemporary History*, vol. 17, no. 3 (July 1982), pp. 459–86.
10 See a good study of Northcliffe in Piers Brendon, *Eminent Edwardians*.
11 Keith Wilson, *A Study in the History and Politics of the Morning Post, 1905–1926*.

CHAPTER 6

1   Philip Magnus, *Kitchener: Portrait of an Imperialist*, p. 302.
2   Elizabeth Greenhalgh, *Victory Through Coalition: Britain and France During the First World War*, p. 8.

3   H. H. Asquith to Margot Asquith, 6 July 1915, cited by Greenhalgh, *Victory Through Coalition*, p. 9.

4   Ibid., p. 9.

5   Hankey, *The Supreme Command*, vol. II, p. 671.

6   William Philpott, 'Unequal Sacrifice? Two Armies, Two Wars?', in Greenhalgh, '1918: The Push to Victory', in Tombs and Chabal, *Britain and France in the Two World Wars*, p. 54.

7   Esher, Diary, 27 April 1918, Haig to Lady Haig, 25 April 1918, 'Notes on the Operations on Western Front After Sir D. Haig Became Commander-in-Chief 1915', 30 January 1920, all cited by Elizabeth Greenhalgh, '1918: The Push to Victory', p. 69.

8   Haig, Diary, 24 April 1915 and 20 February 1916.

9   Lord French, *1914*, p. 32.

10 See Tim Travers, *The Killing Ground: The British Army, The Western Front and the Emergence of Modern Warfare 1900–1918*, pp. 253 *et seq.*

11 Peter Hart, *1918: A Very British Victory.*

CHAPTER 7

1   Quoted by Paul Guinn, in *British Strategy and Politics 1914–1918*, p. 280.

2   Haig to Robertson, 28 May 1917, *Robertson Papers*, Liddell Hart Military Archives, King's College, University of London, 1/23/28. See also David R. Woodward, 'Did Lloyd George Starve the British Army of Men Prior to the German Offensive of 21st March 1918?', in *The Historical Journal*, 27, 1 (1984), p. 245.

3   David Lloyd George, *War Memoirs of David Lloyd George*, vol. V, 1917–1918, p. 147.

4   James E. Edmonds (ed.), *History of the Great War: Military Operations France and Belgium 1918*, vol. I, p. 39.

5   John Terraine, *To Win a War*, p. 32.

6   Lloyd George, *War Memoirs*, p. 207.

7   Ibid., p. 208.

8   Ibid., p. 148.

9   Ibid., p. 6.

10 Hankey, *The Supreme Command*, vol. II, p. 739.

11 Hankey, Diary, 6 December 1917, 1, 3.

12 Woodward, 'Did Lloyd George Starve the British Army ...', pp. 241–52.

13 Lloyd George, *War Memoirs*, p. 147.

14 Ibid., pp. 148–9.

15 Ibid., p. 5.

16 Hankey, *The Supreme Command*, vol. II, p. 743.

17 Charles à Court Repington, *The First World War 1914–18*, vol. II, p. 172.

18 Edmonds, *History of the Great War*, p. 74.

19 Lloyd George, *War Memoirs*, ch. LXXII.

20 Elizabeth Greenhalgh, 'Lloyd George, Georges Clemenceau and the 1918 Man Power Crisis', in *The Historical Journal*, 50, 2 (2007), pp. 397–421.

21 Ibid., p. 403.

22 Ibid., p. 408.

23 Lloyd George, *War Memoirs*, vol. V, 1917–1918, p. 137–8.

24 David French, 'Sir Douglas Haig's Reputation, 1918–1928: A Note', in *The Historical Journal*, 28, 4 (1985), pp. 953–60.

25 David R. Woodward, 'Did Lloyd George Starve the British Army of Men Prior to the German Offensive of 21st March 1918?', in *The Historical Journal*, 27, 1 (1984), p. 242.

26 Edmonds, *History of the Great War*, p. 52.

CHAPTER 8

1 Benjamin Ziemann, cited by Hew Strachan, in *The First World War*, pbk edn, p. 261.

2 John Wheeler-Bennett, *Brest-Litovsk: The Forgotten Peace, March 1918*.

3 Robert T. Foley, 'From Victory to Defeat: The German Army of 1918', in Ashley Ekins (ed.), *1918 Year of Victory: The End of the Great War and the Shaping of History*, p. 71.

4 Richard Watt, *Dare Call It Treason*, p. 10 (Introduction by Cyril Falls).

5 Edmonds, *History of the Great War*, p. 2.

6 Barry Pitt, *1918: The Last Act*, pbk edn, p. 69.

7 Ibid., p. 39.

8 Ziemann, cited by Hew Strachan, in *The First World War*, p. 283.

9 Martin Kitchen, *The German Offensives of 1918*, p. 13.

10 Cited by Kitchen, op. cit., p. 24.

11 Pitt, *1918*, p. 42.

12 But to follow a fascinating evolutionary account, see Kitchen, *The German Offensives*.

13   Pitt, *1918*, pp. 50–1.
14   Dr Christian Stachelbeck, 'The Road to Modern Combined Arms Warfare: German land warfare tactics in the battles of *matériel* on the Western Front in 1916', in Strohn, *The Battle of the Somme*, p. 154.
15   Peter Simkins, 'Co-Stars or Supporting Cast? British Divisions in the "Hundred Days", 1918' in Paddy Griffith (ed.), *British Fighting Methods in the Great War*, 2004 edn, p. 52.
16   Paddy Griffith, *Battle Tactics on the Western Front: The British Army's Art of Attack 1916–18*, pbk edn, p. 96.
17   Cited by Kitchen, *The German Offensives*, p. 35.
18   Rupprecht, *Mein Kriegstagebuch*, vol. II, p. 372.
19   Private communication.

CHAPTER 9

1   Henry Wilson, Diary, 31 December 1917.
2   Brock Millman, *Pessimism and British War Policy 1916–1918*, p. 155.
3   John Barnes and David Nicholson (eds), *The Leo Amery Diaries*, vol. I, p. 168.
4   Stephen Roskill, *Hankey: Man of Secrets*, vol. I, 1877–1918, p. 443.
5   Ibid.
6   See J.L. Wallach, *Uneasy Coalition: The Entente Experience in World War I*, pp. 92–3.
7   Cited by Travers, *The Killing Ground*, pp. 221–2.
8   See Tim Travers, *How the War Was Won: Command and Technology in the British Army on the Western Front 1917–1918*, p. 34.
9   Kitchen, *The German Offensives*, p. 47.
10   Lloyd George, *War Memoirs*, vol. V, 1917–1918, pp. 3–4.
11   Quoted Official History, p. 61.
12   CAB.23/44 Part 2.
13   Lloyd George, *War Memoirs*, p. 313.
14   Edmonds, *History of the Great War*, pp. 85–6.
15   David French, *The Strategy of the Lloyd George Coalition 1916–1918*, p. 218.
16   Hankey, *The Supreme Command*, vol. II, p. 830.
17   French, *The Strategy of the Lloyd George Coalition*, p. 14.
18   Hankey, *The Supreme Command*, vol. II, pp. 779–80.

CHAPTER 10

1 Personal communication.
2 Northcliffe to Sassoon, 13 December 1917, Northcliffe Papers, quoted by Damian Collins, *Charmed Life: The Phenomenal World of Philip Sassoon*, p. 63.
3 Haig to Lady Haig, 14 December 1917, Haig Papers, National Library of Scotland.
4 Lloyd George, *War Memoirs*, pp. 364–5.
5 Sir Hubert Gough, in Walter Shaw Sparrow, *The Fifth Army in March 1918*, pp. 306 and 308.
6 Lord Beaverbrook, *Men and Power*, p. 211.
7 Philip Sassoon to Haig, December 1916, Haig Papers, National Library of Scotland.

CHAPTER 11

1 Wilson, Diary, 31 October 1917. See Greenhalgh, *Victory Through Coalition*.
2 Greenhalgh, *Victory Through Coalition*, p. 183.
3 Hankey, *The Supreme Command*, vol. II, p. 711.
4 Lloyd George, *War Memoirs*, p. 351.
5 Ibid., p. 352.
6 Quoted in Shaw Sparrow, *The Fifth Army in March 1918*.
7 *Daily News*, 9 November 1920, quoted in Shaw Sparrow, op. cit., p. vi.
8 Hankey, *The Supreme Command*, vol. II, p. 782.
9 Greenhalgh, *Victory Through Coalition*, p. 188.
10 Millman, *Pessimism and British War Policy*, p. 242.
11 PRO CAB 25/17, 13 January 1918.
12 Haig, Diary, 7 January 1918.
13 PRO CAB 21/4, 4 January 1918.
14 PRO CAB 27/73, 21 March 1918. See also Millman, *Pessimism and British War Policy*, pp. 176–98.

CHAPTER 12

1 Amery, Diary, 29 January 1918, cited by Winter, *Haig's Command*, p. 178.

2   Gary Sheffield, 'Finest Hour? British Forces on the Western Front in 1918: An Overview', in Ekins, *1918 Year of Victory*, pp. 56–7.

3   WO.158/72 and French Official History, AFGG, vi (1) Annexes, vol. I, No. 287.

4   Ibid.

5   Benson Papers, cited by Winter, *Haig's Command*, p. 179.

6   Hubert Gough, *The Fifth Army*, p. 238.

7   Edmonds, *History of the Great War*, p. 98.

8   Gough, *The Fifth Army*, pp. 233 and 234.

9   Lloyd George, *War Memoirs*, p. 382.

10 Cited by Travers, *The Killing Ground*, p. 226.

11 Report on Doullens Conference, 2 March 1918, WO 256/28, cited by Kitchen, *The German Offensives*, p. 59.

12 Gough to Edmonds, 29 July 1934, CAB 45/192.PRO, cited by Travers, *The Killing Ground*, p. 229.

13 Derby to Haig, 5 March 1918, WO 256/28, cited by Kitchen, *The German Offensives*, p. 52.

14 Anthony Farrar-Hockley, *Goughie: The Life of General Sir Hubert Gough CGB, GCMG, KCVO*, pp. 262–3.

15 Gough in his introduction to the first edition of Shaw Sparrow, *The Fifth Army in March 1918*, p. xxxix.

16 Gough, *The Fifth Army*, London 1931, p. 253.

17 Gough in his introduction to the first edition of Shaw Sparrow, *The Fifth Army in March 1918*, p. xlvi.

A PERSPECTIVE

1   Vera Brittain, *Testament of Youth*, pbk edn, pp. 399–400.

CHAPTER 13

1   German Official History, p. 63.

2   Lloyd George, *War Memoirs*, p. 363.

3   Nancy Maurice, *The Maurice Case* (1972), pt 2 (Diary, 1 Jan. to 20 Apr. 1918), pp. 62–83.

4   Edmonds, *History of the Great War*, vol. I, p. 147.

5   Ibid., pp. 109–10.

6   Lloyd George, *War Memoirs*, vol. V, pp. 2852–5 and see Greenhalgh, *Victory Through Coalition*, p. 188.

7   Gough to Edmonds, 27 May 1945, PRO, CAB, 45/140.

8   Gough, *The Fifth Army*, p. 260, quoted by John Terraine, *To Win A War*, pbk edn, p. 59.

9   Winter, *Haig's Command*, pp. 182–3.

10 NLS Acc 3155/150.

11 NLS, Acc 3155/97 and 375.

12 Edmonds, *History of the Great War*, vol. I, p. 254.

13 Barnes and Nicholson, *The Leo Amery Diaries*, (3 April 1918), vol. I, p. 213.

14 Pitt, *1918*, p. 61.

15 Barnes and Nicholson, *The Leo Amery Diaries*, (21 March 1918), vol. I, pp. 209–10.

16 Gough, *The Fifth Army*, p. 266.

17 Gary Sheffield, 'Finest Hour? British Forces on the Western Front in 1918: An Overview', in Ekins, *1918 Year of Victory*, p. 57.

18 Hankey, *The Supreme Command*, vol. II, p. 785.

19 Greenhalgh, 'Myth and Memory . . .', *The Journal of Military History*, vol. LXVIII, no. 3, p. 786.

20 Haig MS, 21 March 1918, Haig to Lady Haig, 22 March 1918.

21 GHQ cipher telegram to WO OA.561/504 WO.33/920, No.7700.

22 CP.183 WO.33/920, No.7701.

CHAPTER 14

1   OA.561/507 WO.33/920, No.7710.

2   Hankey, *The Supreme Command*, vol. II, p. 785.

3   Paddy Griffith, *Battle Tactics of the Western Front: The British Army's Art of Attack 1916 –18*, pbk edn, p. 91.

4   WO.158/43.

5   OAD.781 WO.158/48, and in AFGG, VI (i), Annexes Vol. 2, No. 530.

6   Adjutant-General GHQ to Adjutant-General WO AA.492 WO.33/920, No.7705.

7   Callwell, *Henry Wilson*, vol. II, p. 73 and IWM, Wilson papers.

8   NLS Acc 3155/97 and 375.

9   Derby to Haig, 5 March 1918, WO 256/28, cited by Kitchen, *The German Offensives*, p. 53.

10 See Fayolle's diary, p. 260, and British Mission, French *GQG*, to WO BM.257 WO.33/920, No.7704, p. 4.

11 Greenhalgh, 'Myth and Memory . . .', *The Journal of Military History*, vol. LXVIII, no. 3, July 2004, p. 788 *et seq.*

12 See Joseph Gies and Herbert Sulzbach, cited in Greenhalgh, 'Myth and Memory . . .', *The Journal of Military History*, vol. LXVIII, no. 3, p. 789 *et seq.*

13 Edmonds, *History of the Great War*, vol. I, pp. 299–300.

14 Émile Herbillon, *Souvenirs d'un officier de liaison pendant la guerre mondiale*, vol. II, pp. 227–8.

CHAPTER 15

1 Edmonds, *History of the Great War*, vol. I, pp. 38–9.
2 Pitt, *1918*, p. 70.
3 Edmonds, *History of the Great War*, vol. I, p. 258.
4 Ibid., p. 123.
5 *Field Service Regulations*, Part 1, War Office, London, 1909.
6 Pitt, *1918*, p. 100.

CHAPTER 16

1 *The Times*, 28 March 1918, p. 6, col. d. It has been suggested that this Order of the Day implies that Haig's morale was beginning to wobble on the night of the 23rd. (See Greenhalgh, *Journal of Modern History*, 2004, p. 801.)

2 See J. Thompson, *Lifeblood of War: Logistics in Armed Conflict*, p. 187 *et seq.*

3 Lady Spears' diary, quoted by Max Egremont, *Under Two Flags: The Life of Major-General Sir Edward Spears*, pbk edn, p. 77.

4 Edmonds, *History of the Great War*, vol. I, p. 392.
5 WO 158/72/4.
6 WO.158/72; French account in AFGG, VI (i), Annexes Vol. 2, No.589.

7 See, for example, David T. Zabecki, 'Railroads and the Operational Level of War in the German 1918 Offensives', in Jennifer Keene and Michael Neiberg, *Finding Common Ground: New Directions in First World War Studies*, p. 174.

8 Cited in I.M. Brown, *British Logistics on the Western Front, 1914–1919*, p. 191.

9 See Pitt, *1918*, pp. 94–5.
10 Rupprecht, cited in Edmonds, *History of the Great War*, vol. I, p. 396.
11 Robert T. Foley, 'From Victory to Defeat: The German Army of 1918', in Ekins, *1918 Year of Victory*, pp. 74–5.

12 Kuhl, Weltkrieg II, p. 380, quoted in Robert T. Foley, 'From Victory to Defeat: The German Army in 1918' in Ekins, *1918 Year of Victory*, pp. 74–5.

13 Rupprecht, cited by Edmonds, *History of the Great War*, vol. I, p. 396.

14 Gough, *The Fifth Army*, p. 281.

15 Kitchen, *The German Offensives*, p. 73.

16 Poincaré and Herbillon, cited by Greenhalgh, 'Myth and Memory . . .', *The Journal of Military History*, vol. LXVIII, no. 3, p. 793.

17 Clive, Notebooks, 18 April 1918, CAB 45/201, PRO.

18 Cited by Greenhalgh, 'Myth and Memory . . .', *The Journal of Military History*, vol. LXVIII, no. 3, pp. 793–4.

19 Barnes and Nicholson, *The Leo Amery Diaries*, vol. I, p. 213.

20 Hankey, *The Supreme Command*, p. 786.

CHAPTER 17

1   WO 158/72/4.

2   Hankey, *The Supreme Command*, p. 786.

3   Paper, 5 July 1915, Kitchener to Sir John French 6 April 1915, WO 32/5591, PRO, cited by Greenhalgh, 'Myth and Memory . . .', *The Journal of Military History*, vol. LXVIII, no. 3, p. 778.

4   Instructions for General Sir D. Haig, GCB, KCIE, KCVO, contained in Edmonds, *History of the Great War*, Appendices.

5   Haig Typescript Diary, 23 June 1915, PRO 256/4 and Manuscript Diary, 26 June 1915, cited by Greenhalgh, 'Myth and Memory . . .', *The Journal of Military History*, vol. LXVIII, no. 3, p. 780.

6   Winter, *Haig's Command*, p. 180.

7   Maurice, Diary, 23 March 1918, cited by Nancy Maurice (ed.), *The Maurice Case: From the Papers of Major General Sir Frederick Maurice, KCMG, CB*, p. 77. See also War Cabinet Minutes 371, 23 March 1918, CAB 23/5, PRO.

8   See Greenhalgh, 'Myth and Memory . . .', *The Journal of Military History*, vol. LXVIII, no. 3, p. 781.

9   See Haig, Diary, 27 April 1918 and 2 May 1918, and Hankey, 2 May 1918.

10 See Haig, Diary, 4 June 1918.

11 C.E. Fayle, *Seaborne Trade*, vol. III, p. 22.

12 Ibid., p. 99.

13 Ibid., p. 162.

14 Ibid., p. 435.

15 Ibid., vol. II, p. 403.

16 Ibid., vol II, p. 404 and vol. III, p. 179.

17 Brown, *British Logistics on the Western Front*, p. 184.

18 Zabecki, 'Railroads and the Operational Level of War in the German 1918 Offensives', in Jennifer Keene and Michael Neiberg, *Finding Common Ground: New Directions in First World War Studies*, p. 168.

19 Martin Kitchen, *The German Offensives of 1918*, p, 143.

20 Edmonds, *History of the Great War*, vol. III, p. 147.

21 See Greenhalgh, 'Myth and Memory . . .', *The Journal of Military History*, vol. LXVIII, no. 3, p. 782.

CHAPTER 18

1 Denis Winter, *Haig's Command*, p. 237.

2 Ibid, p. 237.

3 Edmonds to Lady Haig, *Haig Papers*, pp. 17–28.

4 Cited by Travers, *The Killing Ground*, p. 221.

5 Winter, *Haig's Command*, p. 249.

6 Ibid.

7 Ibid., p. 250.

8 Ibid., p. 252.

9 William Philpott, 'Sir Douglas Haig's Command? The Image of Alliance in Douglas Haig's Record of the War', *Records of the Douglas Haig Fellowship*, 2011, p. 11.

10 G.A.B Dewar and J.H. Boraston, *Sir Douglas Haig's Command, 1915–1918*, pp. 85–6.

11 Duncan, Diary, 29 April and 1 October 1917, cited by Philpott, 'Sir Douglas Haig's Command?', p. 10.

12 Brian Bond, *The Victorian Army and the Staff College, 1854–1914*, p. 288.

13 Elizabeth Greenhalgh, 'Writing about France's Great War', *Journal of Contemporary History*, vol. XL, no. 3, p. 611.

14 C.B. Falls, *War Books: a Critical Guide*, p. 146. See also Andrew Green, *Writing the Great War: Sir James Edmonds and the Official Histories, 1915–1948*, p. 776 *et seq.*

15 Green, *Writing the Great War*.

CHAPTER 19

1　G.S. Duncan, *Douglas Haig as I Knew Him.*

2　Byng on 25 March 1918 in CAB 45/192, quoted by Winter, *Haig's Command*, p. 186.

3　Foch, *Mémoires*, II, pp. 16–17; Foch–Clemenceau, 24 March 1918, cited by David Stevenson, *With our Backs to the Wall:Victory and Defeat in 1918*, pbk edn, p. 63.

4　Louis Loucheur, *Carnets secrets, 1908–32* (1962), p. 178.

5　Greenhalgh, 'Myth and Memory . . .', *The Journal of Military History*, vol. LXVIII, no. 3, p. 790.

6　Loucheur, *Carnets secrets.*

7　Herbillon, *Souvenirs d'un officier*, vol. II, pp. 229–32.

8　C.-in-C. telegram to CIGS, OBC 7865,1800 hrs.

9　WO.158/72.

10　Greenhalgh, 'Myth and Memory . . .', *The Journal of Military History*, vol. LXVIII, no. 3, p. 793.

11　Guy Pedroncini, *Petain: général en chef* and *Pétain: le soldat et la gloire*, cited by Greenhalgh, 'Myth and Memory . . .', *The Journal of Military History*, vol. LXVIII, no. 3, p. 794.

12　Greenhalgh, '1918:The Push to Victory', in Tombs and Chabal, *Britain and France in the Two World Wars*, p. 774.

13　Ibid., p. 775, n. 7.

14　Ibid., p. 796.

15　Charteris, *Haig*, pp. 374–5.

16　Dewar and Boraston, *Haig's Command*, vol. II, pp. 133–5.

17　Greenhalgh, 'Myth and Memory . . .', *The Journal of Military History*, vol. LXVIII, no. 3, p. 813.

18　David French, 'Sir Douglas Haig's Reputation 1918–1929: A Note', in *The Historical Journal*, vol. XXVII, no. 4 (December 1985), pp. 953–60.

19　Ibid.

20　Winter, *Haig's Command*, p. 231.

21　Ibid.

22　Quoted in Shaw Sparrow, *The Fifth Army in March 1918*, p. vii.

23　Clive Notebooks, 21 April 1918, CAB 45/201 PRO.

24　Haig Diaries, 3 and 18 May 1917.

25　George S. Duncan's Diary, 29 April 1917, in Guy, Thomas and de Groot (eds), *Military Miscellany*, Stroud, Sutton Publishing/Army Records Society, 1997, vol. 1, p. 349.

26 William Philpott, 'Haig and Britain's European Allies', in Brian Bond and Nigel Cave (eds), *Haig: A Reappraisal 70 Years On*, p. 130.

27 Greenhalgh, 'Myth and Memory . . .', in *The Journal of Military History*, vol. LXVIII, no. 3, p. 777.

28 Clive, Diary, 24 March 1918, CAB 45/201 PRO.

29 Pitt, *1918*, p. 56.

30 Edmonds, *History of the Great War*, vol. I, p. 471.

31 Ibid., p. 448.

32 Gough, *The Fifth Army*, p. 292.

CHAPTER 20

1 Edmonds, *History of the Great War*, vol. I, p. 454.

2 CAB 23/5 DMO, 25 March 1918, cited by Kitchen, *The German Offensives of 1918*, p. 79.

3 Edmonds, *History of the Great War*, vol. I, p. 488.

4 See Greenhalgh, 'Myth and Memory . . .', in *The Journal of Military History*, vol. LXVIII, no. 3, p. 803.

5 Special supplement to the *New Statesman*, 23 April 1921.

6 Lloyd George, *War Memoirs*, Odhams edition, vol. II, pp. 1730–1.

7 Initialled and dated 2 Whitehall Gardens, SW, 27 March 1918. The Memorandum was printed in full in the *New Statesman* of 23 April 1921, was issued in translation by the French Foreign Ministry that same year and printed in various French works, such as Clemenceau's *Grandeurs et misères d'une victoire*, 1930.

8 Milner's letter to Sir Sidney Low, 18 February 1921, quoted in Sir J.E. Wrench, *Alfred Lord Milner, The Man of No Illusions*, 1958 edn, p. 342.

9 See Greenhalgh, 'Myth and Memory . . .', in *The Journal of Military History*, vol. LXVIII, no. 3, p. 805.

10 Lloyd George, *War Memoirs of David Lloyd George, vol. V, 1917–1918*, Little, Brown, Boston, 1936, p. 376.

11 Wilson, Diary, 25 March 1918.

12 WO 158/72 and AFGG Annexe no. 751.

13 Winter, *Haig's Command*, p.186.

14 John Hussey, *The Times Literary Supplement*, 10 May 1991, p. 13, and *Stand To!*, no. 36.

15 Herbillon, *Souvenirs d'un officier*, vol. II, pp. 232–3.

16 Loucheur, Diary, 25 March 1918.

CHAPTER 21

1 Rupprecht, *Mein Kriegstagebuch*, vol. II, p. 322, cited by Hew Strachan, *The First World War*, pbk edn, p. 286.

2 Robert T. Foley, 'From Victory to Defeat: The German Army of 1918', in Ekins, *1918 Year of Victory*, p. 69.

3 Edmonds, *History of the Great War*, vol. I, p. 532.

4 Ibid., p. 343.

5 Rudolph Binding, *A Fatalist at War*, quoted by Pitt, *1918*, p. 108.

6 Gough, *The Fifth Army*, p. 299.

7 Pitt, *1918*, p. 98.

8 Kitchen, *The German Offensives*, caption to portrait facing p. 91.

9 All these picturesque details are supplied by Loucheur.

10 Edmonds, *History of the Great War*, vol. I, p. 539.

11 Milner, *New Statesman*, 23 April 1921.

12 Not published till 1928 and impressionistic but reliable here.

13 Milner, *New Statesman*, 23 April 1921, cited by Kitchen, *The German Offensives*, p. 91.

14 Barnes and Nicholson, *The Leo Amery Diaries*, vol. I, p. 210.

15 Lloyd George, *War Memoirs*, vol. V, p. 376.

16 Ibid., p. 248.

17 Ibid., p. 295.

18 CAB.45/177 WO.158/72 OAD.795.

19 Pitt, *1918*, pp. 100–01.

20 Milner, *New Statesman*, 23 April 1921.

21 William Philpott, *Anglo-French Relations and Strategy on the Western Front 1914–1918*, p. 165.

22 Pitt, *1918*, p. 112.

23 Haig, Diary, 2 April 1918.

24 Wilson, Diary, 14 April 1918.

25 Wilson Papers, IWM HHW 2/29/1.

26 Millman, *Pessimism and British War Policy*, p. 253.

27 Ibid., p. 256.

28 Henri Mordacq, *Le ministère Clemenceau*, vol. I, pp. 267–8.

29 Letter, 2 September 1919, 414/AP/4, [d] 1, Foch Papers, cited by Greenhalgh, 'Myth and Memory', in *The Journal of Military History*, vol. LXVIII, no. 3, p. 813.

30 Pitt, *1918*, p. 56.

31 Robert K. Hanks, *How the First World War Was Almost Lost*, p. 169.

32   Greenhalgh, *Victory Through Coalition*, p. 196.
33   CAB.45/177.
34   Winter, *Haig's Command*, p. 187.
35   CAB.45/177.
36   Ibid.
37   Hankey, *The Supreme Command*, p. 787.
38   Ibid.
39   Herbillon, *Souvenirs d'un officier*, vol. II, pp. 233–5.
40   Lady A. Gordon-Lennox, *The Diary of Lord Bertie of Thame, 1914–1918*, vol. II, p. 290.

CHAPTER 22

1   French, *The Strategy of the Lloyd George Coalition*, p. 24.

CHAPTER 23

1   Jay Winter, '1918: The Road to Victory', in Ekins, *1918 Year of Victory*, p. 39.
2   Robert T. Foley, 'From Victory to Defeat: The German Army in 1918' in Ekins, *1918 Year of Victory*, pp. 76–7.

CHAPTER 24

1   David T. Zabecki, *The German 1918 Offensives: A Case Study in the Operational Level of War*.
2   Ibid., p. 28.
3   Ibid., p. 311.
4   Lloyd George, *War Memoirs*, vol. V, p. 14.
5   Norman Stone, 'General Erich Ludendorff', in Michael Carver (ed.), *The Warlords*, pbk edn, p. 72.

CHAPTER 25

1   Paddy Griffith, 'The Extent of Tactical Reform in the British Army', in Griffith (ed.), *British Fighting Methods in the Great War*, 2004 edn, p. 2.
2   See, for example, Julian Thompson, *Lifeblood of War: Logistics in Armed Conflict*.

3   Brown, *British Logistics on the Western Front*, pp. 139–51 and *passim*.

4   Elizabeth Greenhalgh, 'A French Victory 1918', in Ekins, *1918 Year of Victory*, pp. 93–4.

5   Diary, 17 and 19 October 1918.

6   Hankey, *The Supreme Command*, vol. II, p. 849.

7   Churchill, *Great Contemporaries*, 1941 edn, p. 190.

8   Quoted Terraine, *Douglas Haig, The Educated Soldier*, p. 461.

9   Greenhalgh, '1918: The Push to Victory', in Tombs and Chabal, *Britain and France in the Two World Wars*, p. 813.

10 Haig, Diary, 29 August 1918.

11 Haig to Sir Henry Wilson, 13 October 1918. He seems to be contemplating the possibility that Britain would stand apart from the Franco-German Peace Treaty.

12 Haig, Diary, 24 October.

13 Wilson, Diary, 24 October 1918, quoted by Callwell, *Henry Wilson*, vol. II, p. 42.

14 Haig, Diary, 19 October 1918.

15 HMSO, *Statistics of the Military Effort of British Empire during the Great War, 1914/20*, War Office, 1922.

16 Alexandre Lafon, in 1914/1918 online: International Encyclopedia of the First World War. See also Brown, *British Fighting Methods in the Great War*, p. 94.

Select Bibliography

Arthur, G., *Lord Haig* (London, Heinemann, 1933).

Barnes, J. and Nicholson, D. (eds), *The Leo Amery Diaries* (London, Hutchinson, 1980).

Barnett, C., *The Swordbearers: Studies in Supreme Command in the First World War* (London, Eyre & Spottiswoode, 1963).

Barnett, C., *Britain and Her Army* (London, Allen Lane, 1970).

Barnett, C., *Haig Fellow's Address, Douglas Haig Fellowship Records* (December 2004).

Bayern, R. von, *Mein Kriegstagebuch* (Berlin, Mittler Munich, 1929).

Beaverbrook, W.M.A. (Lord Beaverbrook), *Politicians and the War 1914–1916* (London, Thornton Butterworth, 1928).

Beaverbrook, W.M.A. (Lord Beaverbrook), *Men and Power 1917–1918* (London, Hutchinson, 1956).

Beckett, I.F.W., *Johnnie Gough VC* (London, Tom Donovan, 1989).

Bidwell, S. and Graham D., *Fire-Power: British Army Weapons and Theories of War 1904–1945* (London, Allen & Unwin, 1982).

Binding, R., *A Fatalist at War* (London, Allen & Unwin, 1929).

Blake, R. (ed.), *The Private Papers of Douglas Haig 1914–19* (London, Eyre & Spottiswoode, 1952).

Bond, B., *Victorian Military Campaigns* (London, Hutchinson, 1967).

Bond, B., *The Victorian Army and the Staff College, 1854–1914* (London, Eyre Methuen, 1972).

Bond, B. (ed.), *The First World War and British Military History* (Oxford, Clarendon Press, 1991).

Bond, B. and Cave, N. (eds), *Haig: A Reappraisal 70 Years On* (Barnsley, Leo Cooper 1999)

Bourne, J.M., *Britain and the Great War* (London, Edward Arnold, 1989).

Bourne, J.M., Liddle, P. and Whitehead, I. (eds), *The Great World War 1914–45* (2v.) (London, Harper Collins, 2000).

Brittain, V., *Testament of Youth* (London, Victor Gollancz Ltd, 1933).

Brown, I.M., *British Logistics on the Western Front, 1914–1919* (Westport, CT, USA, Praeger, 1998).

Callwell, C.E., *Field Marshal Sir Henry Wilson: His Life and Diaries* (London, Cassell, 1927).

Carver, M. (ed.), *The Warlords* (London, Weidenfeld and Nicolson, 1976).

Charteris, J., *Field Marshal Earl Haig* (London, Cassell, 1931).

Charteris, J., *At GHQ* (London, Cassell, 1931).

Charteris, J., *Haig* (London, Duckworth, 1933).

Clark, K., *Another Part of the Wood* (New York, Harper Collins, 1975).

Churchill, W.S., *The World Crisis 1911–18*, vols I–III (London, Thornton Butterworth, 1931).

Churchill, W.S., *Great Contemporaries* (London, Thornton Butterworth, 1937).

Collier, B., *Brasshat: A Biography of Field-Marshal Sir Henry Wilson, 1864–1922* (London, Secker & Warburg, 1961).

Collins, D., *Charmed Life: The Phenomenal World of Philip Sassoon* (London, William Collins, 2016).

Davidson, Major General Sir J., *Haig, Master of the Field* (Barnsley, Pen & Sword, 2010).

Dewar, G.A.B. and Boraston, J.H., *Sir Douglas Haig's Command 1915–1918*, vol. II (London, Constable and Co., 1922).

Duff Cooper, A., *Haig*, 2 vols (London, Faber and Faber, 1935–6).

Duncan, G.S., *Douglas Haig as I Knew Him* (London, Allen & Unwin, 1966).

Edmonds, J.E. (ed. and comp.), *History of the Great War: Military Operations France and Belgium 1918* (14 vols) (London, HMSO/Macmillan, 1922–47).

Egremont, M., *Under Two Flags: The Life of Major-General Sir Edward Spears* (London, Weidenfeld & Nicolson, 1997).

Ekins, A. (ed.), *1918 Year of Victory: The End of the Great War and the Shaping of History* (Auckland, Exisle Publishing Limited, 2010).

Esher, R.B.B. (Viscount Esher), *Journals and Letters* (London, Nicholson & Watson, 1934–8)

Falls, C.B., *War Books: a Critical Guide* (London, P. Davies, 1930).

Falls, C.B., *The First World War* (London, Longmans, 1960).

Farrar-Hockley, A., *Goughie: The Life of General Sir Hubert Gough CGB, GCMG, KCVO* (London, Hart-Davis, MacGibbon, 1975).

Fayle, C.E., *Seaborne Trade*, vol. III, *The Period of Unrestricted Submarine Warfare* (London, John Murray, 1920–24).

French, D., *Sir Douglas Haig's Reputation, 1918–1928: A Note* in *The Historical Journal*, 28, 4 (Cambridge, Cambridge University Press, 1985).

French, D., *The Strategy of the Lloyd George Coalition 1916–1918* (Oxford, Clarendon Press, 1995).

French, D., *British Strategy and War Aims, 1914–1916* (London, Allen & Unwin, 1986).

French, D. and Holden Reid, B. (eds), *The British General Staff: Reform and Innovation* (London, F. Cass, 2002).

French, J.D.P. (Viscount French), *1914* (London, Constable, 1919).

Gollin, A., *Proconsul in Politics: Lord Milner* (New York, Macmillan, 1964).

Gordon-Lennox, Lady A., *The Diary of Lord Bertie of Thame, 1914–1918* (London, Hodder and Stoughton, 1924).

Gough, H., *Fifth Army*, (London, Hodder & Stoughton, 1931)

Green, A., *Writing the Great War: Sir James Edmonds and the Official Histories, 1915–1948* (London and Portland, Frank Cass, 2003).

Greenhalgh, E., *Victory Through Coalition: Britain and France During the First World War* (Cambridge University Press, New York, 2005).

Grieves, K., *Sir Eric Geddes* (Manchester, Manchester University Press, 1989).

Groot, G.J. de, '*The Reverend George S Duncan at GHQ, 1916–1918*', in Military Miscellany I (Stroud, Sutton Publishing for the Army Records Society, 1997).

Griffith, P., *Battle Tactics of the Western Front: The British Army's Art of Attack* (London, Yale University Press, 1994).

Griffith, P. (ed), *British Fighting Methods in the Great War* (London, Frank Cass, 1996).

Grigg, J., *Lloyd George: From Peace to War 1912–16* (London, Methuen, 1985).

Grigg, J., *Lloyd George: War Leader 1916–1918* (London, Allen Lane, 2002).

Guinn, P., *British Strategy and Politics 1914–1918* (Oxford, Clarendon Press, 1965).

Haig, The Countess, *Douglas Haig: His Letters and Diaries* (Moray Press, 1934).

Haig, The Countess, *The Man I Knew, The Intimate Life-story of Douglas Haig* (Edinburgh, Moray Press, 1936).

Haig, D., Lt.-Col. (J.H. Boraston, ed.), *Sir Douglas Haig's Despatches (December 1915–April 1919)*, (J. M. Dent & Sons Ltd., New York: E. P. Dutton & Co., 1919).

Hankey, M.P.A. (Lord Hankey), *The Supreme Command 1914–1918* (London, George Allen & Unwin, 1961).

Hanks, Robert K., *How The First World War Was Almost Lost* (University of Calgary, unpublished MA thesis, 1992).

Harris, J.P., *Douglas Haig and the First World War* (London, Cambridge University Press, 2008).

Harris, J.P. and Barr, N., *Amiens to the Armistice* (London, Brassey's, 1998).

Hart, P., *1918: A Very British Victory* (London, Weidenfeld & Nicholson, 2008).

Herbillon, Émile, *Souvenirs d'un officier de liaison pendant la guerre mondiale* (France, Tallandier, 1930).

Hindenburg, P. von, *Out of My Life* (London, Cassell, 1920).

Holmes, R., *The Little Field Marshal: A Life of Sir John French* (London, Cape, 1981).

Hussey, J., 'A Contemporary Record or Post-War Fabrication? The authenticity of the Haig Diaries for 1914', in *Stand To!*, No. 42, January 1995.

Hussey, J., 'Sir Douglas Haig's Diary and Despatches: Dating and Censorship', in *Stand To!*, no. 47, September 1996.

Jeffrey, K., *The Military Correspondence of Field-Marshal Sir Henry Wilson 1918–1922* (London, Bodley Head for Army Records Society, 1985).

Keegan, J., *The First World War* (London, Hutchinson, 1998).

Keene, J. and Neiberg, M., *Finding Common Ground: New Directions in First World War Studies* (Leiden, Brill, 2011).

Kitchen, M., *The German Offensives of 1918* (Stroud, Tempus Publishing Limited, 2001).

Laffin, J., *British Butchers and Bunglers of World War One* (Stroud, Sutton, 1988).

Lafon, A., in 1914/1918 on line: International Encyclopaedia of the First World War.

Lees-Milne, J., *The Enigmatic Edwardian: The Life of Reginald Second Viscount Esher* (London, Sidgwick and Jackson, 1986).

Liddell Hart, B.H., *History of the First World War* (London, Cassell, 1934).

Lloyd George, D. (Earl Lloyd George), *War Memoirs* (London, Ivor Nicholson & Watson, 1933–36).

Loucheur, Louis, *Carnets secrets, 1908–32* (Turnhout, Belgium, Brepols, 1962).

Ludendorff, E. von, *My War Memories, 1914–1918* (London, Hutchinson, 1919).

Magnus, P., *Kitchener: Portrait of an Imperialist* (London, John Murray, 1958).

Marshall-Cornwall, J., *Haig as a Military Commander* (London, Batsford, 1973).

Maurice, N. (ed.), *The Maurice Case: From the Papers of Major General Sir Frederick Maurice, KCMG, CB* (London, Leo Cooper, 1972)

McEwen, J.M., 'The National Press During the First World War: Ownership and Circulation' in *Journal of Contemporary History*, vol. XVII, No. 3 (July 1982) (London, Sage).

Mead, G., *The Good Soldier: The Biography of Douglas Haig* (London, Atlantic Books, 2008).

Middlebrook, M., *The Kaiser's Battle: 21 March 1918: The First Day of the German Spring Offensive* (London, Allen Lane, 1978).

Millman, B., *Pessimism and British War Policy 1916–1918* (London, Frank Cass, 2001).

Moore, W., *See How they Ran: The British Retreat of 1918* (London, Leo Cooper, 1970).

Mordacq, Henri, *Le ministère Clemenceau* (France, Plon, 1930).

Philpott, W.J., 'Sir Douglas Haig's Command? The Image of Alliance in Douglas Haig's Record of the War', *Records of the Douglas Haig Fellowship* (2011).

Philpott, W.J., *Bloody Victory: The Sacrifice on the Somme and the Making of the Twentieth Century* (London, Abacus, 2010).

Philpott, W.J., *Anglo-French Relations and Strategy on the Western Front 1914–1918* (London, Palgrave Macmillan, 1996).

Pitt, B., *1918: The Last Act* (London, Castle & Company, 1962).

Prior, R. and Wilson, T., *Haig, Douglas, first Earl Haig (1861–1928)* (Oxford University Press, 2004; (online edn) January 2011 edn) (London, Oxford Dictionary of National Biography, 2004).

Reid, W., *Architect of Victory: Douglas Haig* (Edinburgh, Birlinn, 2006).

Repington, C.àC., *The First World War 1914–18: A Personal Experience* (London, Constable 1920).

Robertson, W.R., *From Private to Field-Marshal* (London, Constable, 1921).

Roskill, S., *Hankey: Man of Secrets*, vol. I 1877–1918 (Annapolis MD, USA Naval Institute Press, 1970).

Shaw Sparrow, W., *The Fifth Army in March 1918* (London, John Lane, 1918).

Sheffield, G., *Forgotten Victory: The First World War: Myths and Realities* (London, Headline Review, 2002).

Sheffield, G., *The Chief* (London, Aurum Press Ltd, 2011).

Sheffield, G. and Bourne, J., *Douglas Haig War Diaries and Letters 1914–18* (London, Weidenfeld & Nicolson, 2005).

Sheffield, G. and Todman, D. (eds), *Command and Control on the Western Front: The British Army's Experience 1914–1918* (Staplehurst, Spellmount, 2004).

Simpson, A., *The Evolution of Victory* (London, Tom Donovan, 1995).

Sixsmith, E.K.G., *Douglas Haig* (London, Weidenfeld & Nicolson, 1976).

Stevenson, D., *With our Backs to the Wall: Victory and Defeat in 1918* (London, Allen Lane, 2011).

Strachan, H., *The Politics of the British Army* (Oxford, Clarendon Press, 1997).

Strachan, H. (ed.), *The Oxford Illustrated History of the First World War* (Oxford, Oxford University Press, 1998).

Strachan, H., *The First World War* (London, Simon & Schuster UK, 2003).

Strohn, M. (ed.), *The Battle of the Somme* (Oxford, Osprey Publishing, 2016).

Strohn, M., *World War One Companion* (Oxford, Osprey Publishing, 2013).

Terraine, J., *To Win A War* (Edinburgh, Cassell Military Paperbacks, 2008).

Terraine, J., *Douglas Haig, The Educated Soldier* (London, Hutchinson, 1963).

Thompson, J., *Lifeblood of War: Logistics in Armed Conflict* (London, Brassey's, 1991).

Tombs, R. and Chabal, E. (eds), *Britain and France in the Two World Wars: Truth, Myth and Memory* (London, Bloomsbury, 2013).

Travers, T., *The Killing Ground: The British Army, The Western Front and the Emergence of Modern Warfare 1900–1918* (London, Allen & Unwin, 1987).

Travers, T., *How the War was Won: Command and Technology in the British Army on the Western Front 1917–1918* (Routledge, London, 1992).

Tschuppik, K., *Ludendorff: The Tragedy of a Specialist* (London, Allen & Unwin, 1932).

Wallach, J.L., *Uneasy Coalition: The Entente Experience in World War One* (Westport, CT, Greenwood Press, 1993).

War Office, *Statistics of the Military Effort of British Empire during the Great War, 1914/20* (London, HMSO, 1922).

War Office, *Field Service Regulations*, Part 1 (London, HMSO, 1909).

Warner, P., *Field Marshal Earl Haig* (London, Bodley Head, 1991).

Watt, R., *Dare Call It Treason* (London, Chatto & Windus, 1964).

Wheeler-Bennett, J., *Brest-Litovsk: The Forgotten Peace, March 1918* (London, Macmillan, 1963).

Williams, B., *Pessimism and British War Policy 1916–18* (London, Routledge, 2014).

Williams, J., *Byng of Vimy* (London, Leo Cooper, 1983).

Wilson, K., *A Study in the History and Politics of the Morning Post 1905–26* (Lewiston, NY, Edwin Mellen Press, 1990).

Winter, D., *Haig's Command* (London, Penguin, 1991).

Woodward, D.R., *Lloyd George and the Generals* (Newark, NJ, University of Delaware Press, 1983).

Woodward D.R., *Field-Marshal Sir William Robertson* (Westport, CT, and London, Praeger, 1998).

Woodward, D.R. (ed.), *The Military Correspondence of Field-Marshal Sir William Robertson, Chief Imperial General Staff, December 1915–February 1918* (London, Bodley Head for Army Records Society, 1989).

Zabecki, D.T., *The German 1918 Offensives: A Case Study in the Operational Level of War* (Abingdon, Routledge, 2006).

Index